DEATH ON THE DANUBE

A TRAVEL BUG MYSTERY

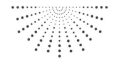

DELEEN WILLS

Life of
Riley
PUBLISHING

COPYRIGHT

ABOUT THE AUTHOR

Deleen Wills loves writing stories that entertain, enlighten, and educate—hopefully encouraging others to realize how enjoyable it is to embrace new friends and gain different insights while discovering our world.

Her passions are writing and globetrotting. Deleen delights in working from her cozy home office creating amusing Travel Bug Mysteries based on her actual explorations with a fictional, clean murder woven in. She also is a travel coordinator organizing adventures for groups, family, and friends.

Deleen lives in south Salem with her gallivanting husband. After three decades as an administrator in nonprofit education, in retirement she enjoys giving back by volunteering for Feed Salem, Habitat for Humanity, and Meals on Wheels.

Death on the Danube is a cleverly plotted mystery set in Central Europe. Join the author who weaves together her winning combination of humor, memories, and a vivid imagination, on this adventure to Hungary, Slovakia, Austria, Germany, and the Czech Republic.

www.amazon.com/author/deleenwills

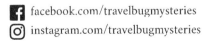 facebook.com/travelbugmysteries
instagram.com/travelbugmysteries

ACKNOWLEDGMENTS

My deepest appreciation goes out to my family, friends, and readers who encourage me to continue writing. They include but are not limited to:

Beth E. Pitcher, for expertly and patiently copyediting.

Jessica Spurrier, graphic designer and photographer. See her work at GreengateImages.com.

Shawn Wood, story consultant.

Sue Christopherson, who encourages and supports me as a true Sisterchick does. Many thanks for letting me borrow your poem on pages 110-112.

Mark Wills, for his ongoing patience helping with technology issues and sales support.

Rob and Debbie, for allowing me to use your names and a bit more.

John J. at Viking Cruises.

To my cheerleaders for their continued encouragement: Beth, Carol, Cathy, Chaille, Davette, Dorothy, Heather, Jeannie, Jenn, Jessica, Joanie, Judie, Julia, Julie, Kate, Kim, Linda, Michelle, Nancy, Patti, Peggy, Shawn, my sweet Mom and both brothers, and many readers of *Murder at Machu Picchu, Murder on Mendenhall Glacier, Murder on the Metolius, Through Colorful Doors, Because of Colorful Doors* and *Behind Colorful Doors.*

DEDICATION

To our treasured friend Rolland who passed away while this book was being edited. He was an integral part of our lives and this story.

We cherish your easygoing fun-loving spirit, enduring friendship, and our adventures together. You are missed.

We will look after Judie for you, dear one.

PROLOGUE

Towing one piece of luggage, a five-foot two woman with a crescent moon smile on her round-shaped face sat down on a wood bench in the bustling train station.

"Isn't this one of the prettiest stations you've ever seen?" she asked in a syrupy, southern US drawl. "Are you traveling alone, sir?"

Replying in the same accent, "Why, yes ma'am, it is, and I am alone. You look vaguely familiar though. Have I met you before?" the man asked innocently. "You surprise me each time I see you," he said, laying down his iPad and removing his reading glasses balanced on the tip of his nose. He bent sideways and gave her a peck on her delicate, smooth cheek. His closely trimmed mustache tickled her.

"That's…different," touching it.

He recognized her favorite perfume, very familiar to him. "I like the matronly, silvery blonde appearance."

Gazing boldly into his flirty, unbelievable ocean blue eyes, she countered, "Nice to see you, too, and don't *ever* refer to me as matronly again." She secretly loved his pleasant laugh, then bantered on, "You seem a bit more *portly* than usual. A new look?"

"You'll see," he intimated.

Yes, she would, just as she had sporadically over several decades. She enjoyed their comfortable repartee; always more amusing, and admittedly more enticing than others she'd worked with over the years. His walnut hair had more silver but she knew not to mention the obvious.

Escaping her solitary, ho-hum life as human resources officer for an international company, she began to unwind on the two-hour train ride through the countryside. The second glass of pinot noir helped. Watching the lush farmland whiz by, she thought about their professional interactions. A smile crept onto her lips as she recalled when, on one assignment, things turned personal. They decided their dalliance would be a distraction and vowed it wouldn't happen again. On their next assignment the vow hadn't lasted. They were much younger and energetic then. She admitted to herself that she loved him but never spoke to him of her feelings. Maybe one day.

"How's the wife and kids?" she joked still sounding like she could be from anywhere in the southern part of the US.

"Divorce #4, and the kids are fine," he chuckled. He remained single which she knew full well.

"Have you been waiting long?" knowing he'd come from Amsterdam.

"Just enough time to get a coffee and catch up on the US news," pointing to his iPad. He purposely neglected to inform her he'd arrived two days earlier.

"Do you have instructions?" She turned solemn.

"It's fluid; we are to make our own decisions."

"Positive ID?"

"Without a doubt."

Her watch read 12:45. "Let's get a taxi for our Danube River cruise, *husband*," she said as they both stood.

"Let's do, *dear wife*," he nodded as he took her hand while walking out of the historic Nyugati Railway Station in Budapest.

CHAPTER ONE

The majestic Canadian Rockies with Mount Robson perched on the Continental Divide reaching about 13,000 feet, gleamed in the sunshine. Anne closed her eyes to the shiny giant mirror reflecting into her oval airline window. Looking out the window from 35,000 feet they were now over Edmonton, Alberta, according to the map on the eight-inch screen embedded in the back of the seat about 11 inches from her. It never ceased to amaze her that they could leave home and nine to ten hours later be somewhere in Europe. Next stop Amsterdam.

Finished with spinach and bacon quiche and some fresh fruit, her next decision with seven hours to—watch a movie or read one of two books she brought. Would it be J.A. Jance's novel *Downfall*, number 17 in a series featuring Sheriff Joanna Brady and her team of officers solving crime in Arizona? She knew from experience if she started this book, she'd never get any catnaps. She didn't sleep much on flights, but a short nap here and there helped. Not so if she opened the first page; she knew she'd be hooked immediately and her mind would race ahead trying to figure who'd done it.

A book of short stories intrigued her about people's discoveries behind a colorful door. Anne loved, loved, loved colorful doors, having probably taken thousands of colorful doors' photos from their explorations. *Behind Colorful Doors* offered a compilation of fiction and nonfiction short stories written by selected authors transporting the reader to several countries over three centuries. Each short story promised escapades brimming with imagination and insight, revealing discoveries behind each colorful door.

Short stories just might be the ticket, she told herself. Read, sleep, drink water, take a loop around the plane stopping at the bathroom and repeat a few times.

The movie selections actually seemed enticing and time consuming, just what she wanted on the nine-hour flight. Scrolling through she found *Wonder Woman* and the comedy *Paris Can Wait*, both acceptable. No disaster or horror flicks for her. Light, fun, nothing serious and if she fell asleep nothing she really needed to rewind. She inserted her ear buds then pushed the button for *Paris Can Wait*, with the promo promising gorgeous scenery including Budapest, perfect since it would be their first stop of the trip. She lowered the window shade and escaped into a world of make-believe.

Her husband of several decades, Peter, in the aisle seat, was already engrossed in *Star Wars: The Last Jedi* with portions filmed in Northern Ireland, one of her favorite countries.

Blurry-eyed Anne squinted at her watch. The hands pointed at 1:10 p.m., nine hours ahead of west coast time at home.

She pulled out her small toiletry bag to check her makeup, then fluffed her chin-length, blondish-silver hair that got smooshed on one side from her restless sleep, finishing up with a disposable waterless toothbrush. "Good as new. Well, almost," she said to her six foot two husband who squirmed in his seat. "Sore butt. Are we there yet?" he joked.

The pilot announced, "We are approaching Amsterdam. Local time is 13:10 and temperature 19 Celsius. We will be on the ground in 20 minutes. Flight crew please prepare for landing."

She recapped with Peter about the temperature conversion: 19 times two and add 30, close enough to convert to Fahrenheit. Sixty-eight degrees, about perfect for Oregonians who were used to cooler temps overall.

Anne peered out the window watching the ground get closer and closer, spotting windmills, lush grasses, and lots of water. She heard a youngster behind them say "Touchdown!" as the screeching tires of the jumbo jet landed on the runway. Peter glanced at Anne with a slight grimace on his face which morphed into a look of relief. Flying wasn't his favorite thing, just a means to an end when it came to adventures around the world.

As wheels made firm contact with Mother Earth, she glanced around their seats where 32 friends were as eager as she was to deplane. Fortunately, it had been an uneventful flight from Portland International Airport.

They'd have three hours to traverse the Amsterdam airport; take a walk, grab a drink, eat some tasty mini pancakes, stop at the restroom, go through security then walk onto another airplane for the two-hour hop to Budapest. They were eager to explore the city before boarding a Viking River Cruise Longship cruising the Danube for one week, then transferring to Prague to finish off their exploration. Anne had been eagerly anticipating this two-week adventure for a couple of years, and now they were practically there.

A female voice interrupted her daydreaming, "On behalf of your Portland-based Delta crew, Welcome to Amsterdam where the local time is 13:30. If Amsterdam is your final destination, we hope you have a good visit in this historic city. If you are continuing, please check the reader board for your next gate or ask any Delta employee. It's been a pleasure flying with you today."

Thirty-four very weary Americans, mostly Oregonians, followed in a row like ducklings trailing their mamma to the water, reaching a long line for nonresidents at immigration.

"A passport stamp!" Anne exclaimed just like a kid in a candy store, one of her favorite things when traveling. They would be in at least one first-time country this trip which meant searching for just the right ornament for their Christmas tree, and a fridge magnet that no longer fit on the fridge. Now her collection had been moved onto newly crafted magnetic boards displayed in their laundry room.

Navigating one of the busiest airports in the world, they had plenty of time to enjoy the yummy pancakes at the Dutch Kitchen, stopped at restrooms, then ambled onto a second jet for a short flight to central Europe.

Miraculously all luggage arrived, and one by one, travelers got onto a charter bus that drove into historic Budapest, a city of 1.5 million. The city has a few nicknames which she'd read: *Heart of Europe*, *Queen of the Danube*, *Pearl of the Danube*, *Capital of Freedom*, *Capital of Spas and Thermal Baths* and lastly, *Capital of Festivals*. She'd heard from several travel friends, and her nephew Brent, that Budapest is still their favorite city and all would return in a heartbeat. It all sounded magnificent to her traveler's heart.

Peter preferred visiting locations of historical value. He'd read about the Celts then the Romans settling and establishing Aquincum, where Old Buda stands today, the Huns arriving from the east, the Romanesque 12th century church, Buda Castle, and bridges.

She'd read that the major religion is Catholic, around 54%, Protestant around 20% and random others. Education is free and compulsory from ages 6-16. Most students go on to secondary school for technical training or study for higher education. They elect a president who is chief of state, and a prime minister who is head of the government. Parliament consists of a 199-seat house called the National Assembly, and they can vote at age 18. Hungary is slightly smaller than Indiana, and slightly larger than Scotland.

Nestled against the window of the bus, Anne felt giddy, and maybe a little travel-dazed, though she wouldn't admit it. She hadn't slept as much as she would have preferred. Between watching movies, eating twice, reading the book about different authors' experiences through colorful doors, drinking lots of water, friends stopping to say "Hi" on the way to the restroom, she'd maybe had 30 minutes of sleep. By the time they go to bed, they'd be up for 28 hours straight.

They learned never to take a nap when arriving but to stay awake by riding a hop on/hop off bus the entire loop to get a lay of the land, or stroll, eat a light dinner, avoid alcohol, and go to bed when it's dark or 8 o'clock, maybe 7, if they could stay conscious that long. After eight to ten hours of sleep, they'd be ready to roll in the morning.

She pinched herself. Fifteen hours earlier she and her husband stepped onto a Delta Airlines plane and now they are in landlocked Hungary, a country of over nine million. It shares a border to the north with Slovakia, northeast with

Ukraine, to the east with Romania, to the south with Serbia and Croatia, to the southwest with Slovenia and the west with Austria.

Anne pulled out a few Hungarian Forint, the local currency. She always brought money of the countries they'd visit for small purchases, taxi rides, tips, and sharing a meal with somebody. On the bus from the airport to the hotel, those awake saw many old and modern buildings. She noticed Peter's eyelids were closed so she didn't point out the People's Park, or a gently swaying national flag atop a museum where she could see three equal size horizontal stripes of beet red, bright white, and grass green. Another flag looked virtually identical except she noticed a coat of arms in the center with limbs of different trees on each side.

On the 30-minute, 13-mile drive, they drove by hundreds of homes and buildings, a large library, and she spotted four bridges before arriving at their hotel, the InterContinental on the picturesque Danube River, an easy walk to the famous Chain Bridge.

Walking into the expansive lobby, Anne noticed marble-swirled tile flooring, modern sofas and chairs for lounging, and floor-to-ceiling windows providing an outstanding view to the river. "I sure hope we have that river view," Anne pointed out to Peter.

Checking in around 3:30, Anne made sure everyone in their party got their room keys first as groups of six rode the elevator to their floor, then found their rooms. She felt responsible as their group leader and organizer of this adventure. While Peter stood patiently off to the side guarding their luggage, Anne was finally checking in. She observed an elderly couple standing about five feet away at the counter. The white-haired man appeared six to eight inches taller than his companion, who Anne assumed to be his wife. They had red Viking luggage tags on their bags just like theirs.

Waiting for the clerk to find their names and keys, movement caught Anne's eye. Something plopped on the floor and the elderly couple hadn't picked it up. She moved four steps to her right, bent to the tile floor and retrieved a face-down but opened burgundy passport with a golden eagle embossed on the front.

She saw the name Dmitry Something then closing it and straightening up, she handed it to the man as he briskly said, "What are you doing with my passport?" in an accent Anne sort of recognized.

At first glance Anne wondered to herself why the somewhat younger looking woman would be with such an older man?

"It fell on the floor," Anne politely replied as the woman jumped in, "Thank you so much. My husband is in his nineties and hard of hearing plus his eyesight is failing." She sounded German to Anne as she'd been to that country several times.

The woman handing his passport to him took him back 70 years when someone else handed him a passport.

It hadn't even taken five minutes for Aleksandr Pushkin to become Dmitry Rudolph. Scrupulous documents prepared by a sympathizer assisting those who had served the Third Reich, or even the SS, had been proudly presented to him like a piece of birthday cake. Dmitry placed a crisp stack of Marks on the black counter and the operative handed him a new birth certificate, proving his newly established Austrian citizenship, and a passport with a photo of him now with dark hair and a beard. Dmitry's hometown had become

Vienna. His backstory would be his Russian father married his British mother and he had spent time in both countries growing up, attending schools where he had learned many accents, inflections, and languages.

He studied and absorbed as much as he could about his supposed hometown, its history, culture, popular coffee houses and even what schools he would have attended in his neighborhood. More than six months after the war ended for Germany, he purposely gained 30 pounds which had been harder than he anticipated. Sandy hair and blue eyes were commonplace in all of Europe, but especially Germany. He dyed his light hair dark brown, and grew a bushy mustache and full beard, dyed to match. And he wore a hat everywhere he went.

Someone suggested going to a tattoo artist who tattooed his bushy blond eyebrows dark brown. Now he had a couple of generic tattoos, one under his left wrist of a black Austrian eagle with a crown on its head, and on his upper right arm a viper with a head at each end ready to strike. His military record would reveal no tattoos if someone checked.

If anything could give him away, it would be his confounded height. He wore shoes with little sole. He started slouching; his shoulders hunched forward. Height he couldn't disguise.

Many former SS and Nazis were disappearing, some kidnapped, and killed. Some of his comrades had vanished, either dead or departed on their own volition. He needed a new home and fast. *I must leave Europe*, he told himself. South America, particularly Peru and Argentina were friendly and sympathetic to Germans. He saw pictures of South American men about five-foot five to eight inches, not a good option for him to blend in.

He picked up accents easily and could speak and write just about any language. After weeks of research, he selected a location where he thought he'd be safe—Cape Town, South Africa. The two official languages were English and Afrikaans.

Tired of looking over his shoulder and knowing if he stayed he could be yet another statistic due to his role during the war, Dmitry bought a ticket on a steamer, then read about South African history. Even though a British Commonwealth country, there was pro-German sentiment dating back generations to the Boer War, when British authorities interned Afrikaner civilians in concentration camps. At the outset of WWII, there was enough of an antiwar movement to make for an extremely tight vote in the South African parliament to join the Allied cause.

Some in South Africa hoped Germany would win WWII. All the deep-seated anti-British sentiment stemming from the South African War in 1898 to 1902, in which the British interned Africans along with many black people in brutal conditions, at least partially accounted for the movement there. These concentration camps would ultimately inspire the Nazi death camps. Others saw what the Nazis offered as a solution for eliminating the control of the British and for initiating white supremacy over black people. Despite their zeal, South African Nazis couldn't disrupt the country's war effort even after informants provided intelligence on shipping from the ports of Durban and Cape Town. Schemes to overthrow the government didn't happen.

Becoming a postwar spy would not be anything he'd be a part of. He would fit in but not get involved in politics or government work.

He packed the newly purchased square-domed steamer trunk with two weeks' worth of his finest clothing, shoes, and two hats. He carried nothing from his past except a gold-framed picture of his mother. Only her.

In January 1947, after a train ride to the coast of France, a bumpy boat ride across the English Channel, another several hours on a train to London, then a cramped bus to Southampton, he finally boarded the *Cape Town Castle*, built by Harland and Wolff Ltd, Belfast, five days later. The ship's first arrival at Cape Town on May 13, 1938, was as mail service. In 1940, she carried 164,000 military troops and everyday passengers before release in July 1946. After renovation, *Cape Town Castle* returned to mail service in January 1947, now accommodating all ages of first class and 553 cabin class passengers. He was one of the fortunate 244 first class travelers.

Sitting down to an elegant table with a linen tablecloth and napkins, multiple pieces of silverware and several glasses of varying size and height, he thought it best to watch what others were using. He hadn't experienced this type of extravagance before. He didn't recognize several items but thought it better not to ask.

The first night the menu choices were:
Consommé Cagliari
Supreme of Brill with lemon Braised Lamb Sweetbreads
Vegetable Marrow with parsley sauce
Purée of spinach
Potatoes steamed

The cold buffet:
Roast Norfolk Turkey with cream corn
Corned Ox tongue
Salad of lettuce, tomato, and beetroot with Windsor Dressings
Chantilly Creole
Sweet American Nanking

Desserts:
Cabinet pudding a la Confiture
Apricot ices and water biscuits

The *Cape Town Castle* program listed opportunities for sports and entertainment. He wasted time playing deck tennis. Contract Bridge didn't appeal to him. He went to the cinema and watched the crime mystery with private detective Philip Marlowe in *The Big Sleep*. He slouched down in the seat watching *Notorious*, where the daughter of a convicted Nazi spy is asked by American agents to gather information on a ring of Nazi scientists in South America. Dmitry felt his heart racing. Cary Grant and Ingrid Bergman were chilling, and he became an instant fan of anything Alfred Hitchcock directed.

He took dance lessons expecting it would be beneficial in British society. Several single young women traveling with their parents tried to coax him to participate in tournaments. He declined their pleas, even though tempted to get involved with one young lady in particular with flirty mossy eyes. There were aquatic sports, but he preferred swimming back and forth the length of the pool. He skipped any contests especially the three-legged race, and further humiliation would be being blindfolded in the insipid sack races. Watching one blindfold potato sack race reminded him of the American vaudeville and comedy team, *The Three Stooges*; their physical farce, and slapstick styles weren't humorous to him. He much preferred a higher-class of humor, dry and witty.

When he arrived 11 days later, Dmitry felt safer in South Africa than anywhere in Europe. He paid cash for two months on a four-room apartment on the second floor close to downtown. Three days after he arrived, he took an entry-level job as a bank teller about six blocks from his new home. He'd bide his time, get familiar with the area, and work his way up at the bank.

"I understand," Anne cheerfully replied to the lady as she moved back, reaching to the outstretched hand of the hotel employee to nab their room key cards. Anne truly did understand, as her parents and father-in-law were in this age group, but they looked much younger and healthier than this frail man. During WWII, her dad served in the Army's 10th Mt. Division, and Peter's in the Navy.

Maybe the woman had been struck by lightning given her shockingly white hair, yet her eyebrows were dark. Anne's immediate thought—she's wearing a wig totally not suited to her complexion or it's a disguise. She should have snow-white brows not black. Anne laughed at herself and her vivid imagination.

Always friendly, Anne asked if they were on the Danube cruise in a few days. The woman said, "Yes," as the antisocial man made no attempt to interact. For a split second, the man's physical stature reminded her of her younger brother Will—tall, lean and six foot five. *Except this stranger is five decades older*, she said to herself.

"Us, too," the outgoing female American replied. The woman politely half-smiled.

The gruff man mumbled something inaudible, and his wife said something back in a foreign language. Anne would never know he'd said, "She's a typical, overly cheerful, busy-body American" and the wife replying, "She's just being kind; you're the one who dropped the passport." He sniffed and grunted something indistinguishable, always needing to get in the last word.

Anne took a side glance at the curmudgeon and thought to herself from her brief contact: Sharp nose, steely-blue cold eyes spaced farther apart than most, with pale grayish complexion. He looked like a shark, similar to ones they'd seen in the Galápagos Islands.

Receiving hotel instructions on all of the amenities: Where breakfast would be provided each morning, that they could use the extensive fitness center, the gift shop location, the concierge always available for assistance, lounge, and bar, and much more, Anne felt quite sure she would not remember much of it the next day. Her glazed-over eyes showed her fatigue and the nice employee said, "If you have any questions, just come back and we will help."

Peter waved as Anne stepped away with their room keys only remembering the most important thing—instructions on where to meet for breakfast each morning.

Pushing open the door of their accommodations for the next three days, Peter gave a sigh, "Now's that a view," standing at the large window taking up the entire wall facing the Danube River and Buda Castle. That'll be something tonight all lit up."

"If we can stay awake that long," she remarked.

"Probably right. Sunset is around 9. Then we'll see it tomorrow night," he agreed.

Anne adeptly unpacked what they'd need for several days and 30 minutes later, after receiving a text from Cathy, they joined her and her husband Casey in the lobby. Casey and Peter had worked together for years at Oregon's Highway Department. More friends, Rolland, that rhymed with Holland, and wife Judie, who two decades earlier were married with Peter and Anne in attendance, traveled together as much as possible.

Mike and Kathy, slightly older than Anne were family friends. Mike's mother, Barbara, was a second Mom to Anne. Phil and Sharon, introduced originally by Mike and Kathy, were retired and now delightful travel mates. Anne looked at her mentor Carol and husband Jim. She and Carol had known each other since 1986 when they worked together at a local law school in the development office. Their daughter Robin and husband Mark were celebrating a wedding anniversary on board.

Then Anne glanced at another pair of Mike and Kathy, who she knew from her current role as administrator at another local university, along with their good friends, Gil and Angie. Along with Anne's longtime friend Julie, who played racquetball with her several decades earlier, all loitered around seeming a bit dazed. Everywhere Anne looked, she could share some story about the people on this adventure with them. All were easygoing, just the kind Anne preferred traveling with.

John and Rebecca, along with Jan and Patti, more friends from their hometown, were already enjoying the hotel's outdoor seating overlooking the Danube. Tired friends filled in empty seats ordering beverages, Margherita pizza, and charcuterie boards of olives, meats, cheese, and pickles. Each selected a light dinner because most were having dessert. The English side of the menu described Gerbeaud Slice: *Bite-size cake under a chocolate glaze lies layers of a sweet dough alternating with a filling of ground walnuts and apricot jam.*

Rolland said, "I'm having that, please. Anything with apricots, I'm in. Or the Rákóczitúrós, meringue and apricot-jam-topped túró cake?" which the server recommended. "The second is my favorite; you could do the other one tomorrow," came the answer.

"Apple Streusel for me with a scoop of vanilla ice cream, please," Peter requested.

Judie pointed to the Kossuth Kifli that seemed interesting.

This half-moon shaped pastry is a flavorful sponge cake, sprinkled with browned almonds. Fortunately, the menu came with pictures of the delectable delights, too.

After a short stroll along the Danube, returning to their room, Anne closed the blackout curtains by using the pants hanger to squeeze them shut as tightly as possible until she found the clothes pins tucked away somewhere. She climbed into bed next to sleeping Peter and joined him in slumber at 7:55 p.m.

She and Peter stood in semi-darkness. Lights shown on a twin-towered bridge. A humongous building seemed to stretch several blocks. Anne recognized the famous Széchenyi Chain Bridge and Buda Castle on the Danube River. There might even be a full moon.

She heard people speaking in a foreign language. Glancing towards the sounds, was it her brother Will? No way. It sure looked like him but why would her younger brother be in Budapest? She knew he didn't speak any foreign languages, yet he'd been a student at the FBI Academy in Quantico, Virginia, some years back.

"HELP! HELP ME!!"

Anne and Peter heard it loud and clear. A man thrashed in navy water.

A rustling drew her attention from the water to the cement walkway. In the inkiness, she saw that Peter had stopped, stripping off his jacket and shirt.

"What are you doing?" she demanded.

"I'm going to save that poor guy." Now his pants and shoes were off.

"No! I'll get help. You don't swim that well." She heard a splash.

Anne felt close to panic because this was her lifetime nightmare. She almost drowned as a child and her fear of water sometimes paralyzed her. Irrational maybe, but she'd not gotten over the trauma of that incident when her younger brother Max found her at the bottom of a swimming pool and pulled her to safety.

To try to get over the fear, even breaking out in a sweat driving along a lake, river, or crossing a long bridge like the Oakland Bay bridge at one mile long, she needed to do something about it. Peter had even tried and although she completely trusted him, unreasonable anxiety took over. Turning 50, Anne took private swimming lessons to prove to herself she could overcome the nonsensical terror. She persevered and could probably, well maybe, save herself if needed, but it wouldn't be easy.

Peter swimming for what seemed forever, plus her life-long nightmare of drowning, she felt about to throw up. She froze on the spot. From the shimmery lights on the water, she saw her husband drop below the water. He disappeared.

She screamed, "PETER!!" but no sound came out of her throat. Snap out of it; get a grip! Anne demanded of herself. "Peter!! Come this way." This time she heard her voice.

Peter heard Anne's firm voice and reached down grabbing at anything he could which turned out to be the collar of the jacket the man wore. Peter tugged with all his strength; he wasn't a body builder, but adrenaline kicked in.

Anne heard her husband's voice, "I have you. Just kick your feet and hang on to me."

"Peter! Peter, swim this way!" she shouted, assuming he'd follow her commanding voice. Fortunately, the men weren't too far from the riverbank.

Together the two reached the cement wall as Anne rushed to them hearing emergency sirens growing louder and louder. Peter hoisted while Anne pulled the man up onto the walkway. Sopping wet, Peter dragged himself out of the river.

Both men lay stunned. "Sir, are you okay? What happened to you?" Anne yelled.

She and Peter heard through the gagging, then spitting water—"PUSHED."

———

Each time Anne awoke from this repeating nightmare, she felt as drenched as both men. She read the numbers on the clock glaring in white, 1:36.

This recurring dream now had become bothersome. Three times over the past month she woke up in a panic. Her breathing and heartbeat slowed slightly as she vividly recalled the scene, like a movie on a big screen playing in front of her. She felt like a cast member in the Bill Murray film *Groundhog Day*, where February 2 keeps repeating.

Yet this time the dream seemed slightly off. Something changed. Maybe the sequence had changed? No, not that. She replayed it in her mind. *Something is different, for sure. But what could it be?* She sat straight up in bed. "Holy moly, I think I recognize the man," she said out loud, her head feeling woozy.

Her feet shuffled along the cool tile floor to the bathroom where she drank a glass of water. The half of Xanax helped her relax and get back to sleep undisturbed for six solid hours.

CHAPTER TWO

S he heard water running as she saw brightness through her eyelids. Squinting one then the other open, the sun blazed through cracks of the heavy curtains of their sixth story hotel room. Peter came from the bathroom, "I'm awake" she said, as he pulled open the window coverings. They stood with the Buda Castle perched directly across from them some 550 feet above the bank of the river.

"I had that irritating dream again last night," she announced to her husband.

"Your imagination is working overtime. We're on vacation, tell your mind to give it a rest," he said looking at the neo-Gothic monument, a huge beige building with a green dome.

"I wish," she replied. "Gosh, the Danube isn't blue like the waltz says but more of a greenish-blue with a tinge of gray."

Peter opened the hotel information notebook and raised his voice while she put on a bit of makeup in the bathroom. "Hey, pay attention. *Buda Castle is the historical castle and palace complex of the Hungarian Kings in Budapest. It was first completed in 1265, although the massive Baroque palace today occupying most of the site was built between 1749 and 1769. The castle now houses the Hungarian National Gallery and the Budapest Historical Museum.*

As Anne got dressed, Peter read, *The building of the Royal Castle began on the Castle Hill by King Béla in 1242, following havoc wrought by the Mongol invasion. Apart from the natural beauty of the place, the central location and the strategic importance of the hill made it an ideal site for a city. In the 1330s, King Louis I set up his court and had its palace built there. After that, it gradually became the permanent royal residence. Major constructions were resumed under Sigismund's rule. King Matthias employed Italian Renaissance masters for the construction.*

"That's it? No more history?"

"Well, my synopsis is this: The Turkish sieges and the 1686 reoccupation destroyed most of the castle, which remained that way until reconstruction during the Baroque period. Maria Theresa restored and enlarged it in the late 1700s before it took its present-day look under Emperor Josef I. Two men, can't pronounce their names, were commissioned to enlarge the palace, and they added the dome. During WWII, the castle completely burned, the roof fell, and furniture was destroyed."

"Let's get to breakfast then hit the streets for Day One of Budapest."

Bowls of fresh fruits, plates of sliced vegetables, various preparations of eggs, skillets of meats, plates of cheese, and flat wood serving trays brimming with scrumptious pastries awaited them: Anne's favorite, fluffy croissants filled with dark chocolate, and Peter's pinwheels with raisins, apples, and cinnamon, with piping hot coffee for him and fresh squeezed orange juice for her. They finished their first of three lavish buffet breakfasts at the hotel's restaurant viewing the castle from the riverside promenade.

They signed up for a tour beginning their exploration on

the hilly Buda side, the west side of the Danube in the Castle District. Their local guide, Davian, met them in the hotel lobby and together they headed to a charter bus. Lions greeted them at the entrance to the Chain Bridge. He told them that the suspension bridge took ten years to build and the ends of the chains, interwoven through the arch, formed portals over the two piers. The chains were secured inside underground chambers on the two riverbanks.

From the west side of the Danube in the distance they could see a statue atop a tall cement column. It looked like a female offering something to the heavens. "Liberty Statue," Davian explained, "was erected in 1947 and commemorates all who sacrificed their lives for the independence, freedom, and prosperity of Hungary."

Continuing on they saw a terraced waterfall, and a lettuce-green statue with an uplifted hand holding a cross on top of Szent Gellért Monument, a 23-foot statue of the saint himself. Driving on Aprod Street past an exhibit from WWI, statues of soldiers hold their fallen comrades.

Stopping first at a relief map on the side of a building, they could see that the Buda Castle District is massive. "Good thing we've got the day for this," Casey mentioned. The sprawling complex in the hills seemed much like its own little village. Anne mentioned it looked like an assortment of styles—Baroque, Gothic and Romantic. Davian replied, "That's because it had been wiped out and rebuilt at least six times over the course of the past seven centuries." He mentioned that what's different about this castle from others they had probably toured is this one doesn't portray what life was like centuries ago when kings were still around; rather, it houses several public institutions.

Julie lowered her voice, "Anne, don't you think Davian looks like a young, clean shaven Bradley Cooper?" "Yes, except with lighter colored hair."

He pointed to an impressive fountain in the main court-yard that depicts the hunting party of King Matthias. The sculpted figures looked so lifelike that Anne thought she could just about hear the dogs barking while chasing the prey. Children scooped their hands, splashing water at each other.

Davian explained that Fisherman's Bastion is a fairly modern structure. The original thick castle walls were built in the 16th century as part of the castle, and over the years it had been attacked, captured, destroyed, and rebuilt. Originally the battlements overlooked a small part of the city called Watertown, a modern-day district by the same name, where the fishermen of the city lived and worked. It's from here that Fisherman's Bastion got its name.

Since the castle had officially lost its function as a mili-taristic structure in 1874, the idea was to build something more communal instead of defensive for citizens to better appreciate the great views over the city and the Danube. It was designed with the intention to create something airier and more accessible, rather than the limited viewpoints and narrow walkways of defensive castles which were no longer necessary.

Another key aspect of Fisherman's Bastion is its seven spired towers, which are intended to represent the seven founding Hungarian chieftains of the Magyar tribes that controlled the land that would become Hungary. The areas have retained this design and structure since its construc-tion. However, in WWII, the Bastian was damaged with the Looking Tower taking the brunt, while the Ministry of Finance building within the courtyard burned to the ground.

Davian pointed out the coat-of-arms with cherubs made of mosaic. He said that the courtyard provides access to the National Gallery, the Ludwig Museum, the Budapest History Museum, and the Gothic 700-year-old Matthias Church in

Holy Trinity Square. The exterior is flanked by the neo-Gothic Béla and Matyas towers with turrets, gargoyles, large geometric windows, and spires.

At Matthias Church named for Hungary's most beloved medieval king, Davian proudly pointed to the outstanding geometric patterns on its gold, brick, black, tan, and cream glazed-tile roof and splendid stained glass windows. It's also called The Church of the Virgin Mary, erected during the 13th to the 15th centuries.

"One of most striking details of the church is the 236-foot-high Matthias Tower in the south. The main western façade faces the Holy Trinity Square. A relief in the ridge of the main gate depicts Mary with her child. The large Gothic rosette is a reconstruction of the rose window bricked up during the Baroque period. The Maria Gate on the south was erected around 1370. The upper part of the gate has a relief showing Maria's death. Let's go in."

It felt welcoming inside with warm lights, shadows, and hues of autumn. They saw frescos reaching from the floor to the ceiling, smooth arches, century old wooden pews, gold-leaf motifs, stunning altars, and plenty of medieval odds and ends. The long stained glass windows that shined dabs of light around the altar at the front grabbed Anne's attention. The arched ceiling glowed in fall tones.

Davian spoke in his church voice, "According to tradition, the first church on site was founded by a St. Stephen, King of Hungary in 1015. This is based on an inscription erected in 1690 inside the church. The current building was built in the latter half of the 13th century. It had been converted into a mosque during the Turkish period; its walls were white-washed, and the windows bricked up. The heavily damaged building was restored in neo-Gothic style between 1874 and 1896."

The dark wood and stained glass windows took Anne's

breath away. Davian continued, "Frescoes and stained glass decoration are the works of several artists, and the high altar depicts the Virgin Mary's rise into Heaven in a wreath of light. This church has been the venue of mass, Matthias' election to king, and both his marriages. Kings Joseph and Charles IV were crowned here in 1867 and 1916. Flags from the last coronation line the walls.

"Hidden behind a wall, they discovered an old Madonna statue. It was originally named after the Virgin Mary, and using names such as the Church of Mary, and the Church of Our Lady, since the 19th century, the church has been referred to as Matthias Church after the king who ordered the transformation of its original southern tower."

They all stopped at the Traceried stained glass window at the southern front of the church. The three windows depict scenes from the lives of St. Margaret, St. Elisabeth of Hungary, and the Virgin Mary. They gawked at the richly carved pulpit where the priest stands.

Anne pointed out a tall man to Peter, "That's the man who dropped his passport at check-in yesterday. Did I tell you his name is Dmitry? I won't forget that because Erica in *All My Children* married Dmitry Marick from Hungary. He's husband number 8 or 9, I don't really remember, but they married twice."

Peter had learned that sometimes it seemed best not to ask many questions about Anne's random comments. Usually, he could figure out her train of thought, but sometimes he didn't follow at all. His usual reply, "Really?" seemed good enough for Anne. At least he was listening. Both watched Dmitry "What's-his-last-name" round a corner alone and disappear behind a marble column.

The wood organ at the back of the church looked massive. "The organ is known as the King's Organ," Davian said as Anne heard a few juvenile snickers behind her, hoping it wasn't anyone from her group. "It has 7,771 pipes and 18 bells," Davian concluded.

As they went down a flight of stairs to the gift shop, Anne heard one boy say he felt like he was playing a character in a *Harry Potter* movie. The entire place felt magical. Carrying her foldable nylon bag she bought in Scotland, she made the first of several purchases of the day. She'd found in their years of explorations that cathedral, churches, and museums offered high quality items at the best value, while she also enjoyed supporting a worthy cause.

Outside, Rolland pointed out the black raven on the southern church tower holding a ring in its beak. Davian said, "History tells us that Hungary had some bad luck when two kings died unexpectedly within seven years. They seemed doomed to lose their hold on their bloodline, and their border. At this dark moment, Hungarians looked to a 15-year-old boy, Matthias, for salvation. According to legend, his mother sent for him with a raven holding a ring in its beak. The raven supposedly flew nonstop from Transylvania to Prague, and thus the "Boy King of Ravens" was crowned. The raven-with-ring motif became part of the family crest. Matthias returned to Buda, becoming the first Hungarian-descended king in more than 150 years."

Walking up the cobblestone road, they entered The Bastion with its elaborate neo-Gothic and neo-Romanesque look. It appeared old but Davian said it had been built between 1895 and 1902. After nearly being destroyed in WWII, the architect's son oversaw the restoration. The expansive wall and sturdy turrets of Fishermen's Bastion overlook the river, the impressive Chain Bridge, and the Pest side of the river. "Absolutely stunning," an awed tourist said.

It stands above a large, modern equestrian bronze statue of Hungary's first king, St. Stephen. Completed in 1906, he's holding a scepter with a double cross at the top, and a gold ring around his crowned head. He's in full armor and flowy cloak, sitting on his horse also decked out in equally impressive finery, which looked to Anne like a lacy tablecloth.

"The name Fisherman's Bastion comes from the guild of fisherman who were charged with defending this section of the castle walls during the Middle Ages," Davian explained, "and the main tower of the Bastion has a multistory tower built over the remains of the former Bastion. The stairways are decorated with the stone statues of chieftains Álmos and Elöd."

The stairs, turrets, and terraces, he pointed out, were built in a blend of neo-Romanesque, neo-Gothic and Romantic styles. "White limestone was used for the construction of the five circular, crested turrets and the main tower at the northernmost point. The turrets are connected by a stone wall and guard over arcaded passages reminiscent of medieval cloisters.

"The crypt of the 15th century St. Michael Cemetery Chapel was unearthed under the Bastion, designed for decorative rather than defensive purposes." From the terraces he pointed out a magnificent view of the Pilis mountains toward the Danube Bend, Gellért Hill, and the entire Pest side.

"This area is where fishermen's wives once sold their wares and today you are here with local families and tourists stopping for snacks and shopping at souvenir stalls. Fisherman's Bastion also adjoins the Matthias Church, and other historic monuments along the Danube Banks, form a large UNESCO World Heritage Site," Davian proudly explained.

"This is why you do a tour with a local guide. You learn so much," Rolland quietly stated.

They went to the far end strolling along the highest level and stepped inside each stone turret with arched windows. "What a vantage point!" a tourist said stating the obvious.

Peter pointed out their hotel and several blocks away, the Parliament Building with Margaret Island farther down the river. "You can see everything from here." Holding a map he continued, "Look, there's Elisabeth Bridge and there are two more bridges after that. See, there's St. Stephens' Cathedral, with the historic railway station several blocks away. We'll visit those places over the next couple of days." Everything looked close together, but they knew better. Turning back to the historic square, the mossy-colored king on his trusted steed stood about the same height as they did.

Cathy alerted them, "Some poor guy is lying on the steps below." Dressed entirely in black, his dreadlocked hair matched. Then they spotted a camera crew down the steps filming him as he got up and crawled, inch by inch, step by step on all fours until he turned dramatically and lay down face up. "Not a program I'm in interested watching," an elderly woman stated matter-of-factly.

On a cobblestone path lined with boxwoods a man sat on a sun-bleached red bench by himself. Peter pointed, "Is that your Mr. Dmitry?" he teased Anne.

"He's not my Dmitry, but yes, it is. All by himself."

She noticed a dark headed stocky man standing close by. A child with a rambunctious leashed short-haired dachshund stopped near Dmitry. He bent over to pet the dog not saying a word to the child. He had a fondness for animals, not people.

He sat quietly in the sunshine, warming his back. Never once had he felt in danger or followed so he no longer colored his hair and facial hair dark brown. Any man over 60 would have gray hair and probably be balding, so at age 70 he stopped. That was 20-some years ago.

A whiff of a floral fragrance transported him 70 years earlier. He looked around hoping to see his mother. He'd been thinking of her more often than unusual. Just her, hardly ever his father. Dmitry didn't have a religious belief, but his mother had some faith, he just couldn't remember what. If there was a Heaven and Hell, she'd certainly be in Heaven. He wouldn't.

As if a character in his own life movie, he watched as his right hand reached out for a brass doorknob. He heard his mother's voice loud and clear, *STOP Son! Do not open that door. Ever!* He turned away.

He disobeyed once over the decades and had opened the door in his mind, telling himself he did what he had been told during WWII. He had followed orders. He'd overheard some prisoners speaking in Polish and he understood the language so he reported the plot of their planned escape to his superior. The next day while patrolling another barracks, he heard the familiar gun shots. Three men did not return to their quarters. He knew he was directly responsible for their deaths yet felt no remorse.

He thought about his mother. She died around his birthday when he turned 62. He really couldn't recall the year his father died. He wondered what happened to his cousins from Finland and his childhood buddies when they moved to Germany. His mother had kept him informed of life happenings but at the time they weren't essential to him. For some reason now it seemed more important, but there was no one left to ask.

True to form, after touring something or a long stroll, not really needing much of a reason, they'd find a place for coffee, pastry, gelato—something traditional. At a bakery about a block from the cathedral, Anne selected a doughnut or fánk, the sign read. It is the Hungarian version of a centuries-old, deep-fried pastry traditionally eaten in the days of Carnival. Anne selected one filled with chocolate custard, a combination she'd never tasted before. Usually, a traditionalist when it came to doughy delights, at home the closest doughnut would be called a Bismarck, filled with real vanilla custard. Peter pointed to strudel or rétes. He passed on cottage cheese, cabbage, or poppy seed types, choosing apple, his favorite.

Going by one- and two-story buildings, one dove gray, one persimmon, the next deep amber, on Fortuna Street, they peered in a window to see the country's first printing press that operated in one of its medieval houses in 1473. A wrought iron black lamppost held an invisible wire basket chock full of rosy geraniums looking like they were suspended in air.

At Holy Trinity Square, Davian explained that the monument at the center of this large square was erected out of gratitude in 1713, following the destruction caused by the Black Death. Depicted among the saints on the walls is St. Roch, patron saint of invalids and of nursing.

Fancy horsedrawn carriages lined the clean manicured square as groomed horses were ready to take tourists on sightseeing tours of the massive castle area.

Judie pointed out a Romanesque mansion that, on further inspection, is the Hungarian National Archives. Colorful two-toned buildings line the left side of the street dead ending at the brick tiled roof and the beige and tan five-story building with arched doorways and windows. "Everything is so quaint and gorgeous," she exclaimed.

On Úri street, they saw the inner courtyards of well-kept apartments and homes. "Look at the uniquely carved sapphire colorful door," Anne exclaimed. She had become addicted to colorful doors since their travels to Scotland. Dense ivy and baby-pink geraniums hung from iron railings, and ferns with colorful plants were bursting from pots on the ground. "I'd love to live on this street," Cath mentioned. Anne and Julie totally agreed.

Davian explained that Sándor Palace, located across from the Buda Castle Complex, has served as the official residence and workplace of the President of Hungary since 2003.

Perched near the corner of Buda Castle and the Habsburg Steps is an impressive statue. "It's huge," a little girl exclaimed. Davian pointed out the mythical *Turul Bird of Prey*, an imposing statue of the national bird. "It depicts a hawk or falcon. The name comes from Turkish 'Turgal' meaning a medium to large bird of prey. It is a national symbol of Hungarians, dating back to the foundations of Hungary.

"According to legend, a turul impregnated Emese, grand-mother of Árpád, the military commander who led the Magyar tribes into the Carpathian Basin around 895 AD. The bird dropped its sword in what is now modern-day Budapest, indicating to the Magyar tribes that the area was destined to be their homeland. The turul became a clan symbol of the ruling House of Árpád in the 9th and 10th centuries. This statue was cast in 1905 featuring a large bird of prey with outstretched wings and a sword in its talons."

"Yikes, that's one scary bird. Wonder if it's the inspiration of the *Angry Birds* app," a jokester added.

They had five minutes to spare before the hourly formal ceremony of the 32nd Budapest Guard and Ceremonial Regi-ment, the infantry unit that performed a Changing of the Guard. Comprised of about a dozen men marching in unison to drums, they wore rather uninspiring brown uniforms, the color of a Hershey's milk chocolate bar. They clicked their heels and performed a full goose step, each foot raised only a few inches off the ground. Each wore a thick, bright emerald rope draped over their arms.

They clomped toward a soldier who stood in a wooden aqua-colored turret. Two faced each other, flipped, and turned their rifles, crossed them, exchanged them, pointed in the air, exchanged several more times, turned around a couple of times doing a complete 360, then drums started again. They marched back together escorting the one soldier who has literally held down the fort for an hour.

Admittedly this is not the Changing of the Guard like at Buckingham Palace in London. Nor do they wear the Bearskin hats the British guards do, but it was still interesting and certainly fit the country and the castle, Anne thought to herself.

They stood in the middle of the Lion Gate and Lion Courtyard, a gate guarded by four lions. This wing of the palace is home of the National Library collection.

Sensing time for another nutritional break, they walked by a life-size suit of armor, complete with a shield, standing beside a sandwich board menu at Arany Hordó Étterem. The House of Franziska, a friendly-looking café, was perfect for their beverage stop. Coffees with foamy leaf patterns appeared. Casey had one with mile-high whipped cream that covered his entire upper lip. Anne, not being a hot beverage person, ordered a pomegranate Italian soda with whipped cream on the top.

They said their thanks and farewells to Davian, Anne giving him an Oregon Marionberry milk chocolate bar. She always carried these flat, easy to pack sweets from home to give to extra special people. He deserved one. She had convinced herself men prefer milk chocolate where women, with more discerning taste buds, usually prefer dark. She rationalized that dark is packed with antioxidants, known for health benefits and can reduce the risk of heart disease and stroke, and can also improve cognitive functions. She read and believed every word from some random health study. And it contains less sugar than milk chocolate. But to her it was all about taste and the rich flavor. She laughed thinking back to her elementary school days when as a Blue Bird, then a Camp Fire Girl, she sold boxes of round mint candy as a fundraiser. It remained her first memory of dark chocolate. Half a box was gone when her mom opened it to have one; only milk chocolate remained.

Sitting outside the hotel in the sunshine, Sandra ate a salad while her elderly husband dozed off and on. Dmitry nearly opened the black door with the brass doorknob in his mind ready to tell Sandra about South Africa and maybe WWII. He heard his mother's voice once again, *Stop son! Do not open this door no matter what*! He woke shaking his head like clearing out cobwebs. "Ready for something to eat?" his wife asked. "No, but I'll have a vodka," he said to a passing waiter.

"Let's take the funicular down," Rolland suggested. "It opened in 1870 and is the second oldest in the world. It's the fastest way down but is slow enough that we can take in the views across the river. It runs on special railway that's a 310-foot-long track with a gradient of 165 feet. Two passenger cars are named Gellért and Margit."

They stepped into Margit, a three-tiered cabin with a *Capacity 24* sign hanging inside. The cars run parallel and Gellért passed them ascending while they descended.

Two large lions greeted them on the Chain Bridge, a 1,246 feet-long and 52 feet-wide suspension bridge. The stone lions guarding the abutments are the work of Marshalko in 1852. Blown up by the retreating German Army in 1945, the rebuilt bridge returned to its original form in 1949. Cast iron chandeliers line the bridge. It's the first bridge to connect Buda and Pest and the western and eastern regions of the country.

Stopping at a few outdoor market stalls, Anne searched for just the right Christmas ornament and paprika, Hungarians' favorite spice. It's considered a national treasure. Some local scientist discovered that it contains seven times as much vitamin C as oranges. Research then led him to win the Nobel Prize in 1937.

She picked up a brochure stacked on the corner of a stall selling decorative small bags, tins and boxes of the red spice and read to Peter, *Though paprika is considered the "red gold" of Hungary, it is actually not a native plant. It was probably exported from central Mexico to Spain in the 16th century. It made its way to the Ottoman Empire via North Africa, and then to the fields of the Hungarian puzsta. Though it had grown there for a few centuries, it did not really become popular in Hungary until the 19th century. Paprika is a ground spice made from the dried and crushed red fruits of the plant known as the bell or red pepper. Its flavor ranges from mild to hot, and the heat comes from the seeds, stalks and calyces that are ground into the hot varieties. Its reddish-orange color comes from carotenoids.*

"So, this is the red stuff you sprinkle on the delicious potato salad and your award-winning deviled eggs?" Peter joked.

"Hush, there's more."

"Oh, there's always more," he teased.

She continued educating him on the wonders of paprika. *The word paprika simply means "pepper" in Hungarian, but the simplicity ends here. There are eight basic grades of Hungarian paprika:*

Erös or strong is the hottest paprika you can get. It tends to have a light brown color.

Félédes is called semi-sweet. Choose this if you want something of medium pungency.

Édesnemese or noble sweet is a bright red type with distinctive strong smell.

Csemege or delicate is a mildly hot paprika with a rich flavor.

Csípös csemege, pikáns, is pungent.

Anne noticed Peter's jet-lagged stare not focused on her litany about this remarkable spice.

"Pay attention," she flicked his left arm with her index finger.

Rózsa or rose has a strong smell but mild pungency.

Különleges or special quality is the mildest paprika. It is very sweet with a bright red color.

Paprika is used to flavor many dishes such as the famous Hungarian chicken paprikash, plus stews, soups, and the equally famous Hungarian goulash.

"I'm getting the mildly sweet kind in those cute cloth bags, with the little white scoop. There's even a recipe for Hungarian goulash," Anne said as she nabbed packages of the red powder.

"Criminy, who knew there are so many types of paprika?" Julie noted.

At the next stall, Julie and Anne selected identical Christmas ornaments knowing when they hung them annually on their trees, it would remind them of their time in Budapest.

Sitting outside back at their hotel, Cathy, Julie, and Anne ordered Aperol Spritzes while others requested iced tea, Hungarian beer called Dreher, and wine. Relaxing and regaining their strength and fortitude to carry on, someone mentioned the river. Anne pulled out a flyer she picked up somewhere. "Want to hear about the river?" barely waiting for anyone to answer before launching into her dramatic readings like she did for Peter.

Flowing east from Germany and Austria all the way to Romania and the Black Sea reaching across the European continent, its tributaries gather water from 19 countries making the Danube the most international river on Earth.

To discover this unique river, we start at the very top. Over 13,000 feet above sea level Piz Bernina Mountain in Switzerland is the highest point of the entire Danube system. Here, almost 900 million tons of water is locked in as ice. The Morteratsch Glacier, 4 miles long and 800 feet deep, is covered in snow for most of the year. When temperatures rise in spring, and conditions are just right, it's an unstoppable force of nature fueling the flow of the Danube River across the continent all the way to the Black Sea. Its journey has only just begun.

A few miles away on the slopes of the valley below, the melting snow makes way for new beginnings. As the meltwaters run on, they join countless other streams and tributaries flowing from all corners of the Danube system.

Huchen, also known as the Danube salmon, can grow over 3 feet long and are the largest freshwater salmon in the world.

As they flow down from the headwaters and alpine valleys, the Danube tributaries finally come together to become this great river. Towns, farmland, and cities begin to line its route. Over thousands of years people have established towns on its banks and have tamed the river, straightened and engineered to help protect against annual flooding.

Having passed through Germany, Austria and Slovakia, the Danube is now at the midpoint of its great journey and arrives in Hungary at the majestic capital of Budapest, a city that owes its existence to the Danube.

In Budapest no less than seven bridges showcase a place that has been the source of cultural inspiration through the ages. Today it is as important as ever. Water might be one of the oldest means of transport, but it's still the cheapest. And Budapest, because of its unique location, is key to the Danube's continued success as the backbone of the European transport network.

"It's easy to see the importance of the river to everyday life in Budapest," Rolland mentioned.

"Time out. I need a drink." Anne took a breath as their friends contemplated what they should do next. Anne handed the flyer to Julie, who continued.

Here in Hungary, the Danube's waters may seem slow and sluggish but by this stage of its journey the Danube has been joined by its major tributaries, the Drava, the Tisza, and the Sava. Combined, they almost triple its flow as it reaches its third and final capital city, Belgrade, in Serbia.

Over half a mile wide and discharging 1.5 million gallons per second, this now mighty river flows towards the border with Romania and one of the last great landmarks on its epic journey, the Iron Gate Gorge in the Carpathian Mountains, the border of Romania and Serbia, 62 miles long and shrinking to just 500 feet wide.

For thousands of years, all traffic on the river had to pass this daunting gateway. The narrow gorge with towering cliffs is infamous for its dangerous rapids and whirlpools making passage in a boat extremely treacherous. The Big Boilers is the strait that separates the Carpathians from the Balkan Mountains.

The dissertation conjured up in Peter's mind cruising through Misty Fjords in Alaska with rock walls bursting from the water virtually blocking the sun.

But in the 1970s, this part of the Danube was changed forever, when engineers harnessed the river's power and created the Iron Gates Dam, one of the largest hydroelectric plants in Europe. This giant feat of engineering produces 5½ million megawatts of electricity, relied upon by 25 million people in Romania and Serbia.

Below the dam, the Danube enters the lowlands of Romania and Bulgaria. At the last stage of its epic journey, the Danube has finally arrived saving the greatest surprise till last: The Danube Delta. Passing through Romania and Ukraine, this mighty river finally breaks free. At almost 2,000 square miles this is the largest undisturbed wetland in Europe. A place that is only accessible in one way, by boat. There are more than 300 species of birds here.

The Great White Pelican with 17,000 breeding pairs is the largest colony in the world outside of Africa. And their numbers are increasing. For just a few months they'll nest here and feed on the Delta's bounty working together in giant flotillas to feast on fish.

The Danube heads into the Black Sea and beyond. The Danube's waters have flowed through more countries than any river on Earth, through a continent separated by borders and changed by humanity, but despite these challenges, always finding a way to keep going, to inspire, and even astonish."

"Whew, who knew all that info about the river? We need to walk. Let's go ride the Ferris wheel," Julie concluded.

Casey mentioned he needed some protein, so instead of making it to the wheel, they stopped at a café ordering mostly a variety of appetizers. Anne and Peter split her favorite pizza, Margherita, with fresh tomatoes, globs of mozzarella cheese and leaves of fragrant basil.

Rationalizing they'd gone over five miles, including stairs, tempting them were scrumptious desserts in the display case: Dobos torte, a sponge cake layered with chocolate butter-cream and shiny, brittle caramel topping; Esterházy torte, a sponge cake alternating layers of ground walnuts and rum-laced buttercream with a white fondant coating. Interestingly, the cake contains no flour.

Kathy asked for something light, and the waiter suggested Gesztenyeszív, chestnut paste treats coated in crackly chocolate cut in the shape of a heart.

"I've got to try these," Mike said, pointing to something interesting, Tepertös-szilvás papucs, prune jam and pork cracklings. He reported after the first bite, "Delicious! Sweet and savory in a light pastry." He wasn't sharing a bite.

Sharon and Phil shared Somlói Galuska and when it arrived everyone howled at the 10-inch mound dessert. The rum-infused sponge cake soaked in vanilla custard, chocolate cream and whipped cream, with a sprinkling of walnuts and raisins, reminded Anne of white glaciers on a mountain in Alaska. The whipped cream portions had dark chocolate sauce streaming down. "We're getting that next time," Anne said to Peter.

They didn't make it to the Ferris wheel that night, back in their hotel room by 8 and fast asleep by 8:30.

CHAPTER THREE

Next morning Buda Castle and a row of light clouds reflected in the water. To the left, the Chain Bridge glistened in the sunshine. Traffic on the river moved along at a brisk pace. They had a new appreciation for this river after Anne's and Julie's informative reading the previous day.

Another quirk of Anne's, cute theme socks: travel, books, penguins, puffins, all her favorite things. Getting ready, she slipped on a new pair her friend Shawn had given her for her birthday. *She had Traveled Far* printed in white on sky blue with airplanes were perfect for today.

The hotel breakfast buffet was another feast of any type of eggs one could wish for, items for a full-English breakfast, and finger-licking pastries. Anne took two of the mini-square croissants chock full of dark chocolate chips, along with a grilled tomato with a slice of provolone cheese, three slices of crisp bacon, and a token spoonful of protein in the form of scrambled eggs. A small plate of watermelon and grapefruit would be plenty to start another day of their vacation.

She eyed Peter's rolled croissant with a thick layer of

cinnamon as he said, "Don't even think about it." "I know, I know," she chuckled.

After a luscious breakfast, today they were on their own for explorations. With their handy guidebook, and downloaded information on their phones, they felt confident they could navigate and learn more about this fascinating city.

It didn't take much to quickly conclude that Budapest has if not thousands, at least hundreds of statues. They stood by a statue of a boy sitting on a fence with a four-pointed cap on his head. Originally the statue was black, but his pant legs were now bronze. Anne took a picture of Julie with her hand on his right shiny knee with Buda Castle in the background.

They came upon another statue of a sweet girl sitting on a planter at the base of a lamppost playing with her feisty dog who securely held on to a ball in its mouth as she tried to pull it away. His ears have been rubbed bronze. Bronze William Shakespeare is taking a humble bow outside the Starbucks, all within a few blocks of their hotel.

Anne knew she might be considered odd by some and didn't care. She always took a photo of a manhole cover in each city. She'd discovered most were intricately designed and Budapest's didn't disappoint, with leaf-patterned scrollwork and *Fovarost csatornazasi Muvek ZRT. EN 124-D400EME A-1004* inscribed around the circular covering for a hole in the sidewalk. Another one read *Budapest Elektromos MUVEK TULAJDONA* with designs of water droplets surrounding a compass, with a shield in the middle.

She normally looked up not down, but manhole covers were cool. Another must-do were pictures of license plate frames on police vehicles for her county-sheriff brother, and the country's flag.

They approached an electric car in a display case on Váci Street. Anne observed Dmitry scrutinizing it through the plexiglass. She pointed him out to Peter and said, "I wonder what people of his generation think about electric cars and all the technical advances in vehicles over the decades."

"Probably the same as our folks being around his age. They can hardly believe it and think gas engines are the only thing that will work for vehicles," he answered.

Dmitry felt out of breath and sat down on the closest bench. Resting, he found himself daydreaming of his times in South Africa. These memories were coming more often recently. Not surprisingly, some of his thoughts had gotten jumbled over the years.

When Dmitry arrived in early 1947, running for his life from the Jewish Revenge Squads, he stepped into Cape Town's enormous growth in both industry and population. The harbor and industrial sites were extended, and modern buildings rose almost overnight. Attractive residential areas spread along the lower mountain slopes and more roadways were being constructed to connect city with the countryside.

The only thing that frightened him after the war were Holocaust survivors who joined Jewish Revenge Squads, sometimes referred to as "Din" squads. "Din" being Hebrew for revenge, they set out to find those who they believed were guilty of crimes against humanity and took the law into their own hands.

The men they found were given no formal trial as their guilt sealed their fate. Teams of three or four operated and were responsible for the deaths of hundreds of ranking Nazi officials. Officially, all captured were under the Geneva Convention. It was made clear by authorities that senior Nazis had to be imprisoned to allow for interrogation. However, the squads had no intention of being held to this order. Dmitry read in an international newspaper that dozens were murdered by squads in the last few months. Only his mother knew his whereabouts.

He assumed his new life would be a solitary one. However, through his job and getting to know coworkers he found himself invited to social events. As it turned out, he liked playing tennis, where he met plenty of women. He easily adapted to his new homeland and stepped into a job where he could use his linguistic skills when needed. He had a head for numbers. Numbers never changed; he could rely on that.

Dmitry thought the banking industry would be a great place to start. He began as a bank teller, a few months later an account clerk, then promoted to a payroll specialist and six months later, billing specialist. He infiltrated British society with his impeccable British accent and average looks. If he found himself in a jam having to share details about himself, his mother was British and father Russian; that's how he got the name Dmitry. His father and the Russian part was true.

To him it felt like yesterday when he stood on the sidewalk dressed in finery along with throngs of Brits on February 17 chanting "God Save the King" which turned out to be a highlight of his life. The Royal Family, King George VI, his wife Queen Elizabeth, and their two daughters, Princess Elizabeth, age 20, and Princess Margaret, 16, disembarked the battle cruiser, HMS *Vanguard*, and descended the gangplank to a 21-gun salute. They were taken to the 14-car *White Train*, dubbed the *Palace on Wheels*, their home for a two-month journey through Africa.

The local press proudly showed a photo of HMS *Vanguard* with Table Mountain in the background. When Princess Elizabeth celebrated her 21st birthday on April 21 in South Africa, page after page in print covered every moment.

He read the daily coverage in the newspaper and saw

pictures of the thousands of people who rolled out the red carpet to greet them. Small girls curtseyed and presented bouquets of flowers. The King could be seen addressing a crowd, as well as the young Princess Elizabeth taking in everything the country had to offer.

For two months every day the newspaper covered the royal family traveling around their country visiting hospitals, schools, national parks, orphanages, charities, museums, attending tribal ceremonies, and inspecting diamonds. Thousands lined train stations as the Royals whistle-stopped their way inland. Commemorative medallions and stamps were made to honor the visit.

He would read later that it had been a momentous year for Princess Elizabeth with the great South African adventure, coming of age, her engagement in July, and marriage to Philip four months later.

A friend from work introduced him to Sarah Bailey, whose grandfather and family came over as British settlers in the late 1800s with groups of people from England. He learned some British history from her. Men came with all kinds of skills: blacksmiths, builders, carpenters, gardeners, millwrights, jewelers, cabinet makers, bakers, farmers, shoemakers, harness makers, horse breeders, plowmen, tailors, painters, teachers, surveyors, surgeons, wine merchants, the captain of the 54th regiment, ministers, one medical student, schoolmasters, master mariners—hundreds of men many times without their wives, who sometimes came later.

Dmitry and affable Sarah dated for 11 months before he thought he should end the relationship or propose marriage. Not sure he knew what it felt like to be in love, this might be close enough. Three years after he'd arrived in Cape Town, he attended his own wedding and purchased his first home, with a loan from the bank where he worked.

When the King of England died unexpectedly on

February 6, 1952, Dmitry recalled five years earlier standing on the sidewalk, seeing the Royal Family. He felt conflicted when hearing the news of the King's death and not confident the young princess could replace her father, himself being only several years older than the young Queen of England. He'd found himself like many others who had said, "The day I met the Royal family…"

1952 wasn't the best year for Dmitry. Sarah divorced him. It was short-lived with little or no explanation, and produced no grandchild, much to her parents' chagrin. It certainly wasn't his fault. Sitting in Budapest, old and confused, he tried to recall what happened to them, but cluttered thoughts evaded an answer.

He recalled selling the house, giving her half the money, moving back into a downtown apartment, and receiving another promotion at the bank, now a financial analyst. Somebody told him he could be president one day: his reply always being, "No thanks."

Sarah's only comments to her mother were that her husband expected to be admired and needed compliments all the time. If he wasn't being showered with praise, he became agitated. The nightmares didn't help, and he drank too much. Vodka straight. He had a few blackouts after being violently sick.

She was mentally and physically exhausted and couldn't even recall why she married him. She told her mother, "He thinks his mere existence is a gift to the world. I'm not perfect and I'm done trying," laughing and crying at the same time as her mother wrapped her arms around her, letting her young divorcée daughter sob.

Dmitry rejected any type of help, constructive criticism, and wouldn't accept anyone's advice. He wasn't the one who needed to change, the rest of the world did.

Yet he continued to work his way up through the bank

with no aspirations to be vice president or to have the responsibilities of being president, overseeing the entire place. Nor did he want people prying into his background, which he thought would be the case should he move into one of those roles.

He'd been in and out of short-term relationships, ending if they didn't fawn over him enough. At a party one night he overheard some blonde he'd spent a couple of nights with say, "He's convinced himself of his superiority and expects that others will recognize his exceptional qualities and tell him so. I didn't." He could have cared less what she thought.

Dmitry started looking over his shoulder more often. Paranoid, he suspected operatives were all over South Africa picking up German Nazi war criminals, as they were called. Anyone who worked for the SS were returned to Germany and were prosecuted at the Nuremberg Trials on a daily basis. Many were sentenced to life, hung, or shot, for doing their jobs, he pontificated, always to himself downing another shot of cheap vodka. He felt righteously indignant but spoke to no one.

One artsy building prompted Peter to recall Gaudi's handiwork throughout Barcelona. This street is known as Fashion Street, the famous shopping and pedestrian avenue packed with stores and gift shops, plus a fountain or two. Hermes Fountain, with a full-frontal view of a nude Hermes with wings on his feet, holds a staff while the other arm points to the sky. He supposedly was a messenger of the Greek gods and attendant of the dead souls. Close by, the four-story Thonet House, an art nouveau masterpiece, is decked out in flowers, ram heads, and colorful blue tiles. The wrought iron banisters separate the residential upper stories from the store below which once sold the famed bentwood furniture of the Thonet Brothers.

Anne's women friends stopped frequently, gawking at the high-end store display windows. A shoe store window with rows of sneakers starting at the top with lemon yellow, cinnamon, cherry red, and raspberry, each with matching laces except the black ones with bright fuchsia laces.

Walking along they came to a stall of souvenirs. Carts of paprika, rows of hard candies, vines of colorful licorice-looking candy, marzipan cookies of all flavors and colors, with the Ferris wheel not far away. Purchases were made; some consumed and some to take home as souvenirs and gifts.

They ambled by one of the large and most impressive fountains, Danubius Fountain at Elisabeth Square, where the marble statue of bearded Danubius represents the river. Supporting the basin are symbols of the three main tributaries, Tisza, Drava, and Sava.

Built in 1883, the tributaries' symbols are strong-looking women. Walking closer they could see three seated women figures. Each of them proudly shows their nice round bosoms, but carefully covering their legs. Above them is a man with almost nothing to hide, rowing on a dolphin with a loose-fitting cape on his shoulders, a paddle in one hand and a seashell in the other.

Anne noticed a group under a tree and recalled reading about free city tours by locals; tips were never turned down. They joined in. Cutting through St. Stephen's Cathedral Square they saw families, children on scooters, bikes, trikes, and babies in strollers. One girl, maybe about eight years old, wore pink strapped sandals, white socks, a bright pink dress with white daisies and purple dots, and a fashionable white hat with a curled rim. Her braided ponytail hung down her back. She carried a water bottle. If it had been April, Anne thought she'd be dressed for Easter.

"What a contrast, that flat, unattractive modern building on the left, then stunning St. Stephen's Cathedral," Rolland observed. Twin towers flank the domed cathedral. "Wonder why it's not very green?" a child pointing to the dome asked a parent. "Good question," Peter agreed.

Almost reverently, they carefully stepped on impressive marble mosaics of swirling patterns, with colors of cinnamon, cream, and a bit of black and tan, before walking up several dozen steps to the sprawling broad front, and massive entrance. Standing on the staircase, each turned to face the colorful square offering a splendid view.

They stepped inside. "Holy moly," Casey murmured looking around at the entrance shaped like an arch. Anne heard the words "enormous," "imposing," "humbling," and she agreed. A pair of Corinthians support the kettledrum. Whole reliefs portray the Hungarian saints paying homage to the Virgin Mary, guardian of Hungary. A mosaic between the columns depicts St. Stephen and the resurrection of Christ. The dome is over 213 feet high and 72 feet in diameter. This is what they saw in the span of about five minutes.

Judie noticed there would be a concert that afternoon. They bought tickets and would return for the 30-minute musical, plus seeing more of the interior.

Casey pointed to a black statue of a life-size sculpture of a hefty policeman named *Rendör, Guardian of Order*, standing on cobblestones outside the Costa Coffee with a view of the cathedral. He wears a long overcoat with his arms folded behind him, which makes his large stomach more prominent in shiny bronze.

Cutting through massive buildings of all types of architecture, the group ended up along the river reaching an unforgettable memorial just south of the Parliament Building.

The guide told them that nearly 80,000 Jews were expelled from Hungary in a death march to the Austrian border, and approximately 20,000 Jews were brutally shot along the banks of the Danube. The victims were forced to remove their shoes at gunpoint, shoes being valuable during WWII, and to look at their executioner before they were shot without mercy, falling over the edge to be washed away by the freezing waters. *Shoes on the Danube* Promenade is a haunting tribute to this horrific time in history. The monument consists of 60 pairs of 1940s-style shoes, true to life and detail, sculpted out of iron. A man's work boots, a businessman's loafers, a pair of women's heels, even the tiny shoes of a child, were chosen specifically to illustrate how no one, regardless of age, gender, or occupation was spared, the guide concluded.

Anne noticed how the shoes were placed in a casual fashion, as if the people just stepped out of them. They didn't stay long; sadness gripped their hearts.

In the river, a half-submerged bright yellow bus with River Ride written in maroon and cobalt on the side, floated down river.

After walking so far, someone suggested it seemed time for a break. Ordering an assortment of teas and coffees, Anne requested iced tea and pointed out something called an Indiáner, puffy black-and-white cake blanketed in chocolate and split by a layer of whipped cream. Cathy ordered a Krémes, a vanilla custard enclosed in a puff pastry, which Anne would have another time. "Those look like a lot of work," one woman appreciatively admired. A man remarked, "So many pastries, not enough time."

Scooting back toward St. Stephen's, they went past thousands of locks, love locks or so they are called, mounted on special structures designed expressly for locks. A specific area has been set up to discourage putting the locks on bridges that become too heavy. A round one stood out, not the usual square lock size. *Agnes loves Paulo* with five hearts. *2016.07.08.* "Oops," Anne said. "There's a black X across it. So much for him."

They had about 30 minutes to take in the magnificent sights of the cathedral by looking up at panels and windows letting in sunlight. One is Moses or Jesus, with outstretched arms in a white flowy robe and dark cape, with blue sky and clouds at his feet like he's floating. Five rays of white shot out behind him. He is surrounded by dozens of cherubs with their wings securing them in a square panel. The next row looked like famous biblical figures.

Another mosaic shows the Holy Father surrounded by the figures of Jesus, the angels, and the prophets. The four evangelists are depicted in the arched triangles under the dome. The central altar and vaulted ceilings with statues, frescoes, and the stations at the cross are remarkable. The flooring could cause some dizziness with the overlapping charcoal and brick-colored square tiles around the room, and various inlaid designs. The designs reminded Anne of the American southwest.

The dark wood organ stands like a guard at the back, watching what's going. It is magnificent with a large window in the ceiling above, letting in light to highlight its brilliance.

Anne poked Peter and pointed to an arched stained glass window of a white-haired and long-bearded man in a red robe trimmed in royal purple, holding a staff in his right hand and a book with a teal cover in his left. Not Jesus, but somebody important. They couldn't get close enough to read the plaque.

Peter whispered, "I think this rivals St. Peter's in Rome." Anne nodded.

Details on the tile work, the gold leafing, the stone carving, intricate paintings, and statues were over-the-top gorgeous. The sun shining through the upper windows illuminated the entire gallery and stunning nave.

Anne stood at the massive altar of the Virgin Mary where the altarpiece depicts St. Stephen offering the Virgin the crown that represents his country. The high altar, with the life-size Carrara marble statue of St. Stephen, gleamed in the sunlight. It looked fluorescent as if someone plugged it in for an even greater special effect. The statue stands in an apse of the sanctuary. The bronze reliefs in the background show scenes from the life of the first king of Hungary. The patches of the semidome above the sanctuary have been covered with mosaics picturing the mass. Everywhere glittered gold, with dabs of celadon and Aegean here and there.

They sat down on uncomfortable straight back wooden chairs assuring that no one could possibly fall asleep during the organ extravaganza. The music pounded from the back echoing around the interior. The numbers selected were unrecognizable to the Oregonians, but it didn't matter. The combination of musical drama left most entranced. Anne couldn't tell if Phil was praying or sleeping with his head down.

Outside, they strolled along an avenue with window displays of leather belts, shoes, purses, clothing, and all types of glassware in clear, light blue and royal blue. Lampposts held iron baskets of trailing magenta geraniums. Hand-painted colorful tiles lined windows of buildings three and four stories high. A Breitling 1884 black clock with white hands showed 3:45 as the aromatic Linden trees in full bloom caused Peter to sneeze.

Two completely different styles of porcelain fountains stood outside of stores, an advertisement of what could be just steps away. One contained gigantic lilac-colored buds about to burst open with chartreuse and soft lime leaves and an eggplant vine winding around and up to the top. On one side, three colorful carved birds sat on the vines.

The other fountain situated in the middle of a stone pool had six spigots shooting water, creating a white foam on the aqua water. A mom held back her toddler who really wanted to take a dip.

Inside the stores were intricately handpainted Hungarian porcelain vases, bowls, pitchers, boxes, cups and saucers, teapots, platters, decanters, and more in uncountable designs.

Cathy drooled over a tall white vase, covered in dainty blue flowers with gold leaves and vines. One display case showed off Vaza design: a pinkish-violet colored flower with moss and gold leaves in vases of all sizes and heights, bowls, squared boxes with matching lids, down to the smallest, a pill box. The hefty shelf below held Mokkakeszlet, which would have been Anne's choice, with aqua, teal, and peachy flowers, also with dozens of vases and boxes. A heart-shaped box, and a tall, elegant teapot with cups and saucers caught her eye. The price tag read 40.900, equivalent to a reasonable $115. Each piece handpainted Hungarian porcelain by Zsolnay Pécs.

Julie stepped into a room with Anne close on her heels. Both sucked in a breath of air, standing in one spot, rotating their heads at the visual eye-candy of shelf after shelf of porcelain caricatures and animals. Owls, ducks, frogs, starfish, geese, roosters, pigs, and a white frosted donut on one shelf were all pink with gray dots. Right above it, in the same design, were hippos, kangaroos, elephants, zebra, rabbits, and much more but in baby blue. The grand finale was a roaring tiger.

In another cabinet the figurines were all white, with carroty triangles, mostly on bunnies of different shapes and sizes, in different stances holding a purple tulip, and one behind a bright pumpkin. Julie pointed out the bunny with a blue cap and matching scarf. The insides of their ears were all white except for some soft aqua. Anne would have purchased the bunny with a teal swath and white design on its head sitting in a colorful hot air balloon if she and Peter still had their hot air balloon, Valley Sunrise. She collected anything with balloons for decades when it was their pastime.

While Julie investigated another display case, Anne found her souvenir. Her infatuation with penguins led her right to one. She and Peter had been fortunate to see the Little Penguins Parade at the seaside haven of Phillips Island on the southern tip of Australia, the tiniest in the world, and the second smallest in the Galápagos Islands. She'd return later to pick it up, not wanting to carry it all day.

They looked but didn't enter the store with a four foot vase painted teal with white lilies, a two foot tall colorful toucan, and a large-as-life seafoam iguana with carroty spikes down its back into its tail. It reminded Peter of the vibrant land iguanas they'd seen in the Galápagos Islands.

Anne spotted an elderly woman dressed in brown slacks and a tan blouse carrying a lightweight jacket and purse walking across the street. She stepped into a store. "Look, that's Mrs. Dmitry. Alone." Anne pointed her out to Peter.

"And that matters to us why?" he asked innocently.

"Umm, just an observation, that's all."

"Uh-huh," she heard him utter.

Across the street outside the Omega store, hands pointed to the three and eight gold chunks on the four foot, peachy gold clock.

A young man pedaled his bike through traffic. He wore a stark white- and bright neon fuchsia-colored shirt carrying a Foodpanda box strapped to his back.

"Treat time," one of their weary shoppers said as they darted into Múvész Kávéház. The outdoor sign read, *Coffee, Tea, Cocktail, Cake, Breakfast, Sandwich. Alapítva since 1898.* Display cases full of sweet treats waited for them. The rich gold interior with dark wood looked like other cool coffee houses. They sat on a long brown leather bench and took turns going to the round tiered case pointing at all of the delights: raspberry chocolate cake, caramel cake with orange slices, lime tart, white chocolate mousse, Belgian chocolate cake, apple walnut tart, plus about a dozen more scrumptious looking treats.

The first bite of rich raspberry chocolate cake tasted divine. Anne closed her eyes, savoring every morsel. Peter's apple walnut tart tasted delicious, minus Anne's more dramatic descriptions and arm gestures. She wasn't the only one in a sweetened euphoria.

After the sweets break, it was time to move on. It was impressive enough standing at the front of the Opera House with its main façade of the statues of four Greek Muses that stand in the corner niches. The creamy white crown molding holds most well-known opera composers like Mozart, Beethoven, Verdi, and others. But stepping inside the main entrance decorated in Carrara marble sphinxes and a magnificent iron candelabra caused several in the group to gasp with oohs and aahs. The marble staircase winds upward, and the ceiling is decorated with vibrant frescoes.

A guide led them into the dimly lit horseshoe-shaped auditorium flanked by four tiers of theater boxes. Their guide pointed out the king's box, as ornate as one would expect adorned with statues symbolizing the four main voices. The ceiling is partly covered by a huge fresco entitled "Mt. Olympus and the Gods." The magnificent hues of gold and copper of the theater is enhanced by an over 6,600 pound bronze chandelier. The black and white flooring all done in mini-mosaic tiles had a dizzying effect on Anne.

Four thespians were practicing on an all-white stage. In the semi-darkness, Anne and friends marveled at the ornate ceiling and huge chandelier, and rows of box seats about three-quarters of the way around.

Between every other seat are golden crowned heads swooping back to a tail with arches of aqua and gold separating groups of boxes.

When somebody turned the lights on, an entirely new room appeared before their eyes. Each box of seats has rich red upholstered fabric on the back wall. There's a chandelier in each arch and alcove. The magnificent chandelier in the middle of the room has countless lights and layers of gold. The medallion is surrounded by floating people draped in colorful capes and gowns, playing instruments. They sat for minutes soaking in the awesomeness of this room.

They walked on red carpeting to the second floor seeing frescoes on the ceiling, more huge chandeliers, and impressive paintings, the party room for sure. The bar stretched the length of the entire hall. Along the back are private rooms for the rich and famous. They all sneaked a peek. Outside they stood on a limestone balcony, looking at ornate buildings and blue sky.

Another level took them to a grand hall, with reddish marble columns that line the corridor and expansive arches above the red-carpeted staircase. The room was packed with busts of famous people. Cathy and Julie leaned against Queen Victoria for a break.

Sitting casually on two sets of stairs covered in plush red carpeting, they were treated to a mini-concert. A soprano with long chestnut hair flowing down her back, dressed in a low-cut cherry-red gown, was preparing herself for a special event. A bothersome man tries to get her attention by singing as she is brushing her hair, applying makeup, and making herself beautiful.

It's playful with a flare of drama and comedy as he does everything within his power in his strong tenor voice to capture her attention. She hands him a mannequin head from her dressing table, and he sings to it while dancing around the room. She indignantly grabs the head as he keeps singing away. She begins singing and he falls to the floor, stunned by her voice and beauty. She puts her hands on her hips like she's telling him he's a drama king, both laughing and thoroughly enjoying their back-and-forth banter in Italian. Their duet ended with both holding hands and singing to each other.

Leaving the Opera House and hopping on the Metro, they got off a few stops later and wandered into the Standrea Wine & Skybar. The view overlooks the Ferris wheel, cathedral, and tiled rooftops. Anne, Cathy, and Julie each ordered the same refreshing beverage, a French '75, a blend of gin, blood orange juice, Prosecco, and lemon juice with a dash of sugar. They watched the mixologist create the peachy-colored drinks, each receiving the exact same amount of this and that. Julie took a picture of smiley Anne holding her peachy concoction. Anne was in her happy place, touring a historic, artsy city with loved ones. They shared potato wedges smothered in gorgonzola, grated parmesan cheese, and crispy bacon bits.

Following the Skybar and strolling by a gelato place, several stepped in. Anne rarely passed up gelato and although the bright blue Smurfs looked revolting, the blueberry, Snickers, Bounty, dark chocolate, Vienna Coffee, raspberry cheesecake, mango passion fruit, strawberry, and several more were tempting. Anne stuck with her favorite—lemon. Walking through the square, gelato in hand, they stood for 20 minutes enjoying a six-person band with their vocalist performing songs in Hungarian.

The group popped into Marty's Kitchen & Bar most ordering a bowl of Hungarian goulash and some dense bread for a light dinner. Julie read the menu aloud: *The origins of goulash date back to the 9th century as a simple meat and onion stew prepared in heavy iron kettles. While the rest of Europe remained lukewarm toward the red chili pepper, Hungary embraced it and paprika has since become a defining element of Hungarian cuisine.*

"It's kind of a mix between a soup and a stew, but not overly packed full of beef and vegetables, a bit more brothy," Peter tasted.

Pulling the curtains closed and saying good night to their castle across the river, the couple recapped their day. Anne jotted down some notes to help her recall what they had seen. It always took her a while to unwind so she kept writing, no longer miffed after all these years that Peter could fall asleep in four seconds.

CHAPTER FOUR

R olland mentioned that if they wanted to walk to Heroes' Square it would take around 45 minutes. Mike said, "We've been on foot plenty the past three days; I'll ask the front desk what they suggest." Moments later all agreed they'd take the train for $1 arriving in 15 minutes.

They stood in front of the famous *BUDAPEST* sign with a tall white column in the background. Heroes' Square is a huge monument commemorating soldiers fallen in the world wars.

A group of men looking very official arrived dressed in black with silver trim and pointy silver hats. They carried swords in their white-gloved hands. This began a parade of men in uniform.

The next troop wore drab army green, but their colorful collars, belts, medals, and patches brightened them up. They carried shiny swords in their gloved hands, too. One carried a pole with a flag.

Then the horse brigade arrived. Four men dressed in navy and silver uniforms, each sitting on black saddles atop a red blanket on their gorgeous brown horses with black manes.

A police car with *Rendörség* written in blue on the hood must have represented the town. Anne did a quick Google search and informed Peter pointing, "It's the National Civil Law Enforcement Agency of Hungary." Travel sometimes offers unexpected opportunities and treats, like this one.

Music got louder and louder as a marching band performed. Young men were dressed in red jackets and black pants with shiny instruments that gleamed in the sunshine. The next band wore black, and two men carried the largest tubas Anne had ever seen. Marching and music, pomp and circumstance, all honoring law enforcement.

The huge *Chariot of War* statue depicts a soldier with two horses running at full speed in the interior nook of the colonnade. Archangel Gabriel, his right bare leg showing through his cape, reaches upward holding the gold Holy Crown in his right hand and a golden double cross in his left. Against the blue sky, he looked ready to be transported to Heaven.

The massive *Chariot of Peace* statue stands on the right. "It's my favorite," Cathy announced. "Look at the difference between the horses from the *Chariot of War*. They are softer, calmer and the soldier's arm is motioning toward people, not like the war soldier ready to whip the horse with that snake-looking rope." Anne always appreciated Cathy's art teacher insight.

The Millennium Monument dominating the square was built for the millennium of the Magyar conquest and the existence of Hungary. The construction began in 1896 and was completed in 1929. The total length of the two parts of the semicircular colonnade is 280 feet designed with an impressive 120-foot-tall pillar at the center. The bronze figure protectively spreading his wings at the top of the pillar is Gabriel. The pedestal carries the equestrian statues of the seven conquering chiefs and Prince Árpád in the middle.

The statues of Hungarian kings, princes, and commanders have been positioned between the columns of the arched colonnade, with seven distinguished people on both sides. They looked at the reliefs below each bronze statue depicting historical scenes from the lives of the respective hero.

During WWII, the decorative pavement was destroyed but restored in 1938 keeping with the original design. For over a hundred years the square has been used as a place for celebrations, rallies, and demonstrations.

Anne poked Peter, "Look, there's Dmitry. Without his wife."

"Maybe she's jet-lagged."

"A youngish woman just approached him. That seems odd."

"Odd why?" Peter asked.

Anne gave him her "Really?" look.

The City Park is Budapest's largest and located just north of Heroes' Square. Sycamores, maples, and horse chestnut trees are scattered about. They read that the City Park used to be a swamp, and where Hungarian kings were elected between the 13th and 16th centuries. It was also a favorite hunting ground of noblemen.

Trees in the territory were planted later. The swamp was drained and the field transformed into an English style park in the 18th to 19th centuries when the emperor declared establishment of a national garden where people could relax and entertain in a nice environment. The City Park was among the first public parks in the world to open for relaxation. Adults were pushing strollers, there were people on skates, and boaters on the pond.

With a choice of riding or walking about one and half

miles back, the map indicated that if they walked straight down Andrássy Avenue it would link them back to Elisabeth Square.

Walking down the avenue flanked by fancy villas built during the 18th to 19th centuries, and sycamore and horse chestnut trees, Cathy said, "This takes me back to strolling the avenues of Paris with the majestic old trees, magnificent homes and buildings, and wide streets with views from one end to the other."

They were in no rush on this lovely day. "It's definitely comparable to the Champs-Elysées in Paris," Anne agreed with Cathy. Reaching the familiar Opera House and St. Stephen's, they detoured, meandering through Vidal Park on their way to the Transport Museum, one of Europe's oldest transportation collections.

An airplane with a bright blue propeller on the top of the building grabs one's attention and interest to go inside. A red train engine poking out from one portion of the building at the entrance, and a train car driving through a wall on the other end, are all great forms of advertising. Peter thought himself sort of a railway connoisseur and enjoyed the unique collection of locomotives and wagons. It showcases all types of transportation, with a railway model and navigation collections.

Thirsty, a few had a beer and sodas at a bar made from a railway carriage on the grounds of the museum. Darting into a café with its windows lined with inviting pastries, they shared a plate of Minyons—dainty, bite-size, delicate French cakes that look like petit fours at home. The color of icing indicates the flavor of buttercream filing: brown for coffee, dark for chocolate. "Is pink for strawberry?" Anne asked.

"No, pink is our most favorite with rum-soaked sponge cake inside," came the reply.

Rolland made sounds showing his appreciation for

Flódni, a rich cake layered with plum jam, apple, ground walnuts and ground poppy seeds. "I wonder what this would taste like with apricot jam. We should try this at home," he suggested to Judie.

Judie and Cathy ordered Punch torte, a rich cake with a striking pink icing enveloping the outside. A layer of apricot preserves and raisins are sandwiched between rows of rum-infused sponge cakes.

Julie had a couple of Linzer and Isler cookies, both jam-filled cookies except there's a chocolate glaze that blankets the Isler. Two women didn't even speak a word eating Rigó Jancsi, a cube-shaped, chocolate cream-filled chocolate sponge cake; chocoholics love this one.

"I've hit the wall," Peter said. "I'm heading back to the hotel." Several weary males agreed, trailing along like a herd of turtles.

"I'll text you a place for you to meet us for dinner in a couple of hours," Anne told Peter.

Anne needed to return to the store where she would purchase a gift for herself with cash her mother had given her earlier, with specific instructions to find something special for herself. After checking out all her options, she had to return for something unique indeed.

Stepping into one of the porcelain shops they visited earlier, she reached for the penguin that would join three others at home that she'd also found in special places: a black and white glass figurine with its wings out on each side like it was steadying itself, from a store in the Galápagos Islands, a mini-mosaic tile one from an art shop near Phillips Island in Australia, and a larger black and white one from her mother. Her new cherished remembrance stood about five inches high, with shiny gold beak and feet. Its wings were trimmed in baby blue with a red swath, and black and lime with matching green under its chin. A red sideways V surrounds its eyes on both sides. Its body is all white with black diamond shapes outlined all over. Now she or he would be secured in bubble wrap and going home with Anne. It spoke to her, like all art or jewelry had to.

Cathy, Judie, Julie and Anne wandered through several more shops picking up treasures from Budapest to take home as gifts. Anne and Judie found matching scarves in beige and coral tones. They waved at Sharon and Kathy darting into a candy store. Kathy was their resident expert in fudge and caramel corn. Lucky for them, she always bought enough to share.

The ladies walked down the promenade looking for an outdoor café for dinner. When Mike earlier mentioned the Hard Rock Café, Anne gave him a disdainful look. "Nothing American, we're on vacation," she warned him.

They had read about the Kiosk Budapest, a casual ware-house-style eatery offering traditional and cool bistro dishes and choices of international fare. Anne texted Peter their whereabouts as they sat outside along the river overlooking the white Elisabeth Bridge, the third newest bridge in the city. It is named after Elisabeth of Bavaria, a popular queen and empress of Austria-Hungary, who was assassinated in 1898.

The Kiosk is housed in a building shared with a Catholic high school upstairs, and its chapel right over the restaurant.

For dinner, one had wiener schnitzel, thin, crisp, and tasty. Others ordered pasta, steaks, and Hungarian classics. Anne went light having goulash with warm brown bread holding out for mákosguba, a traditional bread pudding soaked in vanilla custard and laced with poppy seeds. Or maybe plum dumplings in cinnamon sauce? Or chestnut cake with pear or apricot jam crêpes? Too many decisions, a weary friend observed.

One asked, "Do you realize how many sweet treats we've consumed in the past few days?"

"What a ridiculous thing to ask on vacation," his spouse replied.

"And we're not even on the cruise yet," a friend added.

CHAPTER FIVE

After their luscious final breakfast at the hotel, having a few hours before boarding their Viking Longship, several headed about six blocks to the Ferris wheel for a ride, climbing in two per seat.

The cityscape looked crisp and clean, with perfect views over the roofs of the Pest Side, and Buda as well. They spotted many places they'd been the past few days. Their seat stopped at the tiptop, 213 feet for a bird's eye view making the rotation in about ten minutes.

Purposely eating a lighter breakfast of fruit and multiple pastries, like they'd never get them again in their lives, at 11 o'clock, they stepped onto their floating hotel, Viking *Var*, just north of the Chain Bridge. It would be their home for the next seven days. Their friends made up about a quarter of the ship's population of 180. Each were warmly greeted, checked in, and given their room keys after presenting their passports. "Easy peasy, no lines or waiting," Peter remarked.

Peter opened the door to 227 into their well-appointed stateroom on the starboard side. Anne flung open the curtains on the floor-to-ceiling windows, then opened the door onto their veranda. "Veranda" is the proper term and sounds much classier and suave to her than deck, balcony or patio.

On the king size bed lay two neon orange life jackets. "Just in case we need to evacuate quickly into the river. Much better than an ocean," Peter teased. A bottle of sparkling wine sat cooling in a silver ice bucket with two glasses ready for them.

She picked up the *Viking Daily* that she would consult every night before going to bed. She didn't want to miss a thing. "Hey," she said, *The Nautical Term of the day is As the Crow Flies. When lost or unsure of their position in coastal waters, ships would release a caged crow. The crow would fly straight toward the nearest land, thus giving the vessel some sort of navigational fix. This is also why the tallest lookout platform on a ship came to be known as the "crow's nest."*

Peter joined her as they looked at the Chain Bridge and "their castle" as they'd nicknamed Buda Castle. "Nice view," Rolland announced as he and Judie stood outside next to them. Looking forward and back, friends of theirs stood on the verandas marveling at the view.

"Hallelujah," she exclaimed when their luggage arrived within ten minutes. Timeliness is not the case on all cruises. Anne usually unpacked most of their belongings, informing Peter which built-in drawers his undergarments were in, then which third of the plentiful closet would be his.

He unpacked all the important things: technology items, binoculars, one for each, and video camera, storing them away. He reprogrammed the safe and stowed their passports, wallets, and credit cards.

Anne hung her blouses and pants. Peter was a *folder*; she, a *hanger.* The sizable closet would hold their clothing just fine yet one of Anne's several quirks was that she always brought five wire ones. She'd learned that there were never enough, especially if Peter did want to hang up a few things.

Drawers filled up with pj's and undergarments; shoes were hidden away in the closet. They'd use the complimentary bathrobes they'd signed up for on the *myvikingjourney* page months earlier. She appreciated they could select options making the trip easier for them with less to pack.

Shelves were tucked into every usable corner, nook, and cranny, designed efficiently with every surface usable. Nightstands held drawers on each side of the bed. With everything put away there were several empty drawers left for souvenirs.

They would both end up opening several drawers for a day or two searching for one thing or another that, which at the time of unpacking and stashing, made perfect sense. "I should bring sticky notes on the next trip to label the drawers," Anne announced.

Peter knew Anne was in her happy place, a Viking Longship. "What are you humming?"

"You can't tell?"

"Mmm, no."

"*The Blue Danube*, silly."

"Oh…Right."

She sang, "On the beautiful, blue Danube; these are the only words I know."

Anne taped a list of their friends with their stateroom numbers on the mirror above the telephone that also served as a clock and alarm.

Their room steward Enzo greeted them with a cheerful foreign accent promising to take care of their every need and left his phone extension if they wanted anything.

"He sounds like Franck from *Father of the Bride*," Anne

snickered.

"Embarkation buffet is until 3 when you get hungry. They are doing a leisurely Welcome Walk around the historic heart of Budapest, if you want; it's from 1:30 until 3:00."

"Pass, I think I've done Budapest pretty well," Peter answered.

"I'm going. I need some more postcards. At 3:30 to 5:00, it's cheese and wine tasting in the Lounge. It says we can sample some of the fine wines available through our journey. Cocktail hour is 5:30 to 7:00. But we should go to the 6:15 Welcome Briefing and Port Talk. Dinner is at 7:00, so pace yourself."

Peter mumbled, before closing his eyes for a 20-minute power nap.

"Everything unpacked? Let's go for lunch," Peter's stomach grumbling. Both had poached salmon. Peter added the carrot ginger soup, skipping the spaghetti Bolognese, and beef goulash even though the Cobb salad sounded tempting. Anne always tried to select something they wouldn't necessarily have at home. Carrot ginger soup wasn't anything she'd ever make at home, not liking cooked carrots. Dessert: crème brûlée, one of her favorites. Peter ordered one also, plus a scoop of vanilla ice cream, his favorite, that came with a pencil-thin rolled cookie.

A Viking employee took their navy passports, with a prominent golden seal and United States of America written on the front, as another person said, "Welcome aboard Mr. and Mrs. Smith. I see it's your first time with us and we thank you for choosing Viking. If anyone of us can make your trip more enjoyable, please don't hesitate to reach out. The restaurant is over there, pointing to her right. Your stateroom is just up the stairs, turn left and the Lounge is on your deck to the right, then the Aquavit Terrace."

"Doesn't sound like we'll get lost," Rob grinned. "Where's the bar?"

"As you go into the Lounge."

"Great. Thank you, Miss," Rob said politely.

"We're very excited to be here. We saw a last-minute deal through an ad on Facebook. We called and grabbed one of the last rooms, a suite no less! We're from the south, so it's been a long trip. Are there others from our region?" the friendly female southerner rambled on.

"We've got a large group on board from the west coast, mostly Oregon. I don't recall too many others from America, mostly from Canada and New Zealand—oh, and a few Australians," replied the woman standing behind the counter.

"Come on, Deb, let's get goin,' you can ask more questions later, darlin,'" her winsome husband said. He added a suggestive wink placing his hand on the small of her back coaxing her toward their room.

"Oh quickly, are we on a riverboat, ship or what?"

"Longships are what we call our vessels," came the reply.

Standing on the veranda in stateroom 209, Dmitry looked down the longship and observed the overly friendly American woman pointing to something on the side of the river. He admitted it had been kind that she picked up his passport that his wife hadn't noticed she'd dropped. Nothing was ever his fault. He felt tired at 91, acknowledging he was reaching the end of his life journey. But wasn't he actually 96 years old? His memory jumbled up numbers and dates now. Nothing to be sad about or regrets, just a fact he admitted to himself.

Born in the western part of the Soviet Union, he had heard his mother say repeatedly over the years that the week he was born his parents had watched a black and white, silent drama called *The Overcoat* in the local movie theater.

General Secretary of the Communist Party was Joseph Stalin, who Dmitry's papa knew personally.

A law had been passed that the size of inheritance estates became effectively unlimited. This law helped his family, as his grandfather had been involved in diamond fields.

The Treaty of Berlin was signed pledging neutrality in the event of an attack on the other by a third party for five years.

Dmitry's mother, born in Finland, preferred the arts— movies, music and anything live on stage. She felt proud that they had an original Kandinsky *On White II*, that her husband purchased as a wedding gift to her, hanging in their main hallway, knowing any visitors couldn't miss seeing it. Many considered the artist a revolutionary merely by suggesting that humans could achieve something deeper and more important through creativity, individuality, and freedom through thought.

His papa, born in Tsaritsyn along the Volga River, didn't understand the bold colors and sharp-lined, squares, half and full circles, rectangles, dots, and random swirls of abstract art, but tolerated his wife's indulgence that seemed to keep her occupied. He needed to know what he was looking at and preferred a gray ocean with violent waves slamming against rocks.

But she lit up when discussing Constructivism, an artistic and architectural philosophy that believed artistic endeavor should be a practice for social purposes not merely for aesthetic ends. She also lit up when she spoke of her only son, Dmitry.

Dmitry didn't see his papa much and never heard stories about how his parents met. But he saw a warmth and fondness demonstrated often between his parents.

He did recall how one day his mother explained they were moving as papa got a new job, across the border in Germany. Dmitry didn't remember anything about the Soviet Union but had a faint remembrance of a long train ride that his mother later would tell him went 450 miles south, then turned west through Poland, Czechoslovakia, and Austria arriving in Munich several days later.

In their new country, Dmitry grew up in a two-story home with a balcony on each floor surrounded by white wooden fencing. Years later, he would smile thinking about the staircase and sliding down the slick wooden banister. He also remembered how cold his bedroom felt. The fireplaces in most rooms didn't keep the winter cold out. They seemed to have money but no help in their home. His mother scurried from room to room restocking the fireplaces with wood from outside stacked close to the back door. He couldn't recall how the firewood got there and never imagined his father cutting wood.

Dmitry excelled in school and had just a couple of close friends, Arno and Lukas, brothers down the street. He would have been best friends with his cousin Harald, but he lived hundreds of miles away in Finland.

His teachers perceived early on that Dmitry had an aptitude for numbers. His parents observed something else while on a few family vacations. One time in Poland his mother said to his father, not thinking their son was paying attention, "Do you hear him? He's speaking Polish after just 20 or 30 minutes?" Another time in Romania, his father pointed out how well he spoke to locals. The same thing happened when they spent one week in Sweden.

"How do you do it?" his father asked him.

"I don't know; I just hear and understand."

One day his mother showed him a letter written from her sister in Finland. "Can you read this?"

"No, nothing; should I be able to?" he innocently replied.

Lukas's and Arno's father worked for the government. He became keenly aware of young Dmitry and that his sons admired and bragged about their neighbor who spoke several languages and lived only a few houses away.

One time his family got all dressed up and went to a large building where an important ceremony would take place. His father told him repeatedly not to speak unless an adult spoke to him first. They each went home with a piece of paper identifying them as German citizens.

"Look mother. This is my Hitler Youth membership card." He joined the League of German Worker Youth at the age of 10. She hoped her son hadn't seen her cringe. His father felt proud.

Dmitry felt honored carrying his green paper card for German Youngsters, called *Deutsches Jungvolk* for boys ages 10 to 14 years old. It included his signature and address with a stapled picture of him from the chest up with a big smile on his ten-year-old face. An embossed seal made it look very official. When he turned 14, he became eligible for the Hitler Youth (*Hilterjugend*). He went to after-school meetings and weekend camping trips sponsored by the Hitler Youth from which he graduated at age 18.

He was taught to live a life of dedication, fellowship, and Nazi conformity, and already trained to become faithful to the Party and the future leaders of the National Socialist State. He served in a variety of leadership roles in the program, which prepared him for roles in the military and the German occupation organization. On his 18th birthday he was a member of the Nazi Party and served at a camp where he was assigned until the war ended. After only three years of service, it was over.

Years later, his mother found a professional photo taken one Christmas of their family of three. She stood with her right hand on her ten-year-old son's left shoulder. He wore black pants, a belt, tan shirt with a stiff collar and tie. And a cap. He proudly smiled. Looking at herself years earlier, she hadn't smiled but remembered vividly that she felt frightened and sad. Her son had become part of eight million children who had been pressed by peers and parents to be part of what would be a horrific war effort.

Dmitry's aunt and uncle and their two children, his cousins Eleonoora, called Ella, and Harald, lived hundreds of miles away. Dmitry heard his mother repeatedly suggest to his father that they leave Germany and move to northern Finland with her sister. His mother had a premonition the future would turn out badly, and she felt extremely concerned for her only son.

Her childhood had not been easy but she had fond memories of her parents and sister. As a child, she never realized the hardships her parents went through. One generation later, at 17 years old, Cousin Ella tried not to think back on her early childhood. When she did, her stomach ached and her heart raced. Losing one's home had been deeply traumatic for all family members including the children. She had been barely a teenager the first time they lost their home due to mass evacuation of civilians.

They lived in Lapland, northern Finland, a place where

most of the world thought of people dressing in fur and having reindeer as pets.

They had extended family who were fighting and defending the borderlands against the massive army of the neighboring Soviet Union. Major battlefields were in the eastern and northern parts of the country.

Their family lived in Vuotso, the southernmost reindeer-herding Sámi community in Finland, about 125 miles north of the Arctic Circle. It is known as the Gate to Sápmi: the homeland of the Sámi, stretching across northern Norway, Sweden, Finland, and Russia. Their village had approximately 8,000 households, hosted a major German supply base and military airport, and an anti-aircraft artillery base.

Their father worked alongside German and Finnish military in the anti-aircraft artillery base. Their two-story home offered accommodations to two German soldiers.

But something horribly changed toward the end of WWII. The former friends became enemies, which resulted in the destruction of the lives of local people in profound ways for years to come.

Their family and neighbors left Lapland and their homes twice: first in 1939 during the Winter War against the Soviet Union and again in 1944, due to the so-called Lapland War, a conflict between Finland and their former ally, Nazi Germany.

Many Laplanders would eventually be able to return to their villages but in most cases there were no homes left. The German Army, while retreating to Norway, scorched their homes and forests so there wasn't much to come home to. Dwellings and infrastructure had suffered massive destruction and the German troops also booby-trapped the smoking ruins of villages and roadsides with thousands of landmines. She hated the Germans, thinking that meant her cousin

Dmitry, too, who she knew was one of those boys being used by Hitler.

Dmitry's childhood memories weren't tragic like his cousin's but often full of excitement and adventure. His early life experiences were much different than his cousin's.

He knew Ella would never understand. He'd just done his job, and what he had been told to do. But from a young age they were being taught to hate. He buried any emotions he once had. And memories.

Dmitry wondered why those memories came back to him sailing on the Danube so many decades later.

———

She returned to find Peter sitting on the veranda watching river traffic.

"Oh my, hear those birds chirping? Another reason I love cruising on a river," said Anne, unloading several more Budapest souvenirs into drawers.

"Did you use up all the Hungarian Forints?"

"Absolutely."

"Let's go see what's happening in the Lounge. It's almost wine-tasting time."

"And cheese. Go ahead, I'll be there shortly; just want to change clothes."

Peter and Rolland, drinking Old Fashioneds, Judie a glass of pinot, Julie a Manhattan, Casey a beer, and Cathy a Lemon Drop, they sat in the Lounge comparing notes about their time in Budapest, marveling at how fast their luggage had arrived in their rooms and what was coming up for the week.

A middle-aged couple sauntered by with vacation smiles and beverages in their hands. The man asked, "Mind if we join you folks?" clearly from a southern state of the US.

"Please do," Julie answered for the friends. "We're just saving one for Anne."

"Rob and Debbie Smith from Alabama," the man said sliding comfortably into two vacant chairs as everyone introduced themselves. They were on their first river cruise and decided to come at the last minute. He wore a lapis, lightweight sweater, white-collared shirt, and gray slacks. The tips of his brown hair were just a little darker than the rest, maybe damp like he'd just showered. The streaks of silver suggested he could be middle age. She wore floral pants and a teal blouse that set off her cobalt blue eyes, not hidden by her frameless glasses. When she smiled, dimples appeared below her rosy cheeks.

Across the room an elderly woman observed the interaction in the Lounge. Indistinguishable chatter from groups of three and four friends who hugged each other, greeting for the first time on their vacation together. Others shook hands welcoming newcomers. Some couples sat alone.

Sandra had just turned 80 years old, born in Warsaw as Kassandra Meller. *Where have the past 30 years gone?* She could hardly believe she was 80. She felt 50; most thought she looked 60.

As a toddler living in London, she couldn't recall the horrors of WWII except vague memories of her mother crying and always being frightened, even after the bombs stopped in May 1941, after nine months of continual fear. Her father worked all the time as a fireman.

She only knew London as her home and Sandra as her name. She never had been told about her heritage until both parents were dead and an aunt filled her in. She had been born a Jew named Kassandra. Kah-SAEN-Drah meant "shine upon mankind." Her parents changed her first name and their last, dropping an "e" for an "i," and never stepped foot in a synagogue but instead, the Church of England. The Jewish Meller family from Poland became the Millers from England.

She still didn't know how to feel. Sad, mad, grateful; she still felt somewhat conflicted and spoke with no one about it.

"Excuse me, Madam, can I bring you a drink?" He'd pronounced Mah-dam correctly; she preferred it over madam, the British and English version.

"Yes, please. I'd like a Savoy Affair, please. Do you think the bartender knows this drink…Axil?" quickly reading his name tag.

"Of course, Mah-dam. I know it as a special drink for very particular people. Our bartender Killian's father came from Belfast, and knew Joe Gilmore, the drink's creator also from Northern Ireland. Joe served as head barman at the Savoy Hotel's American Bar in London. Killian's father taught him Joe's recipes and he knows exactly how to make the perfect one for you. It's a specialty of his."

Sandra watched her drink being concocted. Killian first sliced a lime, rubbed the rim of a cocktail glass, then dipped it into sugar. He mixed 2 teaspoons of strawberry liqueur, 2 teaspoons of peach brandy, 2 teaspoons of lime juice, 2 teaspoons of passion fruit juice and champagne and filled the rest of the glass with a small scoop of crushed ice. He added something else that Sandra couldn't see. Killian poured the mixed ingredients carefully into the sugar-rimmed glass, adding a petite sugar-dipped strawberry on the rim.

Axil delivered the pinkish-peach drink and Sandra took a sip. "Delicious!" she declared and raised the glass to the bartender who watched for her reaction. He took a polite slight bow. He'd added his own flare of something that made it probably the tastiest she'd ever had.

Taking a longer drink of her favorite beverage, a smile crept on her lips as she recalled the first time she'd cautiously sipped her first Savoy Affair. Then more memories flooded back to high school when she fell in love with a classmate. John returned her affections. Dating as much as possible, a favorite of theirs was going to the theater to watch American made films. *The Man Who Knew Too Much* sent tingles up Sandra's spine and John laughed when she grasped his arm while closing her eyes. A vacationing married couple in Morocco are dragged into a twisting plot of international intrigue when their young son is kidnapped. She almost fell in love with James Stewart, and John with Doris Day.

John preferred *Moby Dick* and pictured himself as the sole survivor of a lost whaling ship, after the captain's self-destructive obsession to hunt the great white whale.

They both got caught up in *Around the World in 80 Days* and spoke for hours on end about adventures one day around the globe. In the film, a Victorian Englishman bets that with the new steamships and railways he can circum-navigate the globe in 80 days. The following year, they watched the soap opera movie *Peyton Place*, a bit racy for Sandra.

John's all-time favorite adventure-drama was Ernest Hemingway's, *The Old Man and the Sea*, the short 1952 novel about a fisherman off the coast of Cuba who struggled with a hooked marlin bigger than his boat. John put himself in place of Santiago, played by a scrubby old Spencer Tracy.

They both loved seeing films and scrimped and saved to attend live performances at the theater. "The theater is magical and addictive," said Irish-British and American Angela Lansbury, one of Sandra's favorite actresses.

John and Sandra married two years after high school graduation, the summer of 1958. She drank her first Savoy Affair on their honeymoon. She heard an American saying somewhere, "He's the love of my life" or "he's my soulmate." John had been both to her.

Graduating at the top of her high school class, she excelled in mathematics. She appreciated that numbers were finite, true, and never changing. She easily found a job as a bookkeeper in a large clothing factory, and the 8-to-5 job allowed her time to get home and have dinner ready when John walked through the door. John went fishing daily on small boats and gained years of experience.

They were content and happy with their lives, even though both were surprised that they had not been blessed with children. It did allow them more freedom for travel around Great Britain as well as taking the ferry across to Europe.

The couple found themselves celebrating wedding anniversaries along with the changing times during the 1960s and early 1970s. Each anniversary they treated themselves by going for a nice meal, including her annual Savoy Affair and him a pint of Burton Ale. He was a beer man enjoying the well-hopped darker ale. It tended to taste sweeter than bitter, which he preferred. If they had enough money, they'd celebrate their birthdays out with a fine dinner, too.

Fifteen years went by in a flash. They kicked off each new year by watching the Best Picture Oscar Award winners, from 1959-1973: *Ben-Hur*, *The Apartment*, *West Side Story*, *Lawrence of Arabia*, *Tom Jones*, *My Fair Lady*, *The Sound of Music*, *A Man for All Seasons*, *In the Heat of the Night*, *Oliver!*, *Midnight Cowboy*, *Patton*, *The French Connection*, *The Godfather*, *The Sting*, and New Year's Eve 1974 found them holding hands at the violent *The Godfather: Part II*, which she only watched because of their longstanding tradition.

Then one day an opportunity came his way he couldn't pass up, even though it meant leaving Sandra for longer periods of time. John's heart was with the sea, and she knew it. Before they left for dinner and a movie, John had rushed in that evening, "Sandra, it's finally happened. I've been offered a good job on a new supertrawler called the *Gaul*. She was built last year and she's ready to go right out of Hull. And you know, it is very easy to get back and forth to East Yorkshire from here. But Love, I will be gone for longer than a fortnight, could be three to four weeks. They showed me a map of the route along the coast of Norway in the Norwegian Sea, and at the top of Sweden they will veer east into the Barents Sea. If they'd go north and west, they'd skirt the southern tip of Greenland."

"John, why do they call a boat or ship a "She"? Sandra asked, trying to keep the conversation light.

"I really don't know, never thought about it before. Maybe because men love them? I told them that I'd need to speak with you before giving them my answer tomorrow. I know it's New Year's Eve, but I said I'd get back to them. Did I mention it's a 220-foot, 36-person super trawler? The ship has been built for these types of conditions. The size is necessary and designed to fish in Arctic waters and to process, freeze, and store the fish that is caught. It's huge. I can't wait for you to see her." He finally took a breath. "Tell me what you think."

She smiled loving his excitement and adventurous spirit. "Don't worry about me, Love. I'll be here waiting for you each time you return. Of course, I'll miss you horribly." The longest time he'd been away fishing was two weeks. She coped but didn't like it much.

She recalled sitting through the violent *Godfather II* movie, closing her eyes during several parts. Her mind really wasn't on the movie, but on her husband.

Decades later, Sandra held up her empty cocktail glass and when Axil asked if she'd like another, she simply nodded.

She remembered taking the bus with her husband sharing his excitement as much as she could muster. He was right, the *Gaul* was huge and beautiful for a fishing boat, really the size of a small ship to her. She briefly met several crew and John pointed out the captain. The couple kissed like young newlyweds, like a soldier departing for war. She cried riding back home alone looking out at the gloomy countryside.

He called before leaving from a red telephone booth. "How are you, Love? "

"Oh, fine. Busy at work. What have you been doing?"

"It's been a very busy week. We've been through much training, provisions are stocked, and we depart tomorrow at 5 a.m., Love. I'll call you the minute we return. I love you, Sandra."

"I love you, too, John. Please be careful and I'll see you in a month or so."

"Okay, Love. I must go and let others use the phone. Ta-ta for now, my dearest."

When John and 35 others departed on January 22, 1974, the skipper was captaining the *Gaul* for the first time, although he had experience with other fishing vessels of comparable size. They headed to the fishing grounds of the Barents Sea with its full complement of 36 crew on board.

From January 29 onwards, the crew fished continuously and without incident, making radio contact with other fishing vessels in the vicinity, and contacted the home port of Hull several times. Updates were passed along to families, including Sandra.

The telephone rang. She heard an official voice on the other end explain that in the early hours of Saturday, February 8, the weather in the Barents Sea began to deteriorate rapidly with a storm developing with waves around 27 feet. Despite the weather conditions *Gaul* was coping. Crew made radio contact around 11 a.m. with another fishing vessel in the area and with staff at Hull. There was no report that they were in any trouble.

The *Gaul* was fishing north of Norway and close to Russia. Initially nothing seemed amiss but over the weekend of February 9 and 10, concern began to mount when the boat first failed to report in, required by commercial fishing regulations, and then did not respond to radio messages. By the morning of the 11th, an alert had been issued for all fishing vessels in the area to be on the lookout and the Royal Navy began the search.

When the *Gaul* had still not contacted anyone by early afternoon of the same day, a full-scale search began with Norwegian Rescue launching a search and rescue operation, and the UK authorities sending more vessels to the area and preparing to search by aircraft.

Sandra didn't retain a word the man with the deep voice said. She just knew that the *Gaul* capsized. John died while working, and Sandra became a widow at age 36. Yes, there was an ongoing search but she could feel it; John was gone forever.

Frantic wives were on the phone to each other. They could have filled an ocean of tears. Young widows had questions and wanted more information. They discussed the search, but after a few meetings, Sandra just couldn't do it. She could hardly bear his death.

She did follow the news. Sometimes she received updates from a friend whose husband also had been on board. No reports were forthcoming on what actually happened or where the *Gaul* was.

The first year she felt like an actress in one of the many movies they'd watched together. She was playing a part, merely coping. She lived in a nightmare that repeated over and over in her mind. Hours became days, days became weeks, then months, and years.

A decade passed and in 1984 she wondered where ten years had gone. Her job and friends had gotten her through the nightmare. But she felt restless and needed a change. Her company was opening a branch in Munich and asked if she'd like to move. She packed and was on a train three weeks later but she couldn't escape the *Gaul* saga.

With all the publicity about the *Gaul*, in 1997 Sandra read a detailed newspaper article that an inquiry reported that a search was launched once the ship was believed to be in trouble. The Royal Navy aircraft carrier HMS *Hermes* was on its way to Norway to take part in joint exercises with the Norwegian Navy and changed its course to assist HMS *Mohawk* in the search. They were soon joined by a number of other Norwegian Navy and Coastguard vessels. These were later joined by RFA *Tideflow* that refueled and resupplied the other ships. There were also 23 trawlers in the area which broke away from fishing to assist in the large-scale air search. The search ended at 4 p.m. on February 15, after no trace had been found.

Just when she thought she could put the *Gaul* behind her, something else happened. She received a phone call from a widow that a Norwegian vessel found a lifejacket from the *Gaul*, and other trawlers reported snagging their nets on obstructions that had not previously been present. Yet despite all these discoveries, the wreck had not been located.

Even living in Germany, the rumor mill was in high gear that led to several theories explaining what had happened to the boat. The fact that the ship had been relatively close to the Soviet Union during the Cold War meant that many people speculated Russia might have been involved. This idea was strengthened by several factors.

First, the British government refused to search further for the *Gaul*, claiming that the initial search had been so thorough that there was little point in conducting additional searches, as they would only yield the same result.

Secondly, the *Gaul* was a new ship of modern design that had been specifically constructed to withstand the type of storm which had presumably sunk her. Many people refused to believe that the *Gaul* could sink in the type of storm which its identical sister vessel had withstood without major incident.

Lastly, no Mayday call was issued. This was considered very unusual as it would have been standard procedure to issue a distress call.

Despite these claims and theories, the British government continued to refuse to search for the vessel, putting forward the additional claim that the area was littered with the wrecks of WWII ships which would need to be examined with complex specialist equipment to differentiate them from the *Gaul*. In other words, the search would be both too time-consuming and expensive. This reinforced the belief that the UK government had something to hide if the wreck of the *Gaul* was to be discovered.

But it wasn't over for many. With most of the conspiracy theories ruled out, work could begin on figuring out what happened with the findings collated in a new inquiry in 2004. Although this inquiry agreed that the *Gaul* had been hit broadside by a succession of large waves, it did not agree that this had been solely responsible for its sinking. The vessel should have been able to withstand such waves, and there- fore there had to be an additional factor that played a part.

As time passed, the pressure was building on the British government with conspiracy theories and media attention eventually forcing the government to make a stunning admission—British trawlers were used to spy on Russian vessels and gather intelligence on Russian ship movements. The government originally tried to play this down, stating that Royal Navy personnel were sometimes present on fishing vessels but only to gain experience. It soon became clear that trawlers were used for spying. This was done by either requesting trawlers' crews to take notes on Russian ship movements and photograph vessels, or by Royal Navy personnel being on board trawlers as spies while at sea.

The government admission led many people to believe that the *Gaul* had been in fact a "spy ship," a fishing vessel used to collect information and intelligence and may even have had Royal Navy personnel on board. If true, then there would be a clear reason why the *Gaul* could have been the target of the Soviets.

The 2004 inquiry was highly critical of the government's use of fishing vessels for spying, starting with the denial, and then admission, that led to mistrust in the versions of events.

While the *Gaul* remaining undiscovered, and the British government refusing to search for it, several theories began to emerge to explain what happened. One of the main theories was that the ship's crew had been convinced by the British government and Royal Navy to spy on Russian ship movements.

The 2004 inquiry heard further evidence that there were actually 38 people on board rather than the official 36, with the additional two men being Royal Navy personnel. The conspiracy theory puts forward the idea that the *Gaul* had been discovered conducting spying activities by a Russian vessel and was escorted back to a Soviet port. All the crew were then either killed by the Russians or imprisoned in a Soviet labor camp, where they remain.

Then there was the theory that a Russian submarine was believed to be responsible for the sinking. Or that a Soviet nuclear sub launched a torpedo destroying the *Gaul* instantly, therefore explaining why it was unable to send a distress call.

When the theory that the *Gaul* accidentally collided with a Royal Navy submarine and supposedly damaged the *Gaul* so badly that it sank, it became too much for Sandra to follow, repeatedly going through misery. She no longer took calls from well-meaning friends.

She paid attention when an analysis of underwater footage and pictures of the *Gaul* on the seabed revealed that the chutes were in the open position, a key clue in explaining what really happened to the ship.

A report concluded that when the storm began, the hatches and offal chutes were left in the open position, allowing seawater to flood into the boat. As the storm worsened, the crew attempted to turn the Gaul so that it faced the waves head-on, but with hundreds of tons of water inside the *Gaul* its buoyancy would have been seriously compromised. It was concluded that turning the vessel caused the water, which had flooded into the vessel, to surge to one side, causing the *Gaul* to capsize and then sink rapidly.

The lack of any credible search for the *Gaul* by the British government prevented the families from getting closure on what had happened, and it seemed unacceptable that it took a privately funded expedition from a television channel to eventually find the wreck.

The bell of the *Gaul* was recovered from the wreck and rang at two services in Hull in February 2014 to commemorate the 40th anniversary of the loss of the lives and the vessel. She stood in pouring rain with tears streaming down her cheeks feeling very alone remembering their last telephone call as he rushed away.

She didn't allow herself to go down memory lane often. "Hmm, I'll have another please, Axil."

Another memory popped into her mind about the British. One morning during breakfast, Dmitry slammed down the newspaper enough to cause Sandra to jump an inch off her chair. In a huff he shouted, "Those insipid children, the poor Queen. Did I ever tell you I saw the royal family in South Africa? "

"No! Really?" she feigned.

"Yes, indeed."

"Tell me about it."

"Princess Elizabeth was a stunner back then." He recounted their grand entrance, the 21-gun salute and thousands of people cheering "God Save the King." Each time she heard his recounting, many times over the years especially more recently, he told it exactly the same way down to every detail. Some of his memories were muddled but not this episode. She recognized his age or dementia was causing more stories to be repeated.

He had also mentioned his first wives, Sarah and Eliza, more in the last two or three years. Then he'd go quiet. Once or twice, he mentioned leaving after the war and moving 6,000 miles away to South Africa. She asked him why he left. He just looked at her and replied, "It seemed the safest thing to do at the time."

He had more nightmares when they were first married. She moved into a spare bedroom when his left arm hit her hard across the face one night. When she told him, he said, "I didn't do that." Exasperated, she showed him the bruises. He indignantly replied, "I don't recall doing that and if I was dreaming, it's not my fault." Nothing would ever be his fault, she learned quickly.

She recognized his self-centered and egotistical ways, but she was also old enough to know not to take it personally. The bursts of temper had fortunately declined. And she hadn't caused his personality traits. She did pity those younger wives. She'd stuck it out. He could be pleasant enough, now at least tolerable. When she had been irritated with him, or his repeated stories, she was now more patient and understanding. She'd been reading about dementia and Alzheimer's disease at the library. The library had become her refuge.

Anne entered, scanning the crowd for familiar faces. She recognized Mrs. Dmitry sitting by herself drinking something pink.

She spotted her group and as she approached them, she overheard the woman sitting with her husband and friends saying, "He was too highfalutin for our taste. If I had my druthers, we would have left months ago."

"Hi. I'm Anne," she said as she reached out her hand and shook the warm hand of Debbie. Rob's felt rough and strong.

Cathy inserted, "She's our fearless leader. Not only a lifetime friend but she coordinates our travels. There's a bunch of friends on board."

"Oh, you're the big group from out west?" Debbie noted. "They told us about you when we checked in."

"Yep, we are, 34 of us."

"Oh, my goodness gracious, you take up about a quarter of the ship. How do you keep track of everyone, Anne?" Debbie asked sort of in awe.

"They pretty much do their own thing, but I sort of watch out for everyone the best I can. Some are definitely more troublesome than others," pointing at Mike and Kathy across the Lounge, sitting with Phil and Sharon and Rolland and Judie. "Those six, watch out," she jokingly warned.

Debbie replied, "I was just telling Cathy why we left a church we'd attended for years."

Rob and Casey were engrossed in a conversation about sports. Crimson Tide this, A&M Bulldogs that, from football to basketball, leading into favorite golfers.

Rob asked Casey to name three famous sports people from Alabama. Casey rattled off, "Willie Mays, Hank Aaron, and Bo Jackson."

"Right! And others like Bart Starr, Kenny Stabler, and dozens of others, *even some women*," he sort of chuckled looking at his wife who glared at him.

Peter asked, "Didn't Charles Barkley come from your state, too?"

"Hmm, you're correct. Basketball and from *Men in Black*," he laughed.

The ladies spoke about their favorites topics like travel, hikes, evening walks, and gardening. Cathy said, "We are redoing our patio behind our house. I just found two gorgeous mosaic tile birdbaths. I'll use one for some other type of décor."

"We're having some landscaping done in the frunchard," Debbie added.

Anne missed in what context the word was being used. "Excuse me, what?"

"You've got a frunchard and backyard," Debbie answered. The new friends from the west coast just nodded.

Anne scrunched down into a comfy chair rotating towards Peter.

"Is it wine-and-cheese-tasting time yet?" Looking at his watch, "Good timing, five minutes."

They sipped an assortment of wines after a short presentation on the history of winemaking in Germany that dates to the Romans, with evidence of grape growing and cultivation as early as 79 AD. The Moselle was the first established wine region. Most of the vineyards in medieval Germany were run by the churches and monasteries and under the supervision and careful tending by the monks. The quality of the grapes grown flourished.

Anne, you should organize that Paris to Swiss Alps cruise

on the Moselle River, someone suggested. "Will do," came her reply.

They first tasted a yummy Rangen Grand Cru Riesling, a semi-sparkling white wine with a nice crispness and fragrance of flowers and fruit.

Next, they sipped a pinot noir, their favorite red wine from home. The wine is low in acidity and is light in both color and body but there's also another full-bodied variety that is dark red, with higher acidity levels.

Then came a pinot gris, kind of a reddish-gray but usually in the white category that can be gold and yellow, full-bodied with medium acidity levels.

Next came a Muller Thurgau, another famous white grape, but some wine snobs find this German wine to be too plain and sweet. Others enjoy the sweetness as well as the peachy fragrance and mild acidity.

They sampled an assortment of cheeses from the lush Alpine landscapes. The high-quality milk and cheese makes the region the center of the German cheese industry.

The only cheese recognizable to Anne was Cambozola, but others included Butterkäse, about the shape of a cube of butter, it is a semi-soft cheese made with cow's milk, with a mild taste and smooth, creamy texture similar to Dutch Gouda.

Harzer Kase is high in protein and low in fat. This traditional cheese is made from sour milk curd that's just about fat-free and has the lowest number of calories of all the cheeses. The small round balls were sprinkled with caraway seeds and smelled peculiar to Peter. Anne took a nibble but didn't continue because the taste was distinctive caraway, not her favorite.

Bergader Edelpiz is a blue cheese similar to Roquefort, but using cow's milk instead of sheep's milk. Peter wouldn't even taste it. Anne loved it.

Rauchkäse, a semi-soft and somewhat smoky brown rind tasted too salty and spicy for Peter but mmm, so good to Anne. Anne's favorite by far was the Cambozola, the soft blue cheese that is on the one hand creamy and at the same time a sharp blue cheese. Blue penicillin mold is used the same as in gorgonzola and Roquefort, with extra cream to enhance the soft velvety texture.

"What's wrong with you? You're sweatin' like a sinner in church," Debbie teased her husband.

"It's all that wine. I need to stick to scotch and water."

Anne overheard a foursome sitting behind them placing a beverage order with Axil: one mojito, one Old Fashioned, one red wine and the last one, "I'd like a Bombay Sapphire martini, super cold with five green olives, please."

"Certainly. That was five green olives, right?" Axil confirmed.

As Anne took an-over-the-shoulder glance, she saw a knock-out gorgeous woman, with coal black hair, who looked like she could have been a model in her younger days.

"Right, five, please. Did I tell you I'm on an olive diet?" to her friends.

Her companions shook their heads.

"It's going really well. All olives have good amounts of Vitamin E, iron, copper, calcium, and sodium, but I do have to watch my sodium intake; I tend to retain water. Have you heard about it?"

"Alcohol is fine?" the first woman asked.

"Oh yes, the more the better."

"Ahh, my kind of diet," a man muttered.

"What types of food do you eat?" the other woman asked.

"Olive salad with olive oil dressing. Olive tapenade by the spoonful, sometimes with an extra thin, crispy wheat cracker. It's totally cheating, but it's just a few carbs. Did you know they make ones with rosemary and olive oil now? Yep.

Other than that, I've stopped eating meat, fish, dairy, all grains, and most fruits and vegetables with the exception of olives, of course. I eat any type of green olives, and black, brown, purple, salt-cured, oil-cured, marinated. But I don't do stuffed ones, because the foods they stuff them with aren't included in the diet."

"Do you have a favorite?" a polite yet only semi-interested person in her foursome asked.

"Let me think about that one. Probably Cordovil olives from the Moura region of Portugal. I got to see them growing on trees, and when harvested they are whitish green. They are processed when they are small to medium in size, then transition to yellowish to mint color. They taste fruity, slightly bitter with a tinge of spice.

"The Corbancosa olives are from northern Portugal and used mostly for high-quality extra virgin olive oil. The olive tastes a little fruity with a spicy aftertaste, delicious, too.

"But now that I think about it, the Galega variety are the most popular with a soft meat, fruity taste, and cured in a brine and marinated in salt, red wine vinegar, oregano, and olive oil. It's like a party in your mouth. I think any olives from Portugal are yummy.

"But then Spain produces Gordals, soft and plump, slightly salty, and mild. Picual olives are probably the most popular in Spain and grown in the southern region. These are small, partly bitter, and sweet.

"Then there's the Verdial that are fun because they are bright green, bitter, spicy, and firm.

"Manzanilla types are those typical pistachio-green olives usually stuffed with garlic or pimento, which I don't eat because of the added ingredients, illegal to my diet.

"Gosh, you know Spain and Argentina are growing Artuco and I love these because it's like they infuse rosemary flavor. Another one from Spain I really enjoy is Arbequina.

Some South American countries, plus the US and Australia are producing these too. These are small, light brown to orange, kind of firm and fruity."

Peter glanced to his left seeing the olive connoisseur with jet black poufy hair, wearing a black and white outfit and engaged in conversation with three others not-so-enamored. However, his wife, also an olive lover, was engrossed in her eavesdropping.

"When we visited Tangiers, Morocco, we ate Beldi, which are small and fruity and sort of chewy."

"Tangiers? Really, when were you there?" a woman asked.

"About a decade ago. I'd go again in a heartbeat. Alfonsos from Chili are soft and juicy. I drink 1.5 to 3.5 tablespoons of olive oil per day."

The man in the group sort of gagged as he'd just taken a drink from a glass of water.

"All Italian oils are delish. Castelvetrano from Sicily are a bright parakeet-green, medium to large, pitted, salty, sort of buttery yet firm and mild flavor.

"There's Cerignola, The Gaeta, Lugano, and White Olives from Malta; Lucques are small, bright green and stand out because of their unique kidney shape. Picholine, Niçoise, and Nyon are probably the most authentic French olives.

"But back to your question, my favorites are Kalamata named after the town in southern Greece where they originated. They are a pretty, almond shape, smooth, and plump with shiny skin, fleshy, and never mushy. My go-to olive. Then the Castelvetrano. Did I mention I drink about 3 tablespoons a day? I think I forgot a few, hang on, let me picture the world map...oh right, how in the world did I miss the Greeks, oh and Turkey?"

"Mm-hmm, that's okay. You can fill us in on Greek and Turkish olives another time," a fast-thinking tablemate said, thinking to himself, I won't even mention California produces olives, too.

Her trio was dumbstruck. The olive expert's martini and other drinks arrived just as she finished her dissertation.

"In about five minutes we've gotten an around-the-world tour of olives," Peter whispered.

"I agree with her on Kalamata olives, but I sure didn't know about the wonderful world of olives until now. Too bad I didn't think to record her," Anne said, as the snoopy couple were darn impressed.

"Did you hear her mention Tangier? What a memorable day that was for us. I suppose we could laugh about it now."

"Hmm, not quite yet," Peter replied shaking his head.

"Let's not relive that day," his wife replied.

"Agreed."

Around 6:15 the program director introduced himself as George, then the captain. Next the hotel manager, executive housekeeper, Maître d', and executive chef, the last two receiving the most applause. George laughingly admitted this is common. The captain gave them specifics on their vessel, and George told them some things they could look forward to during their time aboard.

Dinner menu read like a five-star restaurant. Anne skimmed it pointing at this and that.

Starters: *Baby shrimp cocktail or Coronation chicken salad.*

Main courses: *Potato-chanterelle Wellington, Roast beef fillet with Yorkshire pudding.*

Dessert: *English teatime celebration of strawberries and cream, shortbread, Eton mess, mini scones, and cupcakes.*

Anything shrimp for Anne, beef Wellington, and the triple tier of desserts.

Rob and Debbie sat with several people from England. They wouldn't make that mistake again. Neither was particularly fond of the British, in general. Fair or not, correct or not, it was their personal prejudice that if admitted, might be deep-seated because of past wars, stuffy monarchy, or history in general.

Cast Off was broadcasted promptly at 8 p.m. The captain announced a surprise for them, a Budapest evening cruise. They stepped up two flights of stairs to the Sun Deck, joining others as they cruised under the Elisabeth and the Chain bridges, past Buda Castle, seeing St. Stephen's Cathedral, and on to Parliament that stretched several blocks long. Thousands of city lights created lines and shapes outlining each structure. Pointy spires, domed churches, and cathedrals, all in white lights. Neon, blinking and colorful lights on restaurants and bars, all created a magical feel.

Two hours later, they eased back into the dock for the night.

Anne woke abruptly wondering why. She'd been sleeping soundly like Peter. A bright flash became her answer. Then a loud boom. A thunder and lightning storm that she, but especially her mother, loved. Her mother spent her early childhood on the plains of Nebraska during the Dust Bowl and Depression era. "There's nothing like a Nebraska lightning storm," Anne heard frequently throughout her life. Her mother, after moving to the Willamette Valley in Oregon as a child, didn't see many, but when there was one, her mom moved a chair to an open window and watched.

Another flash lit up their stateroom, even with the curtains closed. Each flash was closely followed by another boom, "like potatoes dropped on Heaven's floor," her mom would say. Peeking out, it looked like a crackling bolt almost hit the bank across the river. *That's too close for comfort*, she nervously said.

Wide awake, she slipped on her robe, and as tempted as she was, reluctantly did not throw open the curtains. She moved a chair to the right side and pulled the curtain open an inch as another bolt hit about the same place on the bank again.

Probably an hour later she could see a random bolt through her closed eyelids. Even though the storm moved away, she knew getting back to sleep anytime soon wouldn't happen. She hoped not many people would be at the Aquavit Terrace at 2:17 a.m. as she slipped out of their stateroom, Peter still dead to the world.

Good, only one person with his head down, either sleeping or reading, she assumed. As she went by him, she recognized the curmudgeon from the hotel check-in several days earlier. *Dmitry*, she thought.

She made some decaf hot tea, her English version, adding milk and sugar, then sauntered to the opposite side of the room, making herself comfortable, her legs stretched out on a coffee table.

"Now this is a storm," a female employee commented to Anne.

"I love it," Anne replied.

"Actually, me too. Plus, it will rain and that will help the water level of the river. It's become a bit low in some areas of the Danube, and Rhine also," she remarked. "It's a balancing act of too little or too much water. It's much easier for those ocean liners than boats."

Finally feeling drowsy, Anne returned to their stateroom and climbed into bed. The clock read 3:20.

Rob wasn't sleeping well and it wasn't because of the storm. Debbie was driving him crazy sleeping soundly in the same bed. Perturbed, he pulled on his pants and shirt then marched down the hallway straight into the Lounge, heading to the Aquavit Terrace. He noticed an elderly man reading a book at 3:45 in the morning, not fazed by the bright bolts of lightning and rolling thunder.

CHAPTER SIX

Guests were given an opportunity for the Viking shore excursion—a Budapest city tour, that would meet *Var* upriver in several hours. However, having just spent four days in the city, they decided to stay on board to enjoy the scenery. Excursion passengers would rejoin them around 12:30 p.m.

"We cast off for Vienna promptly at 8 a.m. They serve breakfast until 9, so let's watch the river for a little while," Peter suggested.

Joining others who stayed on board, with the city of Vienna awaiting their arrival, Kathy asked if everyone was aware of the history around the Ferris wheel? "Nope," were the responses. She told them that it was built in 1897, and at 212-foot-high, constructing it without scaffolding became a grueling task. It originally featured 30 enclosed cabins, enough room for 12. It burned down in 1944 during WWII but rebuilt along with the reconstruction of the State Opera House and St. Stephen's Cathedral in 1947.

"How do you know all this?" Sharon asked.

"From the *Viking Daily*," she continued. "It's also been in lots of movies such as *The Living Daylights*. You know, the James Bond film with Timothy Dalton? Also, *Scorpio*, *Letters from an Unknown Woman* and probably more. It received upgrades over the years with new lights, paint and they added a café at the bottom. It takes about 20 minutes and has 15 gondolas. We need to make sure we do this. It goes about 1.6 miles per hour."

The other Cathy said, "High on my list is the Swarovski Kristallwelten Store. They have complimentary refreshments at the Moët & Chandon Bar. I want to see if they have any small crystals I can get for my jewelry pieces."

Anne asked the ladies if they knew of Cathy's artistic abilities making unique gorgeous earrings, bracelets, and necklaces, as Anne showed them the one she was wearing made of sterling silver bobbles with a ruby-colored stone between each piece of silver.

"Does she have a website?" Sharon asked.

Anne texted *filigreeandme.com* and added, "She doesn't brag about her fine pieces but she should; she's so talented."

"You know, it's a little confusing having a Cathy and Kathy with us," Sharon observed. "Well, Catherine and Kathleen, what do you prefer?" Anne asked.

"To make it even worse, there's another Mike and Kathy with their lifetime friends Gil and Angie, from Washington. Turns out Peter and Gil grew up in the same south Salem neighborhood but Gil is several years younger," Anne interjected.

"I'll be Cath, and Kathy can stick with Kathy."

The next several hours they saw scenery of castles, crumbled ruins, small villages, and green hills. Peter looked around. People were reading, one woman stitched a design onto a pillowcase, a man dozed in the sunshine, and some, with their feet up, just stared at the river.

They cruised by a town with a massive old fort and an

even bigger stone block building with a round top with what looked like an emerald lid. Bold gold lettering above the door and arched glass window read OVAE SVRSVM SVNT QVAERITE, maybe a science or medical building, but they had no clue. Just another mystery along the river. The printing on the sign with the name of the town, was too small to read and looked to be about 20 characters long.

They spotted quaint villages along the banks, with rolling hills behind, each with a church or two and always a spire. Other boats, some commercial, some pleasure, shared the water with them. Puffy white clouds dotted the sky.

Var sailed under bridges with banners proudly showing they were in Austria. Across the river, a café situated in a boat looked inviting. Tree-filled small islands were jammed with so many it didn't seem like anything else could survive. Homes were built on sturdy stilts, obviously in case of floods. A picnic table sat beneath a stilted two-story brown house with bright white trim, and a man lollygagged in a hammock by the water's edge. They went into a lock where they disappeared between cement walls.

Around 12:15 their ship made a brief stop in Visegrad where Budapest tour guests rejoined them just in time for lunch. Anne appreciated the choice for meals in the dining room, or on the Aquavit Terrace.

At 1:45, for their safety, they paid close attention to what amounted to a mandatory drill on how to put on lifejackets, and where to go in case of an emergency.

In the afternoon they met the captain for a bridge tour hearing more about their longship which he called a vessel, and the waterways they'd be sailing. He pointed out markers and signs explaining what they meant.

Anne noticed Mrs. Dmitry sitting on the opposite side of the ship, close to the front, during the informative talk by the cruise director, George, about the elegant coffeehouses,

Imperial Austria, and the life and works of Mozart. He also showed pictures and buildings, castles and palaces, and the various styles of architecture.

From 1050 to 1200: Romanesque Style buildings typically have symmetrical floor plans and may include simple round arches set on pillars. These structures can appear quite plain compared to many of the more elaborate styles that follow Romanesque.

1150 to 1450: The Gothic Style exemplifies many of Europe's great cathedrals and abbeys as well as in public buildings like city halls. It is characterized by ribbed vaults, pointed arches and flying buttresses that comprise a lacy but strong structural skeleton, often augmented with stained glass and elaborate carvings, and is designed to draw the eye upward.

1450 to 1600: The Renaissance was exemplified in architecture and also art literature and philosophy influenced by Greek and Roman antiquity as well as by new developments in science. The architecture is harmonious, symmetrical, and formal.

1550 to 1775: Baroque Style architecture is structurally of Renaissance style but highly ornamented with elements like frescoes and sculpted plaster decorations. This style exploited dramatic forms and the use of extremes of light and shade to stimulate the viewer's emotions.

1725 to 1775: Rococo Style, or late Baroque, is the 18th century style that abandoned symmetry and became increasingly ornate. Rooms were elaborately designed complete with elegant furniture, small sculptures, ornamental mirrors, and textiles.

1775 to 1875: The neoclassical Style buildings demonstrate a revival of classical elements: symmetry, columned porticos, triangular pediments, and domes that hearken back to the early Greek and Roman architecture.

1890 to 1910: The Art Nouveau Style or "new art," describes a movement in both the decorative arts and architecture that celebrated natural lines in response to the 19th century industrialization.

At 6:30, the captain and hotel manager toasted and officially welcomed them aboard with a clinking of champagne glasses. Mrs. Dmitry also attended, without her husband.

Anne's entire group of friends were on time when the doors opened for dinner. A talented pianist named Tosho played upbeat music on a grand piano. Delicious-looking menu choices made this decision the hardest of Anne's day.

Later they met in the Lounge for *German 101*, a language lesson provided by the hotel manager. Afterwards, they sat around and listened to melodies by their onboard pianist.

CHAPTER SEVEN

The next morning Anne peeked outside at the sunrise at 4:45. The sky looked the color of a glass of orange juice. Getting up and around, dressed and at breakfast by 8, they looked forward to their days in lovely Vienna.

They'd been to Vienna in the past, but would never tire of its history, the hometown of famous musicians, composers, artists, actors, scientists, and probably even more brilliant and talented people.

Standing on their veranda, Peter told Anne that they were in another landlocked country, bordered by eight countries: Czech Republic, Slovakia, Hungary, Slovenia, Italy, Lichtenstein, Switzerland, and Germany. Austria is slightly smaller than the state of Maine. It's full of trees and meadows and more than half the country is mountainous. The government consists of nine independent federal states with their own provincial governments.

Vienna meant several things to her: larger than life statues, music in a concert hall by famous composers like Strauss and Mozart, gorgeous Lipizzaner horses, Viennese delicacies, incredible architecture including beautiful structures like the Hofburg Palace and Vienna State Opera, and the *Sound of Music*, her favorite movie, even though it was filmed in Salzburg.

They'd watched the Vienna Boys' Choir on their PBS station, with their angelic voices wearing their traditional blue and white sailor's uniforms. It was founded in 1498 by the Emperor Maximilian I of Habsburg, to provide musical accompaniment to the church mass. But the tradition predated that by centuries, as boys have been singing at Vienna's Imperial Chapel since 1296.

"Mornin'. What are y'all fixin' to do after the walking tour?" Debbie inquired.

"We haven't decided yet. Probably just wander around."

"I think we'll do that Schönbrunn Palace tour," Rob stated. Peter mentioned they toured the palace on a previous trip, and it was definitely worth it. "It reminds me of Versailles, outside of Paris."

"Remember everyone, we're in Austria now so we're using Euros."

It was one trip where the US dollar and Euros were just about equal. After breakfast, strolling along a pathway between the river and stone wall, Mike decided to impart a new nautical term. Reading from the Viking newsletter it turns out that *A Square Meal* means *In good weather, the crew's mess was a warm meal served on square wooden platters*.

One of the things Anne loved about Viking is that an excursion is included at every stop. This allowed them to plan what they wanted to see and do on their own. Their entire group went on the Panoramic Vienna tour, a morning overview of driving and walking through Vienna. They met their guide and drove into the city, seeing splendid buildings on the remarkable Ringstrasse; palaces, ornate and grand residences line this famous avenue.

They saw Hofburg Palace, winter residence of the Habsburgs and home of the Spanish Riding School with its Lipizzaner horses. They admired the great Gothic St. Stephen's Cathedral, and viewed the Vienna State Opera concert hall, its façade adorned with elaborate frescoes depicting Mozart's opera, *The Magic Flute*.

After the tour ended, they wandered around, stopping at the arched walkway lined with small shops, and where the famous Lippizaners are stabled. The horses were attentive, obviously feeding time. Anne took a photo of lacy iron works, with a steeple in the background and a horsedrawn carriage, buildings, arched ceilings, tiles, and artwork.

She snapped photos of the city walls with purple wildflowers squeezing through the cracks. Windows of stunning purses including a seafoam, ebony and ivory thin-striped one that caught her attention. Also, a solid mint leather one. One window displayed clothing, a beige lacy skirt with about ten layers of petticoats. A small red and white merry-go-round delighted children, riding mini-cars and bikes, going round and round.

Anne looked forward to visiting a favorite coffeehouse for a sweet treat and Viennese coffee, this beverage being a tradition. On the building there was a red sign with gold lettering, *SLUKA, K. & K. Hoflieferant Conditorei Seit 1891 Wien.*

They sat at a small marble tabletop, with an Austrian newspaper showing that day's headlines. The vaulted ceiling, marble columns, and wood-rounded chairs contributed to the coffeehouse vibe. Eye-popping pastries lined an exquisite casc with rows of treats to select from. Apfelstrudel, Linzer Torte, and others made it hard to choose.

Paper cupcake holders held two-bite treats: lemon tarts, a

lime frosted mystery, various shades of chocolate bars, and more lined the displays. Pear cake, sponge cake with vanilla cream, curd cheese and poppy apricot cake, anniversary cake, chocolate truffle cake with a rolled cookie poked in the frosting, strawberry-royal cake, Sluka cake and so much more.

While selecting hers, Anne observed two elderly men playing cards, one younger woman writing in her journal, and a fifty-something woman reading the newspaper. Four older women were talking miles-a-minute between scrumptious bites.

Standing at the counter trying to decide, Anne read a short history on the treat she was leaning towards. *Prince Metternich requested a special dessert to impress his honored guests at the Hotel Sacher in 1832. The pastry chef was ill that night so the task was left to Franz Sacher, the 16- year-old apprentice.* Anne imagined the stress the young man assumed by having to make a dessert for a prince. *But he did create the famous Sacher Torte and over the years, it grew in popularity among locals and eventually went down in history as one of Europe's most iconic confections.*

Little signs described what they were looking at:

Housecake, almond bases with chocolate mousse

Sluka cake, a light and dark sponge cake, orange Cointreau with Parisian cream

Pear cake, shortcrust pastry with crème fraiche, currant jam, pears, and cinnamon

Dobos cake, sponge cake base, chocolate buttercream and caramel

Esterházy cake, hazelnut base with hazelnut buttercream and cherry brandy

Klimt cake, nut base, nougat cream and marzipan

Chestnut cake, sacher base, chestnuts, cranberry, chocolate short pastry and rum

Raspberry chocolate slice, chocolate base with raspberry cream

Anne selected kaffee and kuchen (coffee and cake), frothy, with equal amounts of milk and coffee and Sachertorte, anything chocolate for her: A light sponge cake thinly coated by hand with top-quality apricot jam, covered with chocolate icing, and served with a generous mound of unsweetened whipped cream on the side. The mountainous whipped cream appeared higher than the cake and twirled in a lovely design.

The first bite was a burst of rich chocolate flavors. "This is amazing!" she could barely utter. The cake wasn't light or heavy. The real decadence came from the dark chocolate frosting with a fudge-like consistency, and the thick ganache tasted so sweet and rich that it prompted Anne to pause for a sip of coffee after every bite.

Anne had never been a coffee drinker except somewhere like here. Peter opted for Grosser Schwarzer, a strong black coffee, equivalent to an espresso, grosser meaning with a double shot.

They read the menu of the variety of ways they could order coffee: Judie ordered Brauner, coffee with a dash of cream and cubed sugar. Cath asked for a Goldener, regular coffee with milk. Kathy requested Kaffee Crème, coffee with a small jug of milk on the side. Julie ordered a Kapuzier, cappuccino. Mike asked for Verlängerter, coffee with extra hot water. Rolland requested a Pharisäer, espresso with sugar, whipped cream, cocoa, and a shot of rum. Casey wanted the Fiaker, an espresso with sugar and cherry brandy, topped with whipped cream. It smelled so good and as he took his first sip he confirmed that it tasted as yummy as everyone imagined.

Peter's empty plate looked like he'd licked it clean with not one morsel of Apfelstrudel left. He loved anything apple, especially apple pie made by Anne's dear Sisterchick, Sue, or Anne's cousin Beth.

On *Var*, Sandra contemplated how she'd gotten to this point in her life, and on this longship of all places. Her husband suggested the trip, most unlike him. He became a recluse, content staying in their comfortable five-room apartment, but during the past several years he'd gotten even worse. She agreed to this unexpected trip as a diversion from their humdrum life. He had reacted oddly to a couple of disconcerting telephone calls in the last few months. He wouldn't talk about the calls or why someone reached out to him.

At home, her escape over the years involved volunteering at an elementary school, reading to the youngsters. She'd branched out for about ten years and taught German to English-speaking ex-pats, some from the US and some from Great Britain. Even though British, she found it useful in her thirties to learn French and German and hoped this would get her by. She hadn't traveled except for a few countries. Now one of her regrets.

She loved exploring the public library where she sat for hours looking at pictures and reading articles in periodicals and books about everywhere and anything. When Dmitry announced the trip, she studied up on architecture. If they had a garden area, she would have been able to landscape, combining bushes and flowers from what she'd read. She knew what type of dog was the best for apartment living. She shied away from WWII history; she'd lived it. She'd traveled to over 70 countries, in her mind. Actually, four in real life. She imagined herself inside another person when reading stories.

Thumbing through fashion magazines, she found a new hair style settling on a short look, just above her ears. It worked well back then with her thick hair. She took a photo of it to her hairdresser who gladly fashioned a Jamie Lee

Curtis look. Now it was thinner and all white. She was quite convinced that after nourishment, shelter, and companionship, stories were the thing people needed most in the world. To her, stories became her comfort.

She once read a poem that expressed her feelings about her love for libraries. She copied it down by hand on white lined paper but forgot to write down the author's name; American she thought.

> *Walking down the avenue, my quest not far away*
> *Visions of many books abound, soon to soothe my*
> *soul that day.*
> *As I entered upon the great hall of many written*
> *words at rest,*
> *Excitement arose within me, luring me to books as*
> *their guest.*
>
> *With map in hand, I climbed the stairs to journey*
> *into many stories.*
> *Imagining how I might dive into the jumble of*
> *tempting lore and glory.*
> *Hidden from view, I could hear the quiet call of tales*
> *left untold.*
> *Waiting for me patiently, arms open, with magical*
> *words of old.*
>
> *How very quiet it is, this great hall with far reaching*
> *knowledge,*
> *I think with great ego, that these books wait just for*
> *me in this old college.*
> *How lucky I am to explore like a wanderlust trav-*
> *eling the world,*
> *With the heap of great patience, I can read so many*
> *books and watch action unfurl.*

*My passionate love for books grows as I gaze upon
    them neatly rowed.*
*Who would love an inanimate object? ...might be
    asked by those who scold.*
*A rouge book left unopened looks at me with a
    child's innocence.*
*Cautiously opened, I tumble into a magical world of
    unjust vengeance.*

*"Can you imagine what the mind conjures up," I ask
    my curious self.*
*Every single book in this entire library has a
    wonderful story to tell.*

*It might be an itty-bitty story, a novel, history, or a
    textbook you see,*
*Inspired authors with a desire so deep to write, and
    yes indeed, to read.*
*Heartfelt words burst from their souls, some authors
    well-known, others not so,*
*Who really knows their names and faces, forgotten
    in complex histories of old.*

*Tattered, leather-bound books sit quietly on the
    shelves of many.*
*Adventures await those that love to read stories and
    certainly there are plenty.*
*My hand reaches out and strokes the fine covers of
    hidden gifts for me to discover,*
*Bent pages show the love of a story, so delightful for
    me to slowly uncover.*

*To those who love wonder, excitement, and the sense
    of raw emotion,*

Your choices are many, a gift of discovery sometimes
in slow motion.
My small corner of the authoress world is sparked
with imagination,
Dreams to fulfill the laughter of those who love my
pugs and creations.

As I aimlessly wander along the rows of ideas and
thoughts,
I look like a drunken sailor for those who know
naught.
In this silent world are the storytellers and reciters of
many tales,
I explore the authored stories, poems, and occasion-
ally scary fables.

I sit down and ponder on a dust covered old chair,
of the many tales whispered from the library books
by the stairs.
Imagine my surprise when one special book plops
down at my feet.
"Please open me," it says, as my tears of joy blend
with my loving heartbeat.

While overlooking the Danube from their balcony, Sandra recalled how proud she was of herself after John's death. They'd never purchased a home, renting seemed easier. She had friends from work, and family who helped her get through the rough patches. She wasn't interested in dating and thought she'd be fine alone.

Some years later she needed a change and moved from London to Munich. At age 49, she attended a work-related afternoon event in Munich, and noticed a man alone in a corner looking a little lost. He was maybe six foot, four inches, or taller, with thinning, gray-streaked brown hair that complemented his fair complexion. She boldly went over and said hello. He had a winsome smile, good teeth, which mattered to her, a neatly cropped beard the same color as his hair, and wrinkled skin around his slightly pinched, steel blue eyes. Obviously older than herself, at this point in life, she didn't care much about age.

He spotted her, too, as she came in alone. Probably five-foot, six inches with a medium build, shoulder-length wavy blonde hair with lighter streaks of gray, highlighted by the sun streaming from the windows. She had an engaging, safe smile and her hazel eyes squinted from the sunbeams.

It had taken a few tries to find something he seemed interested in talking about. It wasn't current events such as the dissolution of the USSR, Margaret Thatcher resigning, or unemployment or cost of food, definitely not movies, theater, or books. But East and West Germany reunited, and the Hubble Space Telescope launch piqued his interest. And football. He followed West Germany in the World Cup and rooted for them to beat Czechoslovakia in an upcoming quarter-finals match.

Sandra remembered how Dmitry explained he was an interpreter, knowing several languages, and companies paid him to attend events like this just in case he was needed. He didn't know anyone there. But his lifelong work had been in various positions in the banking industry. "I'm a numbers man," he chuckled.

"Me, too," she exclaimed. "I've been a bookkeeper for years for various companies." For some reason she played down her importance and years of experience. She didn't want him knowing she was more than a bookkeeper, over-seeing an entire department with employees and budgets. Some men could be intimidated by her position at a major company.

"Well, we have something in common then," he added.

She tried to put him at ease with small talk; he seemed nervous, looking often at his watch. Or bored. Or because she was English and he Austrian. She assumed bored until he called a week later. When he called he apologized for not calling sooner, but said he'd been busy at work, and watching the World Cup as West Germany continued to advance. He seemed to think because Sandra was from Great Britain she should care that West Germany would be playing England in the semifinals. She didn't really but celebrated with him overlooking Marienplatz on the fifth floor at Café Glocken-spiel when his team beat Argentina 1-0.

Six months later Dmitry and Sandra were married. The age difference of nine years didn't matter to either of them or being from different countries. It was his third and her second marriage. He deserved some credit for trying out a few things she enjoyed, an occasional movie and museum opening. She didn't know much about him but would glean some tidbits over the years. Now she'd been married to him twice as long as her first love. She felt a fondness towards Dmitry, but not the same love of her soulmate.

She really didn't know much about his first two wives. He told her both died young. She'd never know these were lies made up to make himself look better. He never disclosed that his two wives left him. At random social events over the years, she gleaned snippets of information about his back-ground; true or false, she'd probably never know. WWII was mentioned and Nazis alluded to. He never talked about his past only that he had been, and was to this day, in banking but later as an interpreter.

If she'd known what she now suspected could be true, she never would have married him. And just as secretive as he was about his background so was she. She never wanted him to know her Jewish heritage and how she lost family in the concentration camps, mostly in Poland. Her parents moved to London the summer of 1939, before Poland was bombarded on land, and in air, by Germany on September 1. They had saved their young daughter's life.

After all the sweet treats, Anne and Peter wandered by more windows of clothing, art, and crystal chandeliers. A window of dozens of yellow ducks in a variety of costumes: a nurse, one holding a dumbbell, one under an umbrella, in a boat, holding beer steins, dressed in a sailor shirt, Mozart, police-man, baker in a hat and apron, one with a present and cupcake, all for sale with a sign pointing to The Old Phar-macy Café and Shop. They stopped again where the Lipiz-zaner horses are housed. One white horse watched Anne closely, peering from his Dutch door with the top half open. Turned out his handler was coming with a bucket of food not far from where Anne stood.

While looking at the horses, Anne saw Dmitry strolling at the end of the pavilion. "Look, there he is again, and by himself," she pointed out to Peter.

"Maybe he's a spy," Peter said quietly, like keeping the revelation to themselves.

"You really think so? I thought of that, too," as she lowered her voice. "But decided, no, he's too old. But see how sometimes he uses that cane and sometimes not?"

"Well, maybe that walking stick is hollow and he has some important papers tightly rolled up inside. Or maybe it's like a dart gun," he said in a Scottish James Bond voice.

"You are not funny and don't tease me about him. Some-thing is off with him."

"Let's do the Hofburg Palace especially since we've toured

Schönbrunn Palace, the Habsburg's summer place. Hofburg is their winter house," Peter suggested.

"So remind me, what's the difference between Hapsburg and Habsburg?" Anne inquired.

"I'm Googling it because I'm not sure. Okay, the House of Habsburg or Hapsburg is also known as the House of Austria. Hofburg is the former imperial palace of the Habsburg dynasty. So Habsburg and Hapsburg are the same, just spelled differently."

"Okay, but let's be consistence and go with Habsburg; it's confusing hearing it used both ways."

Peter continued, "So Hofburg is a group of historic buildings with open squares and is pedestrianized so we can just stroll around. We can do the palace and museum, Spanish Riding School, and the Imperial Treasury. It was built in the 13th century and expanded several times afterwards. Since 1946 it is the official residence and workplace of the president of Austria."

"I can't even imagine how they knew to build these buildings all curved this way," Anne observed, while standing in front of one of the most iconic attractions in Vienna. "Just the grandeur and spectacle of the building and the grounds."

Peter pulled out his guidebook and told Anne that six centuries of Habsburgs ruled from Vienna, including Maria Theresa in the late 1700s. She was famous for having 16 children and cleverly marrying many of them into the various other royal families around Europe in order to expand her empire.

Today's palace is furnished as it was in the 19th century from the age of Maria's great great grandson, Emperor Franz Josef. He ruled for 68 years.

They started on the ground floor with tableware, collection after collection of it. Thousands of pieces of silverware and gold flatware, china and glasses, all seemed a bit over the top even though the craftsmanship is undeniable and who doesn't need dishes for every season and occasion?

"Just look at those fancy cake tins," a woman declared to a companion. "She must own a bakery," Anne whispered to Peter going by ornate black stoves. The dining room was set just as it would have been with perfectly arranged golden-ware, and each beverage having a different glass.

Twenty glittery rooms were filled with precious bits and pieces, odds and ends, mementos, and history.

For Empress Elisabeth, nicknamed Sisi, her museum reflects on her private life, her rebellion against the court, her beauty, and sporting aptitude.

"Oh my word it's her bathroom, with hairbrush, comb, mirror, and more," Anne pointed out. "And look at those stunning replicas of dresses and jewelry."

Anne told Peter, "So, Sisi was the wife of Emperor Franz Joseph and married at 16. I've watched several movies and as a teenager she had a fairy-tale wedding that turned sad as the strictness of court life squelched her free spirit. The saga sort of reminds of Princess Diana, unprepared for what was ahead. Everyone thought Sisi unsuitable but I think she felt lost. It didn't help she was at odds with her mother-in-law who took over raising Sisi's daughters. She had a son that improved her standing at court but her health suffered under the stress. Then her son and his mistress died in a supposed murder-suicide and Sisi really never recovered. She withdrew from duties yet traveled, without her family. Then she became obsessive about main-taining her youthful figure and beauty. Get this, she was murdered, stabbed in the heart, by an Italian anarchist in Geneva when she was 60. How tragic is that?" "Very" was Peter's response.

Anne stood glued, staring at an incredible painting of Sisi wearing an off-the-shoulder gown that must have had at least 20 petticoats, creating the puffiness, with her dramatic black hair flowing down her the back.

In the Imperial Chapel they saw an old Bible. The library held thousands of books. In the Treasury they took much more time viewing all kinds of finery. Anne always enjoyed imperial treasuries; it meant crown jewels, swords and scepters, gems and jewelry, relics, and tapestries.

A heavy-looking golden headpiece, more like a cap or helmet than a crown that could cover an entire head, was inlaid with pearls, big rubies, even bigger aquamarines and probably some diamonds. Whoever got stuck wearing it would surely have a headache if their head didn't fall off.

"Now that's a purse!" Anne exclaimed, "just a modest little gold bag." Every stone imaginable was set into gold circles covering the entire bag. Larger stones lined the top and even the clasp was a large light blue stone.

A crown with six scallops and a gold cross on the top was covered in pearls and similar gemstones, but amber had been added.

A red and gold ceremonial robe, with gold on the elegant design and trim, was draped around a headless mannequin.

In another display, looking similarly spectacular, was a blue and gold robe with a third of the fabric draped on the floor. A sword was positioned on the floor as well.

Then there was *THE* crown. It looked like anyone having to wear it would need some practice strengthening one's neck muscles. All gold with pointy bits trimmed with different sizes of pearls, each point completely surrounded by pearls and a huge red stone in front outlined with more pearls, matched the red swath, the only cloth visible. On top sits a large royal blue gem, maybe a sapphire. It's the Imperial Crown of Austria. Laid below is a fancy, bejeweled scepter.

Stepping into the crypt, they were surrounded by black iron tombs decorated with regalia. How the Royals wanted to be remembered is reflected in the tombs they often helped design. Franz Josef is in an austere military tomb. Sisi won the prize for most fresh flowers on any tomb.

"Let's check out the horses on the way out, I'm sort of fading," Anne admitted. The Spanish Riding School is an Austrian institution dedicated to the preservation of classical dressage and the training of Lipizzaner horses.

The riding school was first named during the Habsburg monarchy in 1572 and the oldest kind in the world. Records show that a wooden riding arena was first commissioned in 1565 and named for the Spanish horses that formed one of the bases of the Lipizzaner breed which is used exclusively at the school. Today the horses delivered to the riding school are bred in a village in western Austria.

The horses looked powerful, all with gray coats. They have a long head, small ears, and large eyes.

"Aren't they gorgeous?" Anne gushed, always a horse lover. "They look about twice as big as the Icelandic horses that we rode a couple of years ago."

"You rode, not me," Peter reminded her. He never got on anything that had a mind of its own; only things with a motor or burner, such as when he was a hot air balloon pilot.

The couple hopped on the subway heading back to their floating hotel. A couple of stops later they walked past people lazing in hammocks tied to posts.

"Hard to imagine Schönbrunn as a hunting lodge," Debbie mentioned.

Rob read from a flyer that he was handed when he got their tickets, *Purchased by the Emperor Maximillian II in 1569, the original estate included a house, stables, and a garden and a brook which gave it its name. Various Habsburg rulers used it as a*

summer residence until Empress Maria Theresa enlarged the
palace to its present form between 1740 and 1715. The architect
perfected its neoclassical façade adding pilasters and the distinctive
paint color known as "Schönbrunn Yellow."

The palace garden's Great Parterre is lined with 32 life-size
statues of Greek and Roman deities and culminates at the
Neptune Fountain, where the sea god is surrounded by
nymphs, Tritons, and seahorses. It also includes an orangery, a
facsimile of a Roman ruin, an obelisk, an arcaded gloriette
monument, numerous greenhouses and the Tiergarte, suppos-
edly the world's oldest continually operating zoo. The palace
itself boasts 1441 rooms and the grounds are home to the
Vienna Imperial Carriage Museum. The entire complex has
been designated a UNESCO site for its remarkable baroque
ensemble.

Standing between two columns with gold birds on top,
they saw a huge plot of land with buildings surrounding the
entire square and the palace at the end all painted in the
same shade of yellow.

They bought tickets, picked up their audio headsets, and
toured on their own entering on the main floor seeing the
Palace Chapel, White and Gold Rooms, and Bergl Rooms.
When Maria Theresa grew older she suffered from the heat
during the summer months and stayed in this suite on the
ground floor. The Crown Prince Apartment was where the
only son of Emperor Joseph and Empress Elisabeth stayed.

Ascending the Blue Staircase where the Habsburgs threw
balls and banquets, stucco walls and chandeliers topped by a
ceiling fresco showed the impressiveness of Maria Theresa's
reign.

The Antechamber situated between the Blue Staircase
and the private apartments acted as sort of a buffer zone.
They walked through the Aides-de-Camp Room for army
officers assigned to the emperor's personal service. This

room was next to the Guard's Room, where men were posted to stand guard over access to the apartments.

Next came the Billiard Room, the Audience Chamber, Emperor Joseph's Study then his bedroom. A small room leads into the apartments of Empress Elisabeth. A room with deep red wallpaper called the Stairs Cabinet served as Empress Elisabeth's writing room and her Dressing Room was adjacent to the bedroom.

They strolled around the Imperial Couple's bedroom, the Interior of the Salon of Empress Elisabeth, the Marie Antoinette Room also the family dining room, and the Yellow Salon, which is the first room facing the palace gardens.

The Balcony Room has numerous pictures of Maria Theresa and her children. They stepped into the Hall of Mirrors with red draperies and chandeliers that caused light to bounce from mirror to mirror.

Three Rosa Rooms are named after the artist Joseph Rosa, who painted 15 landscapes in the Large Rosa Room. They looked at paintings of scenery from Italy and Alpine countries in the First Small Rosa Room. The Second Small Rosa Room is one large room and two adjoining smaller rooms full of floor to ceiling art and flowing red draperies. "That a lot of expensive fabric," Debbie said. Located next to the Blue Staircase, the Lantern Room is the anteroom to the palace's ceremonial hall, the Great Gallery.

"Those frescoes in the Great Gallery of all those horses and people floating in the sky, portraits of Joseph I, and naked people drinking and eating, this place is overwhelming," Rob stated. "I've seen enough decadence and overspending. No wonder the peasants rebelled."

"Wasn't that in France? *Les Misérables*, you know." Debbie chuckled.

In the Small Gallery there are two cabinets opposite each

other in mirror-image, both decorated with an array of art from China and Japan.

In the Hall of Ceremonies, a chandelier appeared to be about the size of a Smart Car. Here the monarch received her guests. The Horses Room served as a dining room. The Blue Chinese Salon was stunning and they both spent some time looking at the particularly stunning interiors. A room with black lacquer panels from China blanket the walls of the Vieux Laque Room. Napoleon's Room, probably his bedroom during his stays in 1805 and 1809, has a massive tapestry from Brussels of scenes from a soldier's life.

Debbie particularly enjoyed the Porcelain Room. The small room served as Maria Theresa's private writing room and reflects the monarch's personal tastes that show her appreciation of chinoiserie fashion of the times.

In the Millions Room Rob grumbled, "Well, this is appropriately named, full of extravagance."

"Yes, but *it is* the ceremonial rooms used for the Viennese court. It was originally called the Mirrors Room where she received private audiences," Debbie explained.

Through salons, Princess Sofie's Study, the Red Salon, the Rich Room with Maria Theresa's state bed, and a Hunting Room, they'd reached their limit and completed the tour of the remarkable palace.

"Shall we go for a walk in the park?"

"Yes, that sounds like a great idea, fresh air."

In the gardens they waved to Rolland and Judie strolling under a lengthy trellis of hanging purple wisteria. There were marble statues as far as they could see.

"It's a garden on steroids," Judie stated.

"Getting some ideas?" Rolland asked his wife.

"Ah, no," Judie answered, "too high maintenance."

"What would you say to a cup of coffee back inside?" Rob asked Debbie.

"That's exactly what I'd like right now," she answered as she took Rob's warm hand.

Friends ambled sporadically into the Lounge for a pre-dinner beverage. "The guys are talking sports, *again*," Cath said, as Anne and Peter sat down.

The pianist played the Lionel Richie song "Truly," and Debbie asked, "Do you know Lionel is from Alabama? True. And Helen Keller and Rosa Parks, just to name a few." Rob and Casey were talking about the Crimson Tide. "At home we don't say Hi or Hello, it's Roll Tide or War Eagle," Rob said.

"I'll have a Coke," Debbie requested, "and I'd have a piece of fried chicken if available. Everything fried is best," she chuckled, treating anyone around her like they were her next-door neighbor or family. She proceeded to tell them about the glorious palace and gardens they'd spent the afternoon touring.

For dinner most requested the regional specialties, Alt Wiener Erdäpfelsuppe, a potato soup with root vegetables and bacon. *Everything's Better with Bacon* was one of Peter's favorite sayings. They both selected Wiener Schnitzel, breaded Viennese veal with a warm potato salad.

The sun set on their side of the longship as Anne sat in the warmth reading a fascinating short story from *Behind Colorful Doors* about a woman who grew up from the 1950s to 70s in Yugoslavia under President Tito, then what tragically happened to the nation when Tito died in 1980.

CHAPTER EIGHT

W hen Peter woke his left leg ached. He told Anne that he didn't think he'd go to Bratislava after all. Six months earlier he'd ruptured his Achilles tendon which laid him up for almost an entire month in a cast, then into a boot for two months along with weekly physical therapy. They joked, somewhat now, but it was a traumatic experience for both of them. It also reaffirmed why she hadn't become a nurse. And why they always purchased travel insurance. Even though mostly healed, he didn't have all the strength back. "I'm just going to laze around here for the day."

At breakfast, Mike imparted the *Nautical Term of the Day* and read from the *Viking Daily*, *Let the Cat Out of the Bag. In the Royal Navy, the punishment prescribed for most serious crimes was flogging. This was administered by the bosun's mate using a whip called a "cat of nine tails." The "cat" was kept in a leather bag, and it was considered bad news indeed when the "cat was let out of the bag." Other sources attribute the expression to the Old English market scam of selling someone a pig in a poke (or bag) but replacing the pig with a cat instead.*

Not far from Vienna they crossed the border to Slovakia,

the capital Bratislava, and a new country to experience. On the 45-minute motor coach ride on the D1 motorway, Anne and Julie chatted with Casey and Cath sitting behind them, and Rob and Debbie across the aisle. One other person who had become increasingly familiar to Anne, Dmitry sat about midway, by himself.

Danika, their guide for the day who lived in Bratislava, said she could tell by the age of the group they'd likely remember when Czechoslovakia split in half, creating Slovakia and the Czech Republic. Nodding heads communicated yes, affirming her suspicion.

"Gosh, she sure looks like Reese Witherspoon," Cath observed with Julie in total agreement.

Danika said that the peaceful split came as a result of a nationalistic sentiment and was decided by the federal assembly who voted on the matter. On January 1, 1993, Czechoslovakia separated into two independent states, which is now known as the Velvet Divorce, in reference to the Velvet Revolution, due to its peaceful and negotiated nature. Both countries divided their common goods such as embassies and military equipment, on a two-to-one ratio to reflect their populations.

Although the dissolution didn't lead to any serious unrest, the new boundaries did create a unique situation, inconveniently splitting the border towns in half.

At the time, a widespread storyline argued that the split was purely a political move decided behind closed doors by leaders, the Czechs' Klaus and the Slovaks' Mecair, against the will of the population. There was some truth in that, as the opinion polls showed the vast majority of Czechs and Slovaks were in favor of the preservation of Czechoslovakia, and against the breakup.

Yet the truth is more complicated. Although the Czechs and Slovaks wanted to preserve Czechoslovakia, both sides also wanted reform. There were incompatible versions founded on deeply rooted grievances and frustrations. While Slovak nationalism sentiment strived for more autonomy, Czech nationalism embraced Czechoslovakianism mainly due to their privileged position within the federation.

Slovaks didn't completely adhere to the concept as they often saw Czechoslovakianism as patronizing and paternalistic. Ever since the foundation of the First Republic in 1918, the majority of the people in Slovakia really considered Czechoslovakia as their genuine home, but they wanted more autonomy, more control of their decision-making, and were tired feeling that their fate had been decided by the bureaucrats in Prague. Most felt that the Federal Capital looked down on the less developed Slovaks.

You've heard the saying, They had a lot of baggage? That was the case here, according to Danika. After the split both countries went their own way. Klaus pursued the rapid privatization that made the Czech Republic an economic star of central Europe, but also created public anger as leaders and multinationals benefited unequally from the process.

Mecair tightened his grip and ruled as a semi-authoritarian strongman slowing the process of his country's accession into the European Union, and briefly making it a regional outsider, until he was democratically displaced in 1998.

The demographics also significantly changed. While the Czech Republic became an ethnically homogeneous country, Slovakia was still home to a strong Hungarian minority, with nearly 60,000 Roma communities and between 300,000 to 500,000 Hungarians.

She said despite their breakup the Czech Republic and Slovakia remained more closely linked than any other two countries in Europe, although the dissolution seemed like a defeat and failure for many people. She said that no one is advocating for reunification, and pointed out that the Czechs and Slovaks have been separated throughout most of their history.

Their relationship to the common past remains highly asymmetrical and strained by long-running prejudices on both sides, while the grievances have something to do with it. More current grievances, like the fact that the Czech Republic cunningly stole the Czechoslovakian flag after the breakup, also play a role in the distain on each side of the border.

Danika told them that while the Czech Republic celebrated the century of the foundation of Czechoslovakia in style with great pomp, no event was held in Slovakia. In Slovakia it only qualified as Memorial Day. However, to mark the century, the country instead decided to implement a one day off public holiday on October 30. Meanwhile, January 1, despite being the official independence day for both fails to have any real significance to date partly because neither Slovakia nor the Czech Republic wants to celebrate the 1993 dissolution, and because it overshadows New Year's Day.

Danika asked if some were going to Prague after the cruise. Heads nodded. She said, "You'll get an interesting story when you get there. You'll hear about the history. I think what I've told you is pretty accurate and even though it might be a little boring to you, it's part of our history. As everybody puts it, you'll get a different spin on things. The fact is most of the time we feel like stepchildren, not as important as the people in the Czech Republic."

If someone fell asleep during her history lesson, upon waking they would have seen a noticeable change in the architecture, much different than in Austria. Straight ahead, looming over a double-floor motorway and railroad truss bridge, a metal structure looked similar to the Space Needle in downtown Seattle. Danika told them it's the "New Bridge" meaning harbor bridge.

They crossed the Danube and to the left on a rocky hilltop stood an enormous white building with more red tile roofs. Danika pointed it out and said, "That's where we're headed, the castle." It looked like a fortress guarding that area.

The architecture looked different, statelier, but not over-done. They drove past a soft yellow four-story apartment building with white, curly designed window and door trim. The attached building was painted an off-white with black trim. An aqua building appeared to be the same height, but less wide. The enormous colorful complex stretched out in shades of pink, cream, aqua, and teal, just to name a few.

A stark white, royal blue and cherry-red Slovakian flag rippled in the breeze. The coat of arms consists of a red shield in early Gothic style, with a silver double cross standing on the middle peak of a dark blue mountain of three peaks which looked more like knolls to Anne. The double cross is a symbol of the Christian faith, and the hills represent the three symbolic mountain ranges.

They drove by Grassalkovich Palace and Freedom Square up to Bratislava Castle. Danika assured them that after some time at the castle they'd descend to Old Town, visiting the places they just passed.

On a windy street through a ritzy neighborhood heading to the castle, homes with expansive views of the river and the city below looked custom-built, fancy, and costly.

After disembarking the bus, they walked uphill, reaching a relief map of the castle complex. It seemed massive starting at the Vienna Gate, St. Nicholas Church, Sigis-mund's Gate, Castle Steps, Leopold's Gate restaurants, and gardens, they could be here all day soaking in the new vibes. The immense rectangular white building stands on an isolated rocky hill of the Little Carpathians, directly above the Danube in the middle of Bratislava. Even wearing sunglasses, they squinted due to the bright sunshine reflecting off the white castle.

The Vienna Gate is impressively enormous, made of white stone, with designs at the top of each side. It's the main entrance to the castle complex and stands next to the headquarters of the Slovak Parliament.

Curving around to the back into a courtyard a grandiose statue of the bronze King Svätopluk sitting on his rearing horse greeted them. Called the Yard of Honor, it is also known as Svätopluk the Great, Ruler of Moravia. Casey, standing at the base of the statue, stood about half the height of the cement block, with the colossal king and horse towering above.

Anne and Julie tried taking selfies with the glinting river and boats, red rooftops, and green spaces in the background. Neither being good at it, they ended up with several photos of them crooked, heads cut off, and both laughing hysterically at their ineptness. A miniature red train stopped to drop off and pick up those who didn't want to walk up or down the hill.

Julie nudged Anne, dropping her voice, "Isn't that your guy over there in the trees? That tall man?"

"Jules, he's *not* my guy. He's old and strange and I'm not gonna look."

"Well, you need to look. What's he doing? Where's he going? It looks like there's a drop-off and he's going to walk off the edge."

"I can't watch. It stresses me out but no one even seems to be concerned about him.

"Maybe he has dementia."

"Probably just old age. His wife said he's in his nineties. He's been doing weird stuff our entire vacation."

"Well, what if he gets lost? He could be dead down there and nobody would even know."

"Maybe his wife tracks him with one of those phone apps like *Find My Friends*."

Rob and Debbie were standing close by and he mischievously said, "Now Julie, don't encourage Anne's vivid imagination. She's seen him other places acting suspiciously too." The three of them chuckled, the fourth pouted a little.

Crunching on gravel they sauntered through the manicured gardens of curly patterns made of knee-high boxwood hedges. Mossy-colored leaves with bright magenta impatiens separated the boxy borders. On the steps at the back of the castle, overlooking the gardens, Anne stood by a cute, pudgy, white marble cherub taller than herself, holding a container overflowing with purple flowers.

In the square they saw Roland Fountain, sometimes referred to as Maximilian Fountain, the most famous fountain in Bratislava. Maximilian II, the King of Royal Hungary in 1572, ordered its construction to provide a public water system. The fountain is topped by a statue of Maximilian dressed as a knight in full armor. Anne took a photo to show their Rolland.

"Every building on the main square is worthy of attention but the one that stands out the most is the main landmark, the Old Town Hall. The rebuilt Town Hall on the square began to be fully used in 1434 with the arched underpass built to enable those to enter the Town Hall from the Square. This extraordinary arch has been preserved in all of its beauty to this day," Danika proudly boasted.

The creamy yellow and white square clock tower butts up to Old Town Hall, a complex of buildings from the 14th century. It's the oldest city hall in the country, and one of the oldest stone buildings still standing in Bratislava, with the tower built about 1370. A plaque with a line marking the water level of the Danube during disastrous floods in February 1850 is affixed to the wall.

Sunbeams bounced from the windowpanes above the arched entrance. Under three long windows is a conglomeration of emerald, onyx, copper, and snow-white circled tiles. The dormer style windows are encircled with blocks of cobalt, strawberry, and milky tiles. It all seemed out of place to retired art teacher Cath.

Danika pointed to a cannonball embedded in the Tower Wall, shot by Napoleon's soldiers in 1809 during bombardment of the city. The Hall is the oldest museum featuring an exhibit of its history, and of torture devices. They opted to skip the torture instruments' exhibit and the Old Town dungeons featuring antique weapons and armor.

One by one tourists sat on the bench where a bronze statue of a Napoleonic soldier with his arms crossed rests against the back of the bench. Supposedly he has his backside squarely directed toward the French Embassy building, and the sculptor intended the depiction to be a modern day dig at the French for the siege of Bratislava during the Napoleonic times. However, Danika explained another version. The soldier is supposed to have been going through Bratislava when he fell in love with a local girl, stayed in the city, and became a producer of sparkling wine. His name is Hubert, which is also the name of Slovakia's most popular sparkling wine brand.

Close by, a six-foot plastic waffle cone filled with soft vanilla ice cream easily catches people's attention. Anne took a quick photo of colorful mounds of gelato: strawberry, banana, cherry, dragon fruit, grape, strawberry, salted caramel, Stracciatella, passionfruit, lemon, pistachio, mint and chocolate, lavender, and the most interesting of all, Paul's Smile and Sea Buckthorn.

"Sea Buckthorn?" Anne raised her eyebrows.

A young woman with long pink hair held back by a purple tie-dye scrunchie, obviously had a lot of expertise in explaining something most Americans wouldn't know, at least those from the West Coast. She told them that sea buckthorn, a deciduous shrub can grow up to 25 feet tall. The flowers are greenish-yellow with four petals, and the fruit ripens in the fall, producing peachy coral berries about 1/2 inch in diameter. "It's extremely healthy, too. How about trying a sample?" she asked in a voice sort of daring Anne, who would never turn down a taste of gelato.

"Sure."

"Me, too, please," Cath added.

"Me, three, please," Julie said.

"Gosh, it's so refreshing."

"Well, what do you taste?"

"Yum, it's citrus, sort of like a tart orange."

"With maybe something tropical."

"Sort of a blend."

"Very good. It's orange with mango," the ice cream server revealed.

"Could I please have one scoop of Buckthorn and lemon?"

"I'll have what she's having," Debbie added.

Continuing their stroll through town, Danika pointed to a small alcove within a yellow cement arch. A funny statue of a small naked man, or maybe a sprite, looked to be escaping the confines. Danika said rumor has it that he had been placed there to make fun of a former owner of the building who used to spy on passersby, especially women, through a small window.

At Pressburg Bajgel, Sweet & Local Since 1890, a golden-brown, eight-foot crescent-shaped bagel, with two round saucer-size eyes, tempts bagel lovers. A smile is carved under the big eyes.

Anne heard the familiar bird chirp coming from her purse. A text from Peter: **Having a good time?**

Anne: **Yes, it's a fabulous city. R U feeling ok?**

Peter: **By the pool, living the dream.**

She laughed out loud and read it to Julie, Casey, and Cath, who also chuckled, because they knew Peter was not the laze-around-the pool type of guy, nor was there one on the longship.

Anne sent a laughing face emoji.

Peter: **On our veranda reading the memoirs of retired airline pilot called,** *Unlearning to Fly, Navigating the Turbulence and the Bliss of Growing up in the Sky,* **by Russ Roberts.**

Anne: **You'd love this city. We should move here.**

Peter: **U said that about Budapest, 2.** He saw a winking emoji as her final comment.

They continued to stroll narrow walkways, past outdoor seating of cantaloupe-colored chairs with matching umbrellas, windows chock full of wooden toys, handmade cloth bags with embroidered colorful designs, clothing, blue and white porcelain paperweights, flower vases and glass, glass, glass, everywhere. A shopper's dream come true and all very reasonably priced.

Unfortunately, they didn't have time for the Konditorei Kormuth, or Cake Museum, but the window display showed mannequins in different stages of creating cakes.

Another statue, *Schone Naci*, is a bald man holding his top hat, leaning against a pillar wearing a long coat past his knees, with a contented look and pleasant smile. The old man is the only statue made of silver, the rest are all bronze. He is also the only statue of a real person. His name was Ignac Lamar and he lived in Pressburg, the former name of Bratislava at the turn of the 19th and 20th centuries.

"Everything has a legend," Danika said. "Ignac loved a woman who sadly did not love him back. This disappointed him so much that he went mad. People often saw him giving flowers to random women he met in the streets. He always wore a hat which you can see on the statue," she finished.

Seeing a young man lying on in the street stopped Julie in her tracks. He and other tourists were taking pictures of *Čumil*, a bronze sculpture of a man peeping out of a manhole. He is either resting after cleaning the sewer, or he's looking up women's skirts. The sign reads "Man at Work."

"This is about the prettiest building I've ever seen," Anne exclaimed. "The Primate's Palace, just behind the Town Hall, is a neoclassical palace with a soft pink and white exterior, at least a block long, and three stories high. It houses the famous Hall of Mirrors and is also where the signing of the peace treaty between Austria and France occurred in 1805," Danika told them. "On the roof, the allegorical statues represent the Cardinal's human qualities and achievements. Atop the coat of arms of the cardinal, the first occupant of the palace, is his hat. The iron model weighs 30 pounds. Today it houses the office of the mayor and is the location for city council meetings, concerts, and conferences," Danika concluded.

On a quick walk through they saw a rare collection of English tapestries from the 17th century manufactured in Great Britain. "They were found in the Hall of Mirrors during a reconstruction," Danika told them. Once again Anne appreciated walking through a town with a local guide. How else would they learn all of this cool history, see all the statues, and hear their stories and legends.

The exquisite fountain of St. George depicts the legendary knight slaying a dragon and it stands in the square's inner courtyard.

In Hviezdoslav Square in Old Town, they looked towards the Slovak National Theatre, an eclectic building. Swirling patterns of light and dark stonework on the plaza with wide expanses of greenery, lush trees, benches, and tall flowerpots with coral and tangerine trailing geraniums, created a pristine and a gorgeous sight to behold.

Closer to the theater sits a fountain with a bronze, larger than life-size, slightly bent, mustached man, looking at the waterspouts below. It's none other than the man who the square is named after, Pavol Hviezdoslav, one of the most important poets in Slavic history.

Not far away stands an interesting statue of a man dressed in a suit, while a little man wearing a top hat whispers in his ear, and a snail sits at the base of the statue's feet. It's Hans Christian Andersen.

One of the newer statues is a girl sitting on a Slovenska Posta bronze letterbox while leaning against a pole. The postal box is suspended about three feet off the ground and is attached to two poles. Another girl sits on her skateboard leaning against the other pole. The postal box is a real one.

Their group went into a restaurant, purportedly an institution in Bratislava, called Zylinder. It felt cozy and bright, with floor-to-ceiling windows facing the tree-lined avenue. The white ceiling was interspersed with Kelly-green painted wood beams, the color prominent throughout. The friends shared a large booth, while others in their tour group sat at tables and chairs.

"Thankfully he didn't fall off the edge and die," Julie pointed to Dmitry, sitting with a group of elderly people on the tour. "Look, he's actually talking," Anne observed a first.

Celery-green glasses were filled with water, and wicker baskets of dense bread arrived warm. The restaurant serves local food, including Viennese and Hungarian fare. Anne selected pumpkin ravioli while others ordered entrees of baked chicken, pasta, and a classic Viennese dish—boiled veal served in a mix of minced apples and horseradish. This came highly recommended so Rob ordered it. The stuffed peppers in tomato sauce tasted excellent. Everyone took a bite of the yummy Halusky, potato dough dumplings about the size of a cherry, filled with sheep's cheese and topped with bacon.

Waddling out after the big midday meal, they observed a five-foot-tall pink pig inviting people in to the Pressburg Restaurant and Bar next door. He wears a bronze coat of armor and holds a long-handled wooden spoon in one hand, and a shield with a pig on it in the other.

Next to Pressburg, a polar bear not quite the size of an actual one sits outside ICEBAR waving his paw. An uneven black line under his black nose indicates either a pleased or hungry smile.

Seven colorful umbrellas across and seven down, covered an avenue and were suspended between two buildings. Handcrafted items of birds, suns, and yard art were on display. Everything they saw they wanted to buy. Anne bought an egg-shaped, hand-painted Christmas ornament, and a fridge magnet. They all made purchases, always wanting to support the local economy.

They entered St. Martin's Cathedral, a three nave Gothic cathedral with four chapels and a creamy white tower with a seafoam-colored spire. Danika said that the tower virtually formed a part of the town's fortification and was built into the city's defensive walls.

The interior of the church is large: 230 feet long by 75 feet wide, and 52 feet high. It features a grand internal divided portal. The cinnamon-colored square floor tiles are placed to create a diamond pattern.

Anne sat down so she could take everything in. Stained glass windows were always a favorite and they didn't disappoint. The entire ceiling shimmered in the light, creating a copper hue. The nave of the structure, consisting of three aisles, is divided by two rows of eight columns. The cathedral is constructed in a traditional crucifix shape. Between two stained glass windows, a statue depicts St. Martin in typical Hungarian hussar dress. The saint is dividing his cloak to give part to a man as protection from the cold.

Between 1563 and 1830 the cathedral served as the coronation church for the Hungarian kings and their consorts. It is marked to this day by a 600-pound gilded replica of the Hungarian crown perched on top of the cathedral's 278-foot-tall neo-Gothic tower. Ten kings, one queen, and seven royal wives from the Habsburg dynasty were crowned in St. Martin's Cathedral.

Next to Michael's Tower are three vibrantly painted buildings, one neon pumpkin, lime, and cobalt blue. Mature trees line the streets and the buildings looked vastly different than most painted pastels.

Known officially as the Church of St. Elisabeth, this landmark has been dubbed by locals as the Blue Church, obviously due to its appearance. "It's so elegant, almost dainty looking," Cath said.

Danika explained the Art Nouveau building is painted a unique pale blue, making it stand out. Finished in 1913, everything about this church is blue: the exterior, the interior, the clock tower, and even tiles on the roof are varying shades of blue. "It looks like something that should be in a Disney movie," Anne commented. Danika pointed out the clock tower bears a tube shape, unusual for Slovak-Roman Catholic churches.

Right above the main entrance Danika pointed to an Italian mosaic portraying St. Elisabeth. She's giving alms to the poor while holding a bouquet of roses that, according to legend, she turned into bread, and gave to the poor and the sick.

The interior is mostly blue with white accents and decorated with statues. There are blue-painted pews and blue surrounds the round stained glass windows embedded in white walls. Everything is blue and white with a few splashes of yellow. It looks ornate and classy even with some areas trimmed in gold, but not overly stated, which is different than a lot of Catholic churches.

Anyone sitting on the front pews would be close enough to the altar and to the priest so that they could probably see him sweat. "This is my favorite small church ever," Anne stated. Danika said, "You can see why the Blue Church has a long waiting list for weddings and christenings."

Two neighboring buildings, a matching blue vicarage and the sherbet orange high school gymnasium, were also designed by the same architect, in the same style.

Walking north, they arrived at another of the city's impressive historical sites, the three-story sprawling Baroque presidential palace historically known as Gras-salkovich Palace. Built in 1760, this fancy summer palace has been the residence of the Slovakian president since 1996. French-style manicured lawns with plots of red Impatiens Walleriana, also known as Busy Lizzie, and the other uniden-tified yellow flowers, line the circular drive.

One of the iconic landmarks is Michael's Gate. The 167-foot tower gate at the northern end of Old Town sits at the top of a busy pedestrian street. It's sandwiched between two buildings with five small windows facing Michalská Street. Of the four original gates, only St. Michael's Tower has been preserved.

They hated to leave this historic city. On the return trip to Vienna the sky turned gray and it poured during a cloud-burst. The sound of the drops pounding on the metal roof transported Anne back to her childhood when her family went camping in their tiny 15-foot travel trailer.

Most reflected on the awesome day and of treasures found; Rob and Casey gabbed about the NBA playoffs.

"Sports, sports, sports," Cath said about Casey, and now Rob.

"Rob is a human *Wikipedia*. He's amazing and what a memory," Casey said almost reverently. Cath just shook her head.

"Don't you feel like you've known Rob and Debbie forever?" Julie spoke softly.

"Absolutely," Anne replied. "They're sort of like long-lost cousins. Now we have somebody in Alabama to visit, should we ever get there." Anne encountered dozens of people over the years while traveling, attributing it to serendipity. Some have become lifetime friends like faux Aunties Margaret and Wilma in Scotland, Blue Badge guide Tom Hooper in London, and David and Ellen in the Galápagos Islands, although from North Carolina. No one was a stranger to Anne, not for long anyway. Unless they were a Dmitry-type.

At dinner everyone shared their experiences, some a horsedrawn carriage ride, some into museums, and others shopping.

The storm cleared out just in time for those going to a private Viennese concert only for Viking cruisers in the gorgeous Palais Auersperg, built in 1706, . Stepping into the stunningly decorated rotunda, they saw multiple gold chandeliers, walls covered in tangerine paper, painted motifs, and windows with flowing draperies.

About the 20th row back, Anne pointed out Mrs. Dmitry walking in by herself. "I never see them together," she whispered to Peter.

"Maybe they are hiding something in their stateroom," he said in a Transylvania-ish voice.

"Don't mock me. I'm telling you, there's something really fishy with those two."

"Me? No mockery here."

"Just wait, you'll see," she responded.

Julie said, "Isn't that the tall, weird man's wife by herself? Poor thing, should we invite her to sit with us?"

"Thank you, Jules," just the validation Anne needed. "And yes, it is, and no I don't think so," as the woman made her way forward sitting in a second-row seat.

———

Waiting for the concert to begin, Sandra thought about John. She'd been thinking of him more regularly the past year or so. Maybe it was an age thing, she speculated. She believed in an afterlife and convinced herself they would see each other again someday. She longed for that day. He would have enjoyed a performance like this, just like others they had attended.

———

Sitting on padded red chairs, they excitedly awaited the *Performance by the Vienna Residence Orchestra*, according to the program. Looking around the auditorium, Anne noticed that most of the walls were covered in gold and cream, and floor-to-ceiling pictures. The Vienna Residence Chamber Orchestra has a long tradition, established by pianist and conductor Paul Mosier.

The musicians filed out and sat in chairs or stood depending on their instruments. Men wore black tuxes and women wore original Biedermeier costumes, flowing yellow gowns with scooped necks and poofy sleeves. One singer wore a melon-colored gown and another, robin's egg blue.

Most numbers were not familiar, but it didn't matter. They were treated to solos, duets, instrumentals and dancing. Highlights of the repertoire were Overture to *Marriage of Figaro*, Papagena duet from *The Magic Flute*, *Turkish March*, *The Cat Duet*, *The Emperor Waltz*, Polka Aria from *The Gypsy Baron*, *Vienna Blood*, *The Blue Danube*, and ending with the *Radetzky March*. The appreciative audience was up and down clapping throughout the evening with some shouting "Spectacular!" and "Bravo!" after several pieces.

Afterwards, their bus driver took them on a "Vienna After Dark" tour, but back in time for late-night snacks. They casted off at 11 p.m. Next stop Krems.

Standing on their veranda, the moon was as bright as the streetlight on their corner at home. A duck or maybe a river otter shattered the moonlight on the water.

CHAPTER NINE

A round 5 a.m., Anne peeked through the curtains to see if she could tell where they might be. Nope, just floating down the river past grassy meadows, farmland, vineyards, orchards, and a path where a couple of people rode by on their bikes. They're sure early birds, she thought to herself.

She climbed back into bed for another two hours. When she woke up, Peter was already dressed. "Go ahead to breakfast; somebody else will be up early like you," she encouraged her husband.

Thirty minutes later while perusing the breakfast fare, Anne overheard Debbie speaking with Rob, "This is better than a church potluck." Laughing to herself, Anne recalled many she and Peter attended over the decades.

With the sun rising higher in the sky, sunbeams brightened the water, lightening the shadows from bushes and trees along the banks. Rounding a bend, Peter pointed out the abbey on the hilltop.

They were west of Vienna, and 7:45 according to the tall clock tower attached to a white church with a red roof. Town buildings were mostly obscured by flourishing shrubberies, all secured behind a four-foot-tall stone wall. Under the large clock face are two doors, one with a square top and the other arched, with a wrought iron railing that looked like somebody could come out to clean, wind or work on the clock face.

Anne heard eight churches bells welcoming them to this charming village. Behind the town she could see soft rounded hills groomed with straight terraces and rows of grapes. In 45 minutes they would depart for their morning excursion to Göttweig Abbey.

She sent her lady friends a text in all caps: **DON'T FORGET TO BRING YOUR EUROS AND CREDIT CARDS**. She knew several would appreciate her reminder.

They arrived at a dock where the sign at the end read KREMS, a town of less than 30,000 people. Stores and cafés line the street at the confluence of the Krems and Danube Rivers.

Anne read to Peter from the *Viking Daily*: *Krems is a small university town at the eastern end of the Danube's Wachau Valley. Krems is surrounded by terraced vineyards. In its heyday, during the 12th century, Krems held even more importance than Vienna for its iron, grain, salt, and wine trade. As to the latter, the city has played a long and celebrated part in the popularity of the Wachau's wine culture; the valley's south slopes in Krems are bathed in sunlight all day and create some of the best Riesling and Veltliner wines in the world. The city's cobblestone streets, taverns, wine bars and coffee houses have a timeless appeal.*

Strolling by a stone wall where dainty pink wildflowers shaped like daisies crept from beneath the stones, Peter pointed to a man dressed in a long black robe holding directional signs for pedestrians wanting to get to the ice cream shop on the corner.

"Do you think he's really a monk?" Sharon asked.

"I doubt anybody impersonates monks around here," Phil replied.

Climbing onto a spacious motorcoach, Anne looked at abundant agriculture and farmland, dotted with white homes and red rooftops against a bright cobalt sky. Riding on the two-way roadway, Anne looked up and pointed to a massive complex of white buildings with red roofs on top of a hill. Vineyards on the flat land changed into orchards the higher the coach climbed.

Anne thought of the abbey as more of a "watcher" of the area, not like a fort as a protector. She detected several different colors of green: grass-green, grape-green, then forest-green extending to the abbey. She thought of the many different shades of green in Ireland.

The bus driver told them that Krems was first mentioned in 995 in a certificate of Otto III, but the settlement was apparently in existence even before then. A child's grave over 27,000 years old was discovered here, the oldest in Austria. Krems is ancient and is evident in the squares, old monasteries, ornate houses, and crumbling forts.

Standing in front of the massive gates of the Benedictine monastery, Göttweig Abbey looked impressive with its twin towers and colorful exterior. The guide explained that the complex is huge and includes the main abbey, a walled courtyard, and some gardens.

The abbey is where the local Benedictine monks grow grapes and apricots, practice forestry, and provide sanctuary for those in need of quiet time, reflection, and renewal. Timber harvesting also pays the bills.

A monk stood awaiting their arrival. Since he looked younger than Anne expected, she wasn't surprised when he explained his responsibilities included technology. He said that each monk has a specific job to do.

He pointed to the monk who oversees the summer school

activities herding some youngsters around. Two other monks worked in the apricot orchard, responsible for the upcoming harvest. They all work in surrounding villages as parish priests in addition to their duties running the abbey.

Walking through apricot trees they entered a side door where a host welcomed them at the cellar entrance with trays of short, clear glasses filled with cantaloupe-colored beverages. Next was a sparkling golden, clearer beverage, an apricot wine.

Everyone moved through a stone arched tunnel leading to a room where they sat and watched an informative video of monastic life, what it takes to run a monastery today, and the history of the abbey and the grounds.

After the video, they proceeded to an arched gate painted with yellow trim. Through the gate she could see a rosy building with a red-tiled roof with a gold cross at the top.

They stepped through the church's neoclassical wrought iron door that the monk had unlocked and opened for them. He pointed out its colorful and ornate interior which chronicles its 900-year history as a center of religious life, and its role as a monastic retreat.

Anne felt like royalty as they gracefully ascended the grand staircase called the Emperor's Staircase in the Imperial Apartments. Four-foot-tall marble urns line the wide hand railings. In the immense white walls have many alcoves with statues of either a saint or someone extremely special.

They all gazed up until their necks hurt at one of the largest and most spectacular ceiling frescoes of cherubs floating in white puffy clouds against a sapphire sky. The fresco depicts the Holy Roman Emperor Charles VI in the form of the Greek god Apollo, riding bare-chested in his sun chariot wearing his powdered wig. An angel blows a golden trumpet, another sprinkles flower petals, babies soar with wings and blankets flowing around them. Three cherubs are connected by a vine of greenery. Some of the beings are brown skinned and others white.

Anne couldn't get over all the busts and statues. Marble urns overflow with shapes of the sun, grapes, and carvings of humans.

The adjoining princely and imperial rooms showcase remarkable artwork from the abbey's own collections. The Green Room, in a warm celadon color felt friendly and was painted with birds, small animals, crosses, and gold swirls and displayed several large paintings.

The Blue Room walls were covered with panels of outdoor scenes. Anne observed Dmitry in this room but instead of looking at art, he stared out the window like he was searching for someone.

Julie said, "This has got to be the the most impressive room; the relatively small library is filled to the ceiling with 130,000 volumes. In addition to its collection of books and manuscripts, the abbey houses several antiques and rare coins.

Their guide told them, "The abbey's graphic art collection includes more than 30,000 engravings, making it the largest private graphic holding in Austria. The size of the collection is most likely due to Abbot Gottfried Bessel, who in the early 1700s, began ordering engravings and amassing works.

"Constructed in the 11th century, the abbey was nearly demolished by fire in 1580. In 1718, the monastery burned down again. Its subsequent reconstruction was overseen by Johann Lucas von Hildebrandt, the emperor's architect. Among the few original structures that remain are parts of the Erentrudis Chapel. Wine has been produced by the abbey monks continuously since 1083."

"What, did you say? 1083?" a tourist wanted to make sure he'd heard correctly.

"Yes, 1083." The guide explained that during World War

II, the Germans did not destroy the interiors but stole much of its artwork. When the Russians stayed here, however, they destroyed most of the interior by using whatever they could find to build fires inside the building, causing severe damage to the floors. Many of the pieces of artwork have been returned and restored.

He shared the abbey's past and explained that today 40 monks live and work here, as well as in nearby parishes. He told them that during the 15th and 16th centuries, the abbey declined and that in 1564 not a single monk remained. Michael Herrlich was appointed Abbot and restored the monastery spiritually and financially.

Exiting the building they cut across the courtyard, up several steps through peach-colored columns and a massive door, stepping into the chapel. "Jaw-dropping gorgeous is an understatement," Julie remarked. With arctic white walls matched with a blue and peach arched ceiling, two stained glass windows reflecting colors on the gold altar, and the ornate gold pulpit, all looked spectacular. Anne sat down and wished her head rotated like an owl.

A sunbeam captured the colors of a window, turning the burgundy and gold carpet near the altar into different colors. One corner beamed orange, the opposite to mulberry, with fuchsia, periwinkle, and a pink center with touch of aqua, in another corner. The farthest corner faded to soft, glowing pink. They were in their own magical kaleidoscope.

Six white pots, three on each side of the altar, held hot pink hydrangeas with snowy white ones tucked in.

Turning around she saw the massive pipe organ encompassing the entire mezzanine above the entrance of the chapel.

Back outside they stripped off lightweight jackets, while some stood against the cool stone walls and others under apricot trees, listening to a monk describe the duties of some workers.

Anne looked down and saw a cemetery, farm buildings, and houses in a small valley surrounded by vineyards and trees. It looked idyllic. She turned back to pay attention, taking a picture of a column with a burgundy-red dome and gold cross sandwiched between two trees.

A sign read *STIFT Göttweig Marillengarten*.

While listening to the guide talk about the symbolism of the two colors on the end of the building, Anne noticed Dmitry moving slowly away from the group and towards a path leading into the thick woods. He casually stopped at a fence post with an olive-green baseball cap on the top, picked up the cap and placed it on his head.

"That's weird," she said aloud.

"What's weird?" Peter hesitated to ask.

She told him what she just saw.

"Okay, you're right. That is strange."

"He's peculiar, for sure," she concluded.

"He's going down the path with the yellow markers that the guide told us is the beginning of that famous walk."

"Right, the Way of St. James."

Earlier, they stood in the front of the arrowed sign pointing in all directions. The most significant thing about the sign and path is that it is part of the St. James Trail. A metal sign showing the route was tightly secured between two metal posts as the trail disappeared alongside a stone wall. One would have to bend down under the thick tree branches to follow the path.

Rob and Debbie stood close by, and Anne overheard her say, "I'm goin' to the gift shop. I reckon' this is as good a place as any to get some nice gifts for Christmas."

"I'll sit here in the sunshine," he said.

"How about meeting me inside for a cup of tea in 20 minutes?"

"Okay," Rob waved.

Anne saw Rob glancing toward Dmitry, too. She moved closer to him and said, "That elderly man is odd. I'm telling you, he's shifty."

"Why do you say that?"

"He's always alone. Sometimes he uses a cane, sometimes not. He disappears then reappears; he's just strange."

"Umm, or he's just an elderly man who has a bit of dementia. Do you think someone should check on him?"

"Oh no, he's certainly not the friendly type. I experienced a brief encounter at check-in when he dropped his passport. He was ungrateful and abrupt. The woman with him seemed nice and polite though."

"Don't worry about him; he seems capable enough."

"You're right. I'm going inside to do some serious shopping. You know, Krems is the primary producer of Marillenschnaps, or apricot brandy, and the apricots are used in many items like jams, lotions, makeup, hair products and much more. I'm getting some items to take home as gifts."

"See ya," Rob said as she stepped away. He unfolded a small piece of paper that he carried in his pants pocket. The photograph was of a tall man known to him as Dmitry Rudolph.

As soon as Anne was out of sight, Rob started down the same trail. A group of three fell in behind him so Rob returned to the abbey. Dmitry ambled for about eight minutes on the beaten down path, reaching a well-used wooden bench overlooking the valley. He sat down, reached underneath, and felt around until he touched something and plucked it off.

Dmitry sat quietly. The young girl he'd just seen on the steps going into the chapel took his breath away. She looked like Eliza in South Africa. He'd been in and out of short-term relationships, ending if they didn't fawn over him or admire him enough. Once at a party he guffawed when he overheard some woman he'd spent a couple of energetic nights with say, "He's not the garden-variety snob. He's convinced himself of his preeminence and automatically expects that others will recognize his superior qualities and tell him so. I didn't."

In 1957 he met Eliza while playing tennis at a club he frequented. An acquaintance asked him to complete a foursome and he agreed to play doubles which he normally didn't like. He didn't like to lose and if that happened because of a partner, it would never be *his* fault. Eliza hit the ball so hard it knocked the wind out of Dmitry. He bent over gasping for a breath. Instead of apologizing she announced, "That ball was returnable and it's your own fault you got hit." Dmitry fell in love at first sight. He'd never met another woman with her wit, sassiness, and self-assurance. She could lead him on a leash, and he'd follow.

So, this is what love feels like, he said to himself. Being the second time for both, they married in a quiet ceremony with her best friend and husband as their witnesses. Her parents were pleased with her decision not to have a large wedding. He was not her mother's choice and she saw traits in her new son-in-law she didn't think her daughter could manage.

Like his first marriage, this one ended in a few years. Eliza tried but Dmitry wasn't the person she thought he was —fun yet reserved. Instead, he was selfish and ill-tempered. Eliza foolishly assumed once married, she could change him and he'd want to share everything with her.

She told her family there was darkness, sadness, and hatred in his life. His nightmares were frightening to her and his temperament too unpredictable. He had become too demanding for her. After their divorce it took Eliza a couple of years to return to her upbeat confident personality; he had changed her and not for the better.

In the mid-70s, after 30 years in South Africa, and two young, failed marriages, Dmitry determined it would be safe to return to Europe. Everyone in North America and Europe seemed obsessed with an oil crisis. The Watergate scandal with the American president, and still involved in the Vietnam War kept the US occupied. There was overall economic mayhem, frequent coups and civil wars, plus various political upheaval, along with armed conflicts with struggles between NATO countries.

High intensity conflicts were occurring in the Mideast, Southeast Asia, and Africa. He assumed people and governments were preoccupied with these, and not a former WWII camp guard.

The bank manager sat stunned when reading Dmitry's resignation letter. He packed a few personal belongings and left his apartment. But instead of transiting the ocean like he had 30 years earlier, he booked a one-way ticket on PanAm from Cape Town to Rio de Janeiro, then onto New York. From there he flew to London, and four grueling days later, he stepped off the first-class train car in the station in Munich.

He found a new job within three days, remaining in banking. In his early 50s, his dyed walnut hair was now naturally streaked with some silver strands.

Dmitry stood up after resting on the bench and with the random memories clogging his mind, took off the cap and left it.

Rob returned as the guide continued, "But old doesn't mean it's crumbling and decrepit. The abbey has been singled out as a Model City for Historical Preservations and rightly added to the UNESCO World Heritage List in 2000. You'd think with all its history, the past would dominate but it's clear that modern life with contemporary art and culture plays an important role.

"Much of Krems' old town walls remain intact so hiking around them and exploring the old town center is a great way to see the town and experience local culture. Shops and cafés are tucked away in the structure of some of the walls and many of the old buildings are now used as shopping areas."

Carrying a bag of breakables surrounded in bubble wrap, Anne and friends proceeded to the terrace at the back of the abbey overlooking the roadway ribboning down the valley towards the river. They took pictures of each other with the splendid scenery and the winding Danube in the distance.

She noticed Dmitry alone, as usual. About to point this out to Peter, standing nearby Mike asked, "What's up with you and that old guy? You seem to whisper to Peter about him a lot."

"Really?" she feigned innocence. "Well, he's always by himself. I think he's creepy."

"Why?"

Lowering her voice, Anne told Mike some of the unusual happenings.

"I don't think these are odd at all; purely coincidental."

Mike's wife Kathy joined them, and overhearing said, "Anne has a sixth sense. You DO remember our Alaska cruise when she discovered the body on Mendenhall Glacier?"

"Well, yes."

"As a kid her family discovered a body at the headwaters

of the Metolius, and later all the other campers arrived, including your parents."

"Well, yes," Mike agreed for the second time.

"Anne, I think you should tell somebody," Kathy urged.

"Tell somebody what? That he's done some strange things? He just strikes me as very, very, peculiar."

Dmitry's wife carried a bag of souvenirs meeting him on the opposite side of the terrace.

How had she missed seeing her? Okay, she told herself. *Stop looking for a mystery.*

Puffy white clouds with flat gray bottoms, friendly clouds Peter would say, were mirrored on this stretch of the calm river. He knew clouds from his days as a commercial pilot flying hot air balloons. He learned everything about weather, wind currents, and clouds.

Back on their veranda that faced Krems, Anne put her feet up and took a photo of the sign that read *Auf Wiedersehen*! *Goodbye*! She sat mesmerized by the sounds of the river. People were waving and yelling hello from the bank. All ages were on bikes, dozens of runners, and some kids on skateboards along the sidewalks and roadsides. *Now this is the life*, she said out loud, no one hearing.

That afternoon after lunch they entered the Wachau Valley, a serene green tapestry of forested slopes, charming towns, and castle ruins. This was one of Anne's favorite stretches of the Danube and all 18 miles are a UNESCO World Heritage Site.

Sitting in a lounge chair on the Sun Deck, the Viking

Program Director, George, announced over the loudspeakers, "The stretch of the Danube between Krems and Melk, known locally as "the Wachau," is possibly the loveliest stretch along the entire length of the river. Both banks are dotted with ruined medieval castles, wine-producing villages, and lined with terraced grapevines. Noted for its cultural importance, as well as its physical beauty, the architecture, charming villages, and the agricultural use of the land in the Wachau vividly illustrate a basically medieval landscape, which has evolved organically and harmoniously over time.

"Agricultural cultivation can be traced back to approximately 800 AD, when local monasteries began planting crops along its slopes. However, it wasn't until the 18th century that hillside viticulture was actively promoted in the area due to its favorable ecology. This, combined with the apricot trees, have contributed to the modern Wachau's picturesque character. Though wines from this renowned region can be found in Michelin-starred restaurants the world over, the Wachau produces only 3% of Austria's total wine output. The region's signature grape is undoubtedly its crisp Gruner Veltliner, with its trademark hints of citrus and pepper, and pop of refreshing acidity. This food-friendly wine is best enjoyed with richly flavored foods, such as classic Austrian wiener schnitzel and grilled asparagus."

Sitting next to Kathy, Anne overheard Mike say, *The Nautical Term of the Day is "Leeway." The "weather" side of a ship is the side from which the wind is blowing. The "lee" side is the side of the ship that is sheltered from the wind. A "lee shore" is a shore that is downwind of a ship. If a ship does not have enough "leeway," it is in danger of being driven onto the shore.* Kathy and Anne just looked at each other.

Somebody opened a bottle of Nik Weis St. Urbans-Hof, Bockstein Kabinett as they cruised by quaint little hamlets, each one with at least two or three steeples, and usually one with a clock.

Often above little villages or towns were castles or forts standing like old guardians of the area. Scenery of rolling multicolored emerald hills are layered with amazingly coffered vineyard after vineyard. The only different color than green was something moving among the rows, a red tractor with a person in a blue shirt riding on it. A stone fence lined the road reaching a brick arch, the entrance to another flourishing vineyard.

Sandra paced around the Sun Deck stopping at the herb garden. She bent down and snipped a sprig of rosemary with her fingernail raising it to her nose. It smelled pungent and fresh, like eucalyptus, with a hint of peppermint.

This was the second worse day of any year for her— John's birthday. The first when she received the phone call about the fishing boat going down in the horrible storm. *He would be 82 today*, she said to herself.

She thought about him every day and felt bad if she hadn't. She'd never forget his excited look when he left that day to work on the *Gaul*. But he also felt torn because he'd leave her for longer periods of time. This is how she chose to remember his face. She'd tried to imagine him over the years growing in age as she had, but she couldn't picture him at 50, 60, 70 and now 82.

As they approached a town with a row of pink, green, gold, and blue two-story homes with a more modern-looking church. Carol sighed, "What a spectacular day to cruise the

Wachau Valley," sipping some red wine as Jim snoozed in the sunshine, covered in a Viking signature wool blanket of beige, tan, and coral blocks, and stripes.

Peter motioned to Anne to come quickly, pointing at something. In the yard of a stone house, a giant cement nose rose from the ground, where a cherry red bike lay. An elderly woman sat on the bench waving. A six-foot man could easily stand in the left nostril. "More modern art," Peter said, "doesn't seem to really fit this area."

As they cruised by picturesque Spitz, one of the more easily pronounceable town names, they spotted a bright marine yellow building, probably a restaurant, then a quaint church with a large white cross mounted on its red roof all at the base of emerald terraced vineyards. The impressive Hinterhaus Castle ruins came into view at the outskirts of Spitz. Anne overheard a woman say, "I want to move there." Anne nodded her head in agreement.

The rest of the afternoon they overheard oohs and aahs when seeing castles, ruins, cathedrals, cute villages, and people lazing or sunbathing, some on the nude beach. The longship navigated several locks so close they could touch the coolness of the lumpy gray cement and seeing acre upon acre of grape vines winding its way upwards to the sky. Sunshine sparkled on the river.

Several friends moved into the Lounge for Austrian Teatime and a demonstration by the executive chef learning on how to make Apple Strudel. The rest stayed on the Sun Deck in the fresh air.

Anne picked up movement in a yard and pointed it to out Peter. He said, "It's one of those robot mowers." It moved across, up and down, bumped into a potted plant, turned, and moved elsewhere.

"We soooooo need one of those," Judie poked Rolland. Anne leaned over to Carol and explained, "They live along the Willamette River with massive oak trees, a gorgeous yard, and huge garden; in other words, lots of work."

"Judie, we live on Mill Creek and need one, too," Carol commiserated.

After the port talk about the next day's activities, Anne gasped when she spied kalamata olive bread sticks tucked in the breadbasket on their table. She hoarded two, and the fancy chopped salad she ordered was picture worthy, topped with two plump raisins, a sprig of parsley, shredded white cheese, and chopped walnuts.

"Oh goody," Anne excitedly said. "Crème brûlèe, my favorite. Well, this and Key Lime Pie." Although she was tempted by a triple layered dessert of pressed chocolate and ground nuts for the base, a layer of custard or pudding for the center, and then topped with strawberry purée and fresh strawberries, with a leaf of mint for color, she stayed with her favorite. Extra desserts were ordered as the setting sun created a shimmery spectacle of scarlet, peach, and pink on the river.

They recapped their day mesmerized by the scenery and gentle feeling of gliding along the river. Most were in their own lala land. Casey and Rob were deep in conversation when Debbie said, "Rob, hush your mouth." She admonished him when he started talking about one political candidate in particular. He's not worth a hill of beans."

"We promised we wouldn't talk politics on vacation." Several chuckled and totally agreed.

Back in their room, Peter feel asleep as Anne closed the draperies and climbed into the king size bed. They both slept soundly that night; Anne not waking once.

In the darkness, Debbie squinted. Rob sat across the room. The clock read 4:17. "What are you doing?"

"Couldn't sleep." He wanted to tell her he'd been sitting there for hours recalling their first assignment together in Argentina. They hadn't seen each other for a year, then returned for another job in South America. Each year or two they were in some foreign location working together which led to more personal interaction. Where did those decades go?

He hadn't worked up the courage yet. He couldn't face the possibility of rejection from the woman he loved for many years.

"Once this assignment is complete, let's spend some time alone," he stated not as a question.

"I'd like that," her answer encouraging him. "Now come to bed," she patted the mattress with the invitation he'd been hoping for.

CHAPTER TEN

Around 6 a.m. Anne peeked outside to see Viking *Bragi*, a sistership, pulled snuggly against them. If people from the other longship were on their veranda, they could have shaken hands.

She crawled back in bed for a couple more hours. As the *Bragi* pulled away, they stepped out in their bathrobes, and could easily tell the overall architecture and country flags had changed from Austria now to bold black-, orange- and yellow-striped indicating Germany.

"You know one thing about river cruising is that everyone on the bank can see us in our robes, unlike a cruise ship at sea or nine stories up at a port," Peter noted.

"True, but they'll never see us again," Anne acknowledged.

Buildings along the river were painted in tones from tan to walnut, with brick-colored tile roofs and many with painted designs on the front. Cruising by Obernzell, the butter-yellow twin tower church was trimmed in snowy white with charmingly decorated houses along the river. Sprawling homes were tucked behind trees and bushes with lounge chairs and large umbrellas in their yards.

While getting ready, Peter got the lowdown on Passau, located in lower Bavaria, Germany, as Anne read him the daily ritual from the *Viking Daily. Founded by the Celts more than 2,000 years ago, Passau is one of Bavaria's oldest cities. Known as the "City of Three Rivers," it rests at the confluence of the Inn, Ilz and Danube Rivers. The city has long enjoyed its strategic position and grew to great economic and political power because of it. The legacy of its past prosperity lives on in graceful arcades, colorful houses with Rococo façades and the glorious Baroque St. Stephen's Cathedral, home of one of Europe's largest pipe organs. Passau is also where two nations meet; it is here that the German-Austrian border begins.*

Passau was an important medieval center for the salt trade, the white gold as it was called. Merchants established a powerful monopoly until 1707 when all salt imports to Passau were forbidden and the once flourishing city lost its valuable trade. During the Renaissance, Passau became famous for making high quality knife and sword blades. Local smiths stamped their blades with the Passau wolf and superstitious warriors believe that the wolf granted them invulnerability. The practice of placing magical protective charms on blades became known as "Passau art."

"Isn't this the third St. Stephen's Cathedral this trip? Are they all after the same saint? We need to stop there and compare the others," Anne said.

"You'll have to do some research on that, but this one is spelled with an "a" instead of an "e," "or maybe it's the German spelling for St. Stephen. It reads Dom St. Stephan."

"What's the temperature outside?" Anne asked as it would determine what she would wear for the day.

"Almost 60 degrees."

"Why do Germany and other European countries use Fahrenheit like we do and most others use Celsius?"

"I'm sure there's some explanation but I don't know," her husband honestly replied.

"Look at this map of the Altstadt Peninsula. It shows the point where the rivers merge, Peter pointed out to Anne.

After breakfast, local guide, Catrin, greeted them as they disembarked the longship, leading them along a stone promenade. Anne stopped to smell the fragrant, trailing pale pink roses on an iron fence that created an arch to a large white building with a red spiked roof.

Ambling along a narrow avenue of small buildings, Catrin stopped to speak with a man. They got to meet the last fisherman of the town who still did all his own fishing and sold to his favorite restaurants. He only spoke German. Dressed in a blue and gray plaid shirt, washed out jeans, and black rubber boots to his knees, carrying a wicker basket and two long poles to his gray van, he drove toward the river.

The Old Town Hall called Alte Rathaus is a main feature, and the 14th century neo-Gothic spire can be seen from all corners of the town. Located on the banks of the Danube, the watermarks near the entrance show how high the water has reached throughout the centuries.

They went inside the Great Assembly Room seeing ornate stained glass windows depicting historical events throughout the centuries. Statues hung, suspended like they floated on the corners of buildings.

At Hölgass, known as Artists Alley, they stepped around painted stones of cobalt blue, cherry red, sunshine yellow, and Kelly-green on a narrow cobblestone route leading to artisan shops and art galleries. Some colorful cobblestones veered off the main grouping and led right into a studio.

They could see St. Stephan's Cathedral perched on the highest point of the city's Old Town. She told them that this church has stood in this spot since 730, and it is the largest baroque cathedral north of the Alps at around 328 feet long. It looks mostly light gray with aqua caps on the two towers that hold eight large bells in the bell rooms in each tower.

The bells weigh up to 16,645 pounds. Two of the heaviest hang in the south tower with the other six in the north tower.

Stepping in the entrance to the church through the inner courtyard, Cathrin pointed out tombstones and crypts of people who had been interred there many centuries.

Anne asked, "By the way, is Stephan spelled with an "a" or "e"? I'm confused seeing it in print both ways."

"Either one is fine," was Catrin's answer.

They learned that over the centuries many churches have been built and rebuilt on the site of the current cathedral, which itself was nearly destroyed in the 1662 fire that swept through Passau. With only its late Gothic eastern façade left standing, St. Stephan's was rebuilt between 1668 and 1693, featuring magnificent stucco works and frescoes.

Its famous pipe organ is the largest in the world outside the US. The organ has 17,774 pipes and 233 registers. All five parts of the organ can be played from the main keyboard, either one at a time or all together.

Anne's first impressions of the interior was that a lot of saints and cherubs were gazing down at them from every everywhere. No matter where she looked, something or someone stared at her; a little creepy she thought to herself. The architecture, ceiling art, and massive altar piece were stunning with vibrant colors.

The gold chancel, or pulpit, where the priest stands, is attached to a tall, round gray column. Anne sat on a hard pew, her head back as far as it would bend, staring straight up at fresco after fresco.

Back outside they stepped in the open door of a Wood-carver's Shop, appropriately named, seeing an assortment of local arts and crafts. Several wooden Christmas ornaments were snapped up.

On the hilltop is Veste Oberhaus, built in 1219 and meant

to display the power of the Holy Roman Empire that once extended to this region. Its strategic location over this junction of rivers was an excellent defensive position and the perfect viewpoint.

They noticed the changing styles of the fortress through the times, from Gothic to Renaissance to Baroque. The picturesque buildings are a showcase of the history and art of Passau. Here they easily could see the whirling waters of the three rivers blending together. The Ilz river looked like root beer, evidently from the peat-rich Bavarian Forest that meets the milk chocolate brown Danube, and the soft mint color snowmelt of the Inn from the Swiss Alps, combined to look like a muddy smoothie just out of the blender.

Anne snapped a picture of the round Schaibling Tower with its cream-colored arch and pointed cinnamon-colored roof, an identifiable landmark of the town and a relic from when it was built as a fortified tower in the 14th century. As Catrin explained that it also protected against the waves in the harbor and stored powder and salt for trade, Anne noticed Dmitry not far away. From a distance he looked as tall as her brother Will. "Is that Mr. and Mrs. Dmitry?" Peter asked.

Dmitry raised his hand at his wife who was just about to enter a building, maybe a gift shop. He sat down on a bench.

"Yes. They are finally doing something together," Anne observed.

As soon as Mrs. Dmitry disappeared into the store, her husband nonchalantly got up from the bench and sauntered into a dark alley sandwiched between two tall buildings that blocked the sunlight.

"He seemed unsteady earlier leaning on a cane and now he's not even using it. It's bizarre," Anne stated.

Two men followed Dmitry into the darkness.

"Look at those two men following Dmitry down that dark alley," Anne said concerned.

Peter acknowledged, "I admit, his behavior is certainly suspect. Remember though, his wife said he's in his nineties. He'd old, Anne. My guess is those two men are taking the same shortcut Dmitry is." Anne didn't say what she was really thinking.

The friends headed to the Old Bishop's Palace of Residence. Catrin told them it dates to the 1700s and takes up an entire square. It is where the prince-bishops ruled secular and religious life for hundreds of years but is now a museum. They viewed art ranging from the Romanesque period to the present. Anne was really interested in seeing the exquisite Rococo stucco work above the magnificent staircase. The ceiling showed off paintings of the Olympian Heavens with its gods and goddesses watching over the people of Passau.

Residents could make their way to St. Stephan's Cathedral via a covered passage to reach the doors to the palace. Anne imagined herself living in the palace, maybe as a wealthy daughter. She'd enter through the heavy ornate carved doors and once inside she wouldn't take for granted the exquisite baroque moldings, or the frescoes of hovering angels above the rounded balcony where she imagined the Pope stood blessing his people down below. She could see herself gliding down the magnificent staircase dressed for a ball.

Napoleon is said to have visited and stayed at the residence. She would have looked him right in the eye. They were same height at five foot, six inches. They expected to see signs proudly boasting *Napoleon Slept Here*. There are over 40 major rooms filled with antiques, but none of Anne's group had the willingness or energy to take on such a building.

The area also boasts the oldest and largest vineyard. The

square is filled with pastel-colored buildings. Catrin said that in the past many people couldn't read so the colors of the buildings then linked citizens to the places they wanted to visit. A yellow brewery with chimneys, the butcher shop is red, and the bakery is green. In the center square is a fountain with Mary at the center and three children, who represent the Three Rivers which meet in Passau.

Anne took a photo of the city's manhole cover showing a dramatic lion. Thanking Catrin for the informative tour and her expertise, they entered a restaurant with the Bavarian colors of blue and white cloths covering wooden tables, with the Bavarian Lion on the flag. They wanted traditional cuisine and found it here. Weisswurst, schweinshaxe, spätzle, and more were listed on the menu, along with Loöwen, Brauhaus, Passau, and several shades of beers served in different-sized glasses.

Anne ordered four sausages and kraut. When the waiter looked at her and asked, "That's everything?" she replied, "Yes thanks. This combo is my favorite."

Doughy, golden-brown pretzels speckled with rock salt quickly appeared. Anne's normally talkative group fell silent except for *umms*, *so good* and *delicious* utterances.

Rob leaned back in the chair saying, "I'm so full I'm about to pop." Most agreed.

Around a corner, they all heard Anne exclaim, "Oh my word, it's Dackelmuseum. I've heard about this dachshund museum!" Growing up with two miniature red doxies, as they referred to them, the first one named Duke, followed some years later by Duke II, Anne went in to purchase a few things for her brothers and their wives. Will and Michelle have two different types named Bosley and Smokey. Max, who currently is dog-less, also had one named Daphne. He and Lola now have cats, Joyce and Gordon.

The flyer read, *The world's first and unique dachshund*

museum Kleine Residenz or Small Residence. The dachshund—a philosophy—is shown in an exhibition that contains the world's largest collection of a total of more than 45,000 exhibits.

No other dog seems to be as world famous as the dachshund. The 100th anniversary of the Free State of Bavaria, the dachshund in nobility, or the dachshund in hunting, as well as "Waldi" the dachshund of the 72 Olympic Games, are focal points in the museum.

The collection was compiled by the two master florists, Seppi Küblbeck and Oliver Storz, over the last 25 years and is now shown to the public for the first time. A large number of exhibits are lovingly presented in showcases, with a wink of an eye, and a great passion for dachshunds, which represent Bavaria like none other.

Anne gladly paid the 10 Euros and while others milled around the store at the front of the museum, she entered the world of her childhood furry friends. She saw figurines galore: A clay-looking thing that looked like a Gila monster; a painting of dachshunds running beside horses chasing deer; wooden puzzles; magazines; children's books; and pictures of nobility holding their short-legged, long-bodied, short hair brick-colored dachshunds. *Der Wiener Dog* is completely gold with a crown on his head. There are miniature ones that one can buy for cake toppers. Also stuffed toys, dogs that proudly display an Olympic gold medal around their neck, and wind-up plastic versions that will waddle across one's countertop.

Some are dressed in police uniforms, in Scottish kilts, and firefighter uniforms. They're in baskets; they're in wagons. One sat at a base of a lampshade. They are engraved on boxes; there are postcards; Christmas cards; and a picture of a man sitting in his chair holding his sleeping doggie. There is every size and color of figurine imaginable called the *Dackelparade*, Anne assumed a parade of doxies.

In a revolving multitiered showcase, there's a shelf of

silver dogs, a shelf of white ones, black ones, and various multicolored ones. Doxies around the world in various positions standing around a world globe. There are Christmas tree ornaments, one for every holiday including ones with shamrocks for St. Patrick's Day, and a red one with hearts all over it.

Outside they saw Catrin across the street who waved and rejoined them. "I'm on my way home but I had to tell you that this is a great place for coffee, tasty cakes and schnapps." Comments bounced around from their friends.

"Schnapps midafternoon?"

"It's after 5 somewhere," came a quick reply. The group headed into the café.

Anne said, "I've had peach in some drinks before and it's delicious. Oh, and peppermint or butterscotch in hot chocolate usually in winter or on an Alaska cruise."

Julie added, "Look, gingerbread; the city is famous for it." It smelled spicy.

Bottles of schnapps lined the shelf behind the counter: apple, caramel apple, blackberry, black cherry, coconut, orange, pear, pomegranate, plum, raspberry, strawberry, tropical fruit, and watermelon pucker, all seemed sensible.

Then there were flavors that they had never seen such as cinnamon, Long Island Iced Tea, Maui Blu Hawaiian, pumpkin spice, root beer, vanilla, and whipped cream, to name a few.

"Mango chili. Fire water. Hot cinnamon?" Casey asked.

"Do you have apricot?" Rolland inquired.

"Of course; it's hiding behind the apple," the server answered.

The server explained that schnapps is flavored with fruit or herbs and spices either through the distillation process or by mixing ingredients with a neutral spirit. Some tried sips and some gulped down a shot, some two.

Peter ordered root beer. "Not vanilla?" Anne asked shocked.

"When in Rome...but I'm not sure why anyone would waste perfectly good root beer."

Outside, Anne suggested they go their separate ways for an hour and meet back at the longship. The other ladies heartily agreed.

"We'll need to head to *Var* around 3," Peter reminded everyone.

Debbie said, "I reckon it's time for me to do some more Christmas shopping for our grandkids."

"No more t-shirts," Rob jogged her memory. "They all mentioned it before we left."

The men departed as Cath heard Rob and Casey talking about some football team.

Hearing reports from previous travelers, the ladies knew that Passau was a fine place for shopping. They stepped into Marmeladen-Haus, and sampled delicious marmalades, and supported the local economy, one of their favorite things to do. Adept clerks covered the glass jars in bubble wrap.

Next door Gewürz Depot offered an array of spices and sweet mustards for sale. Anne whispered to a couple of friends, "Did you know you can buy this at home at World Market and not have to pack it? It is a trick I learned years ago. Like when going to Canada, don't haul all the maple syrup home. They have it in a maple leaf bottle there. You don't have to tell anybody you didn't buy it here. As long as it reads *Made in Germany*, that works for me. 'Don't ask, don't tell' is my travel motto."

Strolling back along the banks of the Danube, Cath pointed out a bronze bust perched on a white cement block. *Emerenz Meier* was a local writer and poet in Passau. Cath squatted down and summarized an inscription:

"Born in 1874 to a poor family, she enjoyed all the things

169

relating to nature. She worked with other artists in Passau but immigrated to Chicago with her family in 1906 and died there in 1928. She continued to write in Chicago but wasn't well received. *Daily life, housework, and earning a living often interfered with artistic ambitions* was one of her famous lines explaining why women are too busy to have time to write because of household chores."

"Unfortunately, this is probably the case for thousands of artists who'd like to follow their calling but don't have the time," Cath empathized.

Anne stood nose to nose with Emerenz peering into bronze eyes and her pleasant face. Her hair is pulled back and her head is covered in a scarf that wraps around her hair, then splits in half with the material flowing down in the back. She even has pierced ears wearing little round baubles. Her jacket flares at her waist and her right arm is tucked behind her. Her left hand is on her belt. Her jacket, or maybe a blouse, has a high neck with a round brooch that leads to frills down the front.

Continuing to their longship, they strolled by sweet-smelling scarlet roses creeping toward a bright red canvas awning of a restaurant. Droplets sparkled on just watered leaves. A black dachshund stopped to sniff a post as it led the way for its human. By a large red planter of blooming purple lavender, a neon yellow bike's wire basket held a loaf of French bread and a bouquet of flowers. Quacking mallards paddled away from the bank. The cobblestones were slightly damp from sprinklers.

"Magical," Julie said appreciatively. "I could live here."

"Me too, especially with this view," Anne agreed.

"Oh, isn't that little girl just as pretty as a peach?" Debbie pointed to a child about three years old in a stroller.

Back on *Var* at 3:30 they were going under a bridge with a fort towering above. Steep steps led along stone walls to homes balanced in thousand-year-old rock walls with a highway below. Criss-crossing sets of stairs climbed another hill, with Judie remarking, "I wouldn't want to carry groceries up there."

They cruised by a row of colorful two- and three-story homes in shades of terracotta, pink, periwinkle, light peach, and lastly, a plain white accentuated with cornflower blue trim, all tucked behind four-foot high stone walls.

Relaxing on their veranda drinking iced tea with feet propped up, Peter showed Anne the four-page article and chart in the complimentary *EXPLORE* magazine. "Look, this chart identifies each lock by name and kilometer marker along the river. The gray bar represents the elevation at which our ship enters the lock and the red bar represents the height our ship rises or lowers while in the lock. The total height of the bar is the total elevation at the highest point of this process.

"Looking at this map, we're going into another lock soon and this one is different because it's also a power plant. After this one, there are only two left before Regensburg. That's a total of 12 this trip and most have been during the night while we were sleeping. This one is called Jochenstein." He stood pointing, "There's a small rock island and looks like the lock splits it in half. This is so cool, it's like mini-Panama Canal locks. Instead of taking hours to transit, these don't take long at all; an elevator on water."

Peter continued, "Simply put: 1. The first door opens, and we enter the lock compartment. 2. The door closes behind us. The lock compartment is filled with water, raising us up. 3. The far doors open and then we depart at the new, higher or lower level of the river. In our case, we are entering low and going out higher."

Approaching an especially wide curve in the river, they could see a hydroelectric plant. The lock they would go through was on the far-right side just past the town.

The captain slowed down and they went up one floor to the Aquavit Terrace for a bird's eye view. On the opposite side, there was a closed gate and behind it an empty lock with a second closed gate at the other end. Looking past the lock gate down the river they could see they would be curving to the right. They were in a river valley of hills and mountains covered in dense firs. The historic Jochenstein lock at milepost 2.203 straddles the border of Austria and Germany, with a length of 744 feet and width of 78 feet. The drop height of the lock is 32 feet.

"The soft green hue of the river is so pretty," Anne mentioned. *Var* entered the right lock slowly inching forward. Passing by the gate that would soon close behind them, there is a small tower in the middle that separates the two locks with the name *Jochenstein* on a round gray stone tower with a sign reading "7.7 meters," which Peter explained is about 25 feet. Anne already figured out meters to feet being nearly triple.

"How high are we?" Anne inquired.

"Under 25 feet I'd say because they are not roping off the Sun Deck like a couple of other times." Staff didn't have to scamper around lowering the hydraulic bridge where the captain hangs out, nor fold all the lounges flat and remove chairs. It was a common occurrence through locks and under bridges.

Anne held her breath watching the top of the longship's bridge miss the bottom of the breezeway between the two compartments of the lock. "Jeez, that looked close," she said to an employee. "Not as close as some," he said. "We didn't have to remove furniture."

The captain gingerly moved forward toward the gate and

stopped not quite touching the left side of the lock. Anne reached out touching the damp, cool cement. Inching forward came the sistership *Bragi*, scootching in alongside.

Both captains saluted each other and looked calm like they'd done this plenty of times. Guests with rooms on the starboard side like theirs, and those on the port side of the *Bragi*, could stand on their balconies and shake hands. Anne snapped a photo of two people doing just that.

With both Viking sisterships maybe 10 inches apart, the gates closed, and water started pouring in. The vessels began rising. Closer to the top, Anne saw a dandelion growing out from a crack in the wall. When the gates were open wide enough the captain inched *Var* forward and quickly they were out of the lock and back to cruising up the river. The next lock called Kachlet, would be much smaller. People fished, canoed and a water skier created unriver-like waves.

As the river narrowed, two white swans swam close to shore. Once *Var* was away from civilization, scenery changed to grasses, random buildings, and homes scattered among a few castles. An assortment of islands covered in shrubbery dotted the river close to the banks. In the flat area, a bicyclist rode on a straight path through the countryside. They cruised by a vintage locomotive where people sat under three red umbrellas. One man hoisted a glass of beer and others waved.

In the Lounge, Axil brought around a tray of fluted glasses offering orange juice or Prosecco. Snacks of pretzels and nuts sat on the small oval tables.

A guest lecturer told them about the daily life of a modern German citizen, covering topics such as average salaries, taxes, housing prices, education, public transportation system, and cultural idiosyncrasies.

Mike asked if they'd read today's *Nautical Term, Dressing Down? Thin and worn sails are often treated with oil or wax to renew their effectiveness. This was called "dressing down." An officer or sailor who was reprimanded or scolded was also said to have received a "dressing down."*

That evening they were treated to a Taste of Austria. Olive wood carved bowls held dense white bread. Anne purchased one that was safely tucked away in her luggage. Browned pretzels dangled from wooden holders above sizzling skillets of several types of sausage in different shapes and colors. Five types of desserts were conveniently cut into 2-inch square bites. The menu included *Pumpkin Seed Chicken Thigh, Braised Beef, Grilled Chicken-filled-sausage, Potato salad, Bread dumplings, Red cabbage and sauerkraut, or Grilled char fillet, Roasted potatoes, Sautéed vegetables, and Whipped herbed butter.* Or they could select the German Buffet: *Braised red cabbage, kraut, Bratwurst, smoked sausage, salads, scalloped potatoes, cheeses.* The feast seemed endless. All staff were dressed in authentic Bavarian attire, and waiters delivered tall thin glasses of beer.

Some chuckled when Rob announced, "My eyeballs are floating," and they could only surmise what that southern saying meant, as he trotted to the restroom conveniently located outside the Lounge.

Anne looked at Peter and said, "Let's move to the terrace and watch the sunset. It's such a lovely evening." Scissor-like silhouettes of birds turning among apricot-colored clouds painted a serene picture as dusk stole across the sky. They returned to their party as friends were recapping their day.

Rob said to Anne, "I think I heard somebody say you are celebrating a birthday or something?"

"Our anniversary in March. We use any excuse–an anniversary or birthday–to celebrate with traveling instead of more stuff."

"How did you meet?" Rob asked.

Peter and Anne looked at each other and she nodded saying to her husband, "Feel free," sort of laughing.

"Well, it was December 1, several decades ago, and I was attending college but living at home. A buddy and I were riding in his new Mach 1 cruiz'in *The Gut*."

"*The Gut*? Seriously? Where's that?" Mike butted in. "I haven't heard this story."

"Portland Road in north Salem, a cool straight stretch with a few stoplights back then. My buddy Dan noticed a red Vega and said a past girlfriend owned one similar, and as we got closer it was his old girlfriend, Betsy. We cruised up and down a few times and so did she and somebody else with her. Dan pulled up alongside and rolled down the window to get Betsy's attention. He asked if they wanted to go for a ride in his new Mach 1. We met them behind a restaurant and the friend climbed in the back seat with me, and Betsy up front with Dan." Peter pointed at Anne smiling at the memory.

"She did have some explaining to do because each time we saw them Anne would drop down into the seat like she was hiding. Turned out we were in the car in front of her boyfriend and she didn't want to see him that night. So down she'd go hoping he didn't see her.

"We drove through the countryside and ended up going through a historic cemetery on D Street. Gates were open so why not? It was scary for the girls but we promised to protect them from whatever."

"A huge snarling black German Shepherd with a mouth full of fangs charged my window," Anne interrupted.

"Well, it wasn't confirmed how big or what it actually was since only Anne and Betsy saw it on their side of the car but as it lunged, Anne screamed and jumped into my lap."

"Well, not quite jumped, but it's *his* version," she grinned as she relived that moment.

Peter continued, "Then we ended up at a restaurant, open

24 hours, and talked and got to know each other more. She lived in Albany, about 25 miles south, and Betsy was going to drive her home, but we offered since now it's 1:30 in the morning."

Anne added, "I knew I was in big trouble because I'd never come home that late and didn't find a phone booth to call my folks. I also thought I didn't want to wake them. My rationale."

Peter continued, "We dropped her off and I took her to the door. Then drove back to Salem in about 15 minutes with no real speed limit back then. I told my mom that morning that I'd met the girl I was going to marry."

Anne said, "My mom just said, 'We will talk in the morning, Anne.'" Everyone laughed.

"Holy moly," Kathy said knowing Anne's Mom.

"That's it? Obviously, something else happened." Judie asked.

"Well, he didn't ask for my phone number and Betsy said he didn't ask her for it either when they got back to Salem."

"Okay, Anne, you do the next part," Peter took a breather squeezing a quarter of lemon into his iced tea.

"Well, we met on *The Gut* that Friday night. I didn't sleep much that night or Saturday night thinking about this cool, funny guy, and the boyfriend I needed to break up with.

"I was attending business college in Salem and rode back and forth with an Albany guy. When he picked me up Monday morning, I told him I wouldn't be going back that night. I was staying overnight with Betsy, because we were doing posters for a position we were running for at school.

"Then it started snowing. It continued all morning and classes were cancelled. I had packed two dresses, mandatory attire back then, a few toiletries and pj's as I planned to stay just one night. It snowed about two feet in two days, so I couldn't get home and was stuck at Betsy's. Fortunately, her mom and I were about the same size, so I borrowed some clothes from her. Her parents spoke with mine assuring them it would be fine for me to stay however long because buses weren't even running.

"By Thursday we were getting stir crazy and decided to go for a walk. We hiked about three miles south and found Peter's house but didn't see his silver Chevy Impala he'd told me about. We weren't bold enough to go knock on the door. The return trip wasn't so much fun and we stopped by Fred Meyer to warm up.

"Low and behold who comes around the corner but Dan. We were floored and he wanted to know what I was doing in Salem. We explained the snowed-in saga. He asked what we were doing the next night and having no social agenda, we replied 'nothing.' He said he'd find somebody, and they'd come up and play in the snow, maybe go for a ride in his four-wheel drive Jeep, or a movie.

"Also, the boyfriend had been calling my home and my personal answering service was growing weary of fibbing to him about me being out of the house or not available. My mother firmly said I needed to tell him and break it off. I agreed and the next time he called, Mom gave him the number where I could be reached in Salem, about five miles from his house. I agreed to see him Saturday night knowing that I needed to put an end to it.

"Dan was due around 6:30. Betsy squealed that Peter is with him. Both came in and met Betsy's folks, and off we went to a horrible movie which we all walked out of. We went back to Betsy's and hiked up the hill to where a water tower is, had a snowball fight, and made snow angels. Then we went probably a half mile downhill to Dunkin' Donuts for hot cocoa and sweets. It was so romantic and better than a movie.

"Snow melted to a point where in the next day or so I

could somehow get home. My dad said he'd come get me. Peter asked if I was staying, and my reply was, 'If I have a reason.' He suggested he pick me up and I'd go to church with him, then dinner with his parents, and he'd take me home. Could I stay two more days? Parents all agreed.

"On Saturday evening the boyfriend came and we repeated the snowball fight and snow angels, but it was nothing compared to the night before. A neighbor guy went along as a fourth for Betsy. We went to Dunkin' Donuts and I told him I needed to take a break. He disagreed and asked if it was that new guy I'd met. I didn't even ask how he knew but I said, 'Maybe.' It was over but he kept calling and writing; I didn't reply.

"So, Sunday came, and I went to church with Peter, met his folks, then drove to my house early evening. We parked by the back door, family and friends always used it not the front, and he came around to open the car door. Here's the Hallmark movie part. I got out and reached for his gloved hand, slipped toward him where he caught me, and we kissed. It was magic."

"Yep, she's right," Peter agreed.

"He met both my younger brothers and folks that night. When he left, I told Dad, I'm going to marry him."

"Yes, I know but let's not tell your mother just yet." He suggested.

"There you go and now several decades have passed," Peter concluded.

"You must have been really young." Judie commented.

"Indeed, 20 and 21," Anne replied.

"Well, technically 19 and 20."

"What? Really?"

"Yes, really. We were married in March and our birthdays are both in June, so 19 and 20," Peter replied. "Babies. And

Dan and Betsy were both in our wedding." Anne concluded their story.

The group conversation continued including food, drink, sights they'd seen and what was in store for the following day.

"I have a splitting headache. I am going to retire," Debbie announced.

Rob asked nicely, "Do you want me to come with you darlin'?"

"No, stay for a while. I'm just going to bed."

"Hope you're not coming down with something. See you in the morning," Casey consoled, as they'd set 8 o'clock for breakfast and doing some touring on their own.

"Do you smell that? It's the aroma of burning logs," Anne asked.

"Uh-huh; someone along the shoreline built a campfire. I can hear the crackle of the wood from here." Feet up on their veranda, they waved at kids on the riverbanks. Boats displayed various flags most German—black, red, and yellow.

Out of the blue Anne said, "I'm just saying that something's fishy; just not right with Dmitry."

"You've been watching way too many mysteries."

"Well, I do have a bit of a history when it comes to discovering bodies."

"Yes, you do but that doesn't mean you should go looking for trouble. It seems to find you on its own."

"Maybe I should be a detective," she pondered.

"Uh, no Anne, stick with fundraising."

"I could be though; maybe a new line of work for me.

Remember how I tracked down that creep who stole my wallet years ago? I got video surveillance from the gas station showing the license plate and what the guy looked like. Then a friend at the DMV kindly, but illegally, ran the license plate and gave me the perp's address. I tracked him down. All because the police didn't have time for a petty crime like this."

"Ahhh, yes, but that was also dangerous, and your sheriff brother, Will, told you never to do anything like that again. "

"Fine. But *There's something rotten in Denmark*, or rather on the Danube. Did you know William Shakespeare coined that phrase in *Hamlet*? It's true, I'm not making this one up," she closed the discussion.

Dmitry smelled the same bonfire. It reeked and reminded him of something decades earlier. He kicked a chair across the veranda, startling Sandra who sat inside reading.

"Are you all right?" she asked.

He didn't reply. Clearly the subject wasn't open for discussion. Typical, she thought.

Several hours later, Debbie said quietly, "Probably cleaner than when we arrived," observing her partner's simple nod. His convivial personality morphed from happy-go-lucky to quiet and serious. The first piece of luggage already lowered followed by the second, including the rope. Neither would speak another word. They'd done this before and knew what they needed to accomplish.

What woke me up, Anne wondered. Not Peter, he was sound asleep. The time on her phone showed 3:17 a.m. Her parents' smiling faces popped into her mind. Her intuition told her something could be wrong at home. Living on the west coast of the US, her folks were eight hours behind. She slipped on her white Viking bathrobe and stepped out to the balcony to call them.

They were eating dinner. The caller ID showed her name.

"Anne? Is that you darlin' daughter? Where are you?" Her Dad answered the phone with a mouth full of pot roast.

"Hi Dad. We're cruising between two little towns. The Danube River is incredible. How are you and Mom?"

"Fine, Anne. Honey, aren't you ahead of us eight hours? What's wrong? Why are you calling in the middle of the night?"

"I woke up thinking of you both and thought something could be wrong."

"We're fine and here's your Mom," said her normally talkative Dad although not so much especially when eating one of his favorite dinners. "Anne, is something wrong with Peter?"

Now Anne grinned. "No Mom, I thought something might be wrong with you and Dad because I woke up from a dead sleep thinking of you two. Are Max and Will and their families, okay?"

"Yes, Anne, we are all good, dear."

"Have you heard anything from Peggy lately? Is she okay also?" Peggy and Anne were childhood friends and Peggy had gone through a couple of memorable experiences with Anne, including the Metolius River and Mendenhall Glacier dead body incidents.

"Yes, she, Rich and the girls are doing well, too; she called the other day to chat. Are you enjoying your vacation? Everything going well with your big group of friends?"

"Yes. It's dreamy, Mom. You and Dad would *love* this mode of transportation."

"This phone call must be costing you a lot. Everyone is absolutely fine, dear, I promise. Anne, really now, how are things with you?" her mother asked from 6,000 miles away.

"Fine," Anne replied, but it was an outright lie because things weren't fine, not even close. "Well, actually, not really fine; I keep having these really strange dreams. Remember those during my childhood?"

"Yes, dear, but as I recall, nothing ever came true," her mother tried to reassure her middle-aged daughter.

"True. You're right, as always, Mom. Thanks."

"Tell me about what you've seen and done so far." Anne filled her in briefly on strolls through parks, museums, castles, and after ten minutes or so concluded, "Well, that's probably enough for now. I love you Mom, tell Dad, too, please."

"We love you too Anne. Don't worry about anybody here, just enjoy the rest of your vacation," her mother softly replied.

As Anne's mom hung up, she turned to her husband of sixty-some years and reported, "That daughter of ours is having those odd childhood dreams. I sure hope something doesn't happen like at Mendenhall Glacier and Machu Picchu. She doesn't need that again. She'll begin to think she's jinxed."

"Well, if you think about it, it's really all the way back to the murder that we discovered at the Metolius River headwaters when she was a kid, too."

"Hmm," Anne's mother concluded.

Tea. Maybe hot tea would help. But I don't even like it or most hot beverages, except hot chocolate but that's caffeine; no caffeine, Anne said to herself.

Hoping no one else would be prowling around the ship at

this time of night, or really early morning, she quietly closed the stateroom door, and headed straight past the reception area. A dim light shown over a desk with an employee sitting in an office gently tapping on a keyboard, probably catching up on paperwork, Anne thought.

Anne went up a flight of stairs to the upper deck, through an alcove area offering coffee, teas, and sweet treats. Some fresh yummy treats were there 24/7 and were switched out depending on the time of day. Croissants and pastries in the morning, cookies in the afternoon, and assorted sweets at night. She proceeded into the Lounge heading to the Aquavit Terrace just in case something tempting might be there.

Darn! There actually was somebody up as she recognized the back of Dmitry. As she approached, she thought it best not to startle him, so in a loudish whisper mumbled, "Sorry." She wasn't really sure why she'd said it, but oh well.

He didn't reply while turning a page in his book.

"What's she doing here?" a man across the room raised his hand to stop his companion crashing into the back of him. He smooshed her against the coffee machine in the alcove area on the opposite side of the room.

"I don't know. Maybe she can't sleep," she whispered.

"We'll wait here until she leaves."

Anne spotted pastries and jars of yogurt as she poured hot water into a white cup and selected chamomile tea because she'd heard it's supposed to be soothing and caffeine-free. *Shoot*, Anne said out loud, even though no one heard her. She grabbed five napkins cleaning up the tea that she spilled. Normally not klutzy, she blamed it on being tired or because maybe she'd become preoccupied with Dmitry. *Get a grip*, she told herself. She balanced the second hot water-filled cup on a matching saucer, with the tea bag floating on top, and went back past Dmitry. She repeated, "Sorry" and added, "Good night."

Anne heard a "humph." *Americans*, he thought to himself, *insipid and overly friendly*.

She thought that he's the most unsociable man she'd ever met. Probably felt entitled with his air of superiority. She witnessed other men act like him, but they were mostly politicians, or wealthy, who thought they were better than everyone else. He's probably narcissistic and rich, she concluded.

She was correct. He did think himself better than her and most others. And clever enough to stay under the radar, so to speak, for decades.

Anne left the Lounge juggling the hot tea in her right hand while going down the stairs, being careful to not spill, with her left hand on the handrail. As she reached the main floor a staff person at the reception desk greeted her, "Anything I can do for you?"

"No thanks, just can't sleep. Hopefully this will help."

The employee glanced at her watch reading 4:10. Poor woman, probably jet lag or the time change.

The couple hidden from view watched as Anne departed, looked around and saw no one. The man mouthed, "All clear," then wordlessly they zigzagged through the Lounge's stuffed chairs, retracing Anne's steps just moments before. Silently and professionally, the man stopped to the left of Dmitry. The elderly man felt a pin prick in his neck. He heard a female voice in a Polish accent say, "Zemstra. Sprawiedliwość. Aleksandr Pushkin."

It happened so fast, Dmitry sat stunned. He hadn't heard anyone say his birth name in seven decades. He looked up as a couple moved forward to the Aquavit Terrace.

The couple knew Dmitry was one of the last remaining WWII Nazis living comfortably at home in Germany, leading a normal life, hiding in plain sight, and in some instances, still proud of his participation in one of world history's biggest atrocities. Believing they were workers rather than war criminals these former medics, SS officers, and concentration camp guards were able to return to their communities after WWII as if nothing happened. Most Germans of that era said they knew nothing of the cruelties.

A major break happened some 20 years ago, which Dmitry would have never known. A family moved into a two-story home that needed much repair. The elderly home-owner died some years earlier. Working in the basement, the owners found a trunk tucked in a corner under a stack of wood. Opening it they found a treasure trove of documents. Thumbing through, they discovered records proving a Nazi sympathizer had forged documents helping war criminals escape by creating new identities for them.

Page after page of birth names changed to fictitious characters. The couple turned the originals over to the German government, and a complete duplicate was sent to a Jewish organization. That group sent information to operatives hunting down the criminals. They found proof that the nefarious Nazi guard Aleksandr Pushkin became Dmitry Rudolph.

There was no need to glance back. **Retribution**. **Justice**. Her only regret—too bad it wouldn't take longer for Aleksandr Pushkin to suffer and die for his part in a war that murdered thousands of innocent Jews and others from foreign countries. Dmitry could linger for a few hours. If anybody discovered him, they would not have enough time to determine the poisoning. No antidote exists. It was failsafe.

Dmitry coughed. His chest felt tight. He couldn't catch a breath. He thought his head might burst and his heart raced. He tried to stand up but didn't have the strength. He felt thirsty and hot. He was sweating. He heard an odd sound, himself gurgling. It felt like the fluids and blood in his entire body were drying up.

———

Returning to their room, Anne clearly hadn't disturbed sleeping Peter who punctuated the room with a random snore. She slipped back onto the balcony holding the cup of tea carefully. She heard a motor start up close to their long-ship. It sounded like a lawn mower or maybe like a leaf blower. No wait, more like the zippy rubberized black Zodiacs they rode in the Galápagos Islands from the ship back and forth to the islands. Anne heard a whooshing sound, and thought she saw a couple of people in one of those types of Zodiacs.

"Huh, that's peculiar at this time of night," she said out loud. Then thought, maybe an employee or the jazz pianist just had a very late departure.

———

"Once again, well done," Debbie whispered to Rob as a third person guided the Zodiac easily across the river. Within five minutes, they arrived at one of dozens of docks easily acces-sible to land. "We do make a great team," he replied.

They stepped out of the watercraft and as it pulled away, the Zodiak glided easily in the current down river, disap-pearing in the darkness. She looked at their floating hotel as it motored upstream aglow with lights on the Sun Deck. What a lovely working environment for this assignment, she thought.

A man stepped out of an idling sedan and opened the back door for his two passengers, not saying a word. He may have questioned his assignment to pick up a couple from a dock in the wee hours of the morning, but he'd never divulge anything. Instead, he chauffeured them away. Some would call it murder; they considered it justifiable retribution.

The couple prided themselves on righting the wrongs from WWII. They were affiliated with the next generation of what was loosely called *Jewish Revenge Squads*. The groups started around 1944, going through 1960, and were made up primarily of about 6,000 Jewish Allied soldiers. Teams of three or four operated for 16 years and were responsible for the deaths of about 1,500 ranking Nazi officials.

Winston Churchill said, "It seemed to me indeed appropriate that a special unit of the race which has suffered indescribable treatment from the Nazis should be represented in a district formation among the forces gathered for their final overthrow."

The next people to encounter Debbie saw a shorter woman with walnut hair to her neckline and brown eyes. Just before they left, she removed the blue contact lens and flushed them down the toilet.

Rob tossed the mid-waist pillow form he'd worn for too many days into the closest garbage bin he could find, saying "Good riddance. That thing made me sweat."

Debbie and Rob were actually Goshia and Nelis. They were aware of the history of the squads first-hand from his grandfather who barely survived a camp, and what became of the rest of his family.

Supposedly one of the last killed by the revenge squads was a man who ran concentration camps in Estonia. Under his rule 100,000 were murdered. He thought himself safe in Canada, but a revenge squad found him and hanged him.

People discovered through much research that some high-ranking Nazis escapcd detection and lived around the globe even though most were likely 90 years and older. Nelis and Goshia, one of several European units, felt genuinely gratified to assist with these random missions, and considered it their obligation to their family and countrymen. The work continued and would as long as they and others, were still alive.

———————

Death hadn't come as quickly as the couple expected, but they'd never know what transpired. One sat reading a magazine on a train heading north, and the other was on a flight to London instead of going directly home to Amsterdam.

Dmitry's pulse dropped dangerously low until he could no longer speak, not even an utterance even if he wanted to. Did he hear a voice? Maybe his wife? His hazy thoughts were of the pesky American woman, but why would she want him dead? His final thoughts were of his mother. He could smell her perfume. He perished two hours after the needle had been inserted in his neck.

CHAPTER ELEVEN

Dressed and sitting in a corner chair with her feet up on the oval glass table, Anne stared, trancelike, out their open veranda glass doors as she saw white churches with red steeples, villages, and bridges, with some sort of a castle-like structure dead ahead.

Peter woke at 7. "Tell me you haven't been sitting there all this time. I left you in that chair last night."

"No, but I sure didn't sleep well. My head feels like cotton batting," she informed him.

"Are you distracted by things at home?"

"Maybe, but Mom said everything is fine at home. I probably just need some protein. Since I'm ready I'll get a plate of nibbles and bring it back."

Entering the Lounge on the way to the Aquavit Terrace, she noticed Dmitry in the same chair where she'd observed him several hours earlier. He must have fallen asleep because the book he'd been reading lay on the floor.

She waved to Judie and said, "Good morning." Pointing to the elderly man she said, "He must be a sound sleeper," then told her about the nighttime tea escapade, and call to her parents.

Carefully balancing two small plates of food, Anne returned to their room and the couple stood on the veranda anticipating the excursion and activities in Regensburg.

Ten minutes later she said, "I'm going to run these plates down and get a glass of OJ, do you want some?"

"No thanks, I'm getting in the shower."

Walking by Dmitry she said to herself, *He's still asleep. It sure seems odd with all this commotion. Should I check on him?*

She approached and said, "Sir, are you okay? Sir?"

No answer. Her blood pounded in her ears and her palms were clammy.

An employee came by and Anne stopped her and explained the situation. The employee said, "Thank you Mrs. Wellsley, you enjoy the day. I will check on Mr. Rudolph. He's polite and reserved, and a bit of a night owl," she noted. She knew all the passengers' names.

"Oh, that's his last name. I didn't know. I've seen him twice in the middle of the night this past week; guess you are right about the night owl." Anne thought the "polite" comment was overly kind.

Reaching the Lounge doorway, Anne turned back as the employee picked up the book on the floor and spoke loudly to Mr. Rudolph. He did not respond and she called out for assistance.

Anne may have appeared calm, cool, and collected to anyone going by her but inside her nerves were on fire. She opened the door and heard Peter in the shower. She stepped forward and fell back onto the bed facing the ivory ceiling, her left forearm covering her eyes. She lay there just a few minutes until Peter came out and said, "You're back so soon? What's up?"

"You will not believe this. Never in a million years. Close

the curtains, quick. I just can't… I don't understand…Why me?" she mumbled still not removing her arm.

"Anne. What's happened?"

She spoke rapidly. He deciphered most of the convoluted story as she went off on this tangent and that. "First the Metolius River, then Mendenhall Glacier, next Machu Picchu and now here? I'm going back to the lobby; I can't stay here. I need to know what's going on."

"Maybe you should stay here. We don't want to get in the way. How about the daily reading? You need to fill me in on Regensburg."

"Coming or not?"

"NOT—oh wait—I'm going with you. Two minutes."

———

While some of Anne and Peter's friends stood outside waiting for their guide, an ambulance arrived at the gangway, and personnel pulled out a gurney and equipment, rushing to board Viking *Var*.

Kathy remarked, "Gosh, I hope no one is seriously ill."

"Seems like it could be," came the reasonable observation from Phil.

"Considering the ages of some on board, there certainly could be some medical situations." Mike noted calmly.

———

He tapped his foot, "They are 15 minutes late. Did you try texting Debbie?"

"Yes, Casey, after I called their room phone twice," Cath replied, more patient than her husband.

"We agreed just last night to meet them for breakfast and do the excursion together."

"I know. I wonder where Rob and Debbie are."

"They're the ones who suggested the whole thing."

"Well, she did have that horrible headache last night. Maybe they turned their phones off and they're sleeping in, or maybe they don't feel well. Let's not bother them."

Off they went minus Rob and Debbie, catching up with the others.

Judie mentioned, "I thought you were going with the southerners this morning."

"She must be sick. They never showed for breakfast, and after calling and texting, we decided to leave them alone."

The new friends had all exchanged phone numbers and friended each other on Facebook at the start of the trip. Cath texted Debbie, **Sorry we missed U at breakfast and the excursion. Hope U R feeling better soon. Maybe C U at dinner.**

Employees moved through the guests in the Lounge, requesting they make room as emergency personnel rushed in.

"Do you think he's had a stroke?" "Maybe a heart attack?" "He is quite elderly, could be any number of things" were overheard comments.

A paramedic shook his head. "No pulse," he said. "Look at his skin. It's suspicious because the color of the man's skin is very red."

"Something's off, call the police," a young medic directed.

Police arrived dressed in navy, with a sky-blue stripe down the outside of the pant legs. One wore a sky-blue shirt, with his sleeves rolled up, and another a jacket with the word *Polizei* in gold above the right chest pocket. **POLIZEI** was written along the side of the white and blue van, with matching colored light bars on the roof.

Chief of Police Arno Haas had been only four minutes away, en route to his office. The medic said, "Sir, there's something you should see."

Someone checked for a wallet. The patient had nothing in his pockets. "Do we know who this is?"

"Yes," replied Erik from Guest Relations. "Dmitry Rudolph, stateroom 209."

"Is there a wife?"

Erik nodded.

"Please ask her to come here."

Erik knocked loudly. "Mrs. Rudolph? Mrs. Rudolph?" Sandra heard someone at the door. Opening it a man said, "It's your husband. Please come with me now and hurry."

This could be the end, Sandra thought. He'd been declining for the past year, more rapidly than she would have guessed. Whether old age, cancer or whatever the case, Dmitry refused to see any doctor.

Anne scootched up beside two employees standing by the beverage alcove, looking into the roped-off Lounge. She heard, "I wonder if they might need Gina."

"Who's Gina?" Anne wondered if she'd actually said it out loud without realizing the question popped out of her mouth.

"Aren't you the woman who found him?" One asked.

"I guess I am. Who's Gina? "

The two female employees looked questioningly at each other. "Tell her; she's *involved*."

"The medical examiner."

"I'm not sure, but there's been a lot of activity in there with the paramedics and police."

Anne saw Dmitry's wife standing with officials.

"*Gina's* probably coming," Anne emphasized Gina to Peter as he stealthily moved in closer beside his wife.

"Who's Gina?"

Three women simultaneously answered, "The medical examiner." Anne laughed nervously and Peter glared at his wife.

"Gina? I wonder if she's from Russia," Anne said in a church quiet voice.

An employee whispered, "From Romania—matter of fact, detailed, precise. Do you know of her? She has quite a reputation."

"*No*, we don't," Peter pointedly clearing up the questioning.

"One of my favorite TV programs out of New Zealand is *Brokenwood Mysteries*. The ME is no-nonsense, dry-humored, extremely detailed, and thorough. She's my favorite character on the program. She's from Russia," Anne anxiously rambled.

The two female Viking employees glanced at each other; one raised her eyebrows.

"I need to go back to our room and pick up my purse. And take a couple of ibuprofen. I have an instant headache," Anne said.

Standing next to her husband of over 30 years, Mrs. Rudolph let out a sob. A kind woman put an arm around her.

Sandra heard the police chief say, "Call Gina. Something's not right here." Long ago he learned to trust his gut, and his gut was telling him this was highly suspicious.

"Sit down, dear. Please bring Mrs. Rudolph a cup of tea, Axil," a female said softly.

Within ten minutes, when the Regensburg Gina arrived both Anne and Peter stood dumbfounded. This Gina had long, strawberry-blonde hair pulled back and secured with a scrunchy. She stood about five-foot-five, maybe six, a light complexion, and looked much like the Gina on the fictional *Brokenwood* series.

"Okay, that's uncanny," Peter acknowledged.

"I'd say weird if you ask me," Anne uttered. "First, Dmitry is unconscious and now he's dead? That's enough for me. Let's go take a walk. Maybe we can catch up with the others."

"Well, we haven't heard for sure if he died. Maybe they're just covering their bases, just in case."

"I don't think they call for the ME unless they have a body; only from watching all the murders on TV, you know."

One quick-thinking employee asked if they could get Anne's cell phone number. Anne answered, "Sure, and it's on my guest registration form."

Gina knew her role. Medical Examiners research and study the nature, the cause, and development of diseases, and the structural and functional changes resulting from them. They diagnose from body tissue, fluids, secretions, and other specimens. They identify the presence and stage of disease utilizing laboratory procedures. MEs advise other medical practitioners and law enforcement.

She did her normal preliminary once over and noted two tattoos, not German. She spent some time looking at the side of the man's neck. "I call tell you that it's suspicious. See the mark?" she pointed out to Haas. He couldn't see it. "This could be the work of professionals. I'll have details for your tomorrow after a thorough postmortem examination at my office. It might be later than sooner."

"What *can* you tell me now, Gina?"

"It's not the Russians."

"How do you know?"

"They are much cleaner and accurate. This is messy, but not as messy as a knife, of course. Still too messy. If a Russian had done it, the prick would be hidden at the top of the vein, which would only be found with a microscope or a looking glass, making it extremely difficult to find. They are meticulous murderers. If I can see this puncture wound, it's not them." Gina pointed to a nearly invisible spot on the side of the man's neck. Haas slipped on his reading glasses still not seeing the tiny dot.

"Are you're saying it's homicide, not just some elderly man passing away from natural causes? Can you give me an estimate on time of death?"

"Most likely. Not really. Since it's 9:30 a.m. now, and no rigor mortis has set in, it was likely two to five hours ago."

"Any guesses how?" Police Chief Haas watched Gina, her eyes still sparkling blue although there were now more lines around those gorgeous eyes and her brow showed permanent creases, all disclosing their middle-age. She was truly brilliant, and he never wanted to work with anybody but her on problematic cases.

She was never wrong. It could take her some time, but her work was meticulous. The only time he could recall she'd been accused of being incorrect was years earlier. It had been documented she hadn't come up with the right time of death. She stuck by her findings. Turned out the witness lied to cover his tracks. No one ever doubted her again.

"You could help by finding out some answers for me. I need to know his medical history, any underlying illnesses. It's most likely murder, and you get to solve why. I'll take him back to the mortuary. Once I determine exactly what was used and the time of death, I will contact you. Don't rush me. I'll call you when I'm done. I'm backlogged, my assistant is sick."

Anne slipped on her sunglasses just in case somebody might see she was weepy. They caught up with the others not indicating anything was awry. A guide named Karl met them at the end of the dock and told them that Regensburg dates to Roman times and was the first capital of Bavaria.

She and Peter had toured the town on a prior trip, and now was at the top of Anne's favorite quaint, charming city list. She perked up slightly knowing professionals were caring for the man she believed for the past ten days to be very strange.

Mike mentioned the *Nautical Term of the Day, Over the Barrel. The most common method of punishment on board a ship was flogging. The unfortunate sailor was tied to a grating, a mast or "over the barrel" of a deck cannon.*

Cutting through Old Town Square, they followed cobblestones through an iron gate into Villapark. The plaque at the entrance was printed in German but Anne could understand the date 1856/57. Karl mentioned that this city survived the bombing in WWII because no one thought it was that important. Most of the buildings are many hundreds of years old.

Strolling along a colorful, charming narrow street lined with two- and three-story buildings painted in earthy shades of brown, coral, pine, and plum, they stopped at a dragon fish hanging from a curly iron display jutting out from a building. The fish had its mouth open about to swallow a man. "Thoughts are it's a sturgeon," Karl said, telling the story about the giant fish.

They went by an open-air market, just as the cathedral bells rang ten times. Bulging baskets of pink and red geraniums sat atop pillars. Gazing up, Cath pointed out trailing flowers tumbling from Juliet balconies. One cement planter held a family of rusty metal quail.

Strolling through an arch at the base of a tall building they were on the way to St. Peter's Cathedral. "No St. Stephen's Cathedral?" Anne asked.

"Not in this town," Karl chuckled. Just about anywhere in the city one could see the Gothic twin towers. The guide told them that anyone who gets lost usually can find their way here. It is known as Dom St. Peter or Regensburg Cathedral. The church has existed since around 700 AD but due to several devastating fires, it was rebuilt, and the current Gothic-style building was completed in 1320. It is 279 feet long and 115 feet wide. The nave is 105 feet high, and the twin towers are nearly 350 feet high. One tower was covered in see-through scaffolding, a monumental task to keep it in good repair and clean, he explained.

Stepping inside, it took their eyes a few seconds to adjust from the outside brightness to the dim interior. Craning their heads back they saw that the exterior features many statues. What grabbed Anne's attention were the spectacular kaleidoscopic stained glass windows. The windows show apostles, saints, the life of the Virgin Mary, and scenes from the legend of St. Catherine. Then there is the silver-sheathed main altar. An impressive bouquet of tiger lilies, miniature scarlet roses, and bright tangerine-colored daisies, about five feet tall, sat on the third step. "This is my favorite so far," Anne stated. "This stained glass rivals Sainte Chappelle in Paris." The cathedral is also the home of the Domspatzen, a 1,000-year-old boys' choir that accompanies the 10 a.m. Sunday service during the school year.

Outside they rounded a corner and came to a full stop seeing a colorful mural of a giant Goliath and David created in 1573. Smaller David is bent over putting a rock in his slingshot at Goliath House.

They passed an ice cream shop, an apothecary, and a golf store where clubs were displayed in what looked like an umbrella stand. The sun brightened a line of peach, lime, apricot, and slate-blue fronts of four-story buildings.

Several from their group darted into a kafféehaus for a beverage. While waiting outside, Anne noticed a tot on all fours heading down the middle of the pedestrian avenue. He wore a blue shirt under a mustard yellow sweater, eggplant knickers with snowy dots, lime socks, and terracotta shoes. He stole the limelight from the quaintness of the area. People stepped around him; moms pushing strollers split their path going by him; a pair walking their dog stopped so he could pet their pooch; bikers rode by and waved. His mom finally retrieved him, putting an end to the street entertainment.

Karl told them that the city is famous for its patrician towers. The tall towers are monuments to the wealthy and powerful people of medieval times. The goal was to lay claim to the tallest tower in the town. The tallest is the Golden Tower, or Goldener Turm, with a clock on the top.

He led the group to Old Town Hall. It looked uninviting and boring except for the buttery building next door which happens to be the Tourist Information Center. Climbing up about ten steps into a tall ornate doorway leading directly into Town Hall, Karl told them to keep in mind it welcomed dignitaries from the 13th century, and princes from the Roman Empire gathered to discuss and solve crises and vote on important issues of the day. They passed by the basement which contained remains, and an old torture chamber with racks and other scary, painful devices.

Café Prinzess is Germany's first coffeehouse. Established in 1686, the dark, hot beverage made its debut here. The window shop was filled with chocolates in all flavors, shapes, and sizes. Several stepped through the door and were welcomed by the divine scent of chocolate and coffee.

Others stopped at CremaGelato, admiring the selection of tasty cool delights. Anne didn't vary much from lemon; on this she was predictable, much like Peter and vanilla. She tucked a dozen I LOVE GELATO napkins in her pocket. These would generate fun remembrances when serving a favorite chilly dessert that she first devoured in Inverness, Scotland. In her version of the modified Lemon Meringue Sundae, she uses two types of gelato, lemon and vanilla, slathered with generous amounts of lemon curd on top. Along with another layer of lemon curd, blueberries or raspberries separate the lemon and vanilla layers. She added a thin ginger cookie wedged into the top of the mound of this scrumptious indulgence.

They went by the Irish Harp Pub stepping through the pedestrian arch onto the Old Stone Bridge. Strolling across the Danube, Peter pointed out the line of longships with theirs at the very end. Glancing back at the picturesque Old Town it looked lively, bright, and colorful. They strolled by a papier mâché giraffe and racks of handcrafted cards and artsy napkins, straw flowers atop succulents and cactus, two long-haired dachshunds leading their people down an alley, a bakery display of trays and bins of sweet treats, and a statue of a sitting dog, like a retriever, at the dog store. Julie went in to get Ollie a treat, her four-legged family member at home.

The Old Stone Bridge is a medieval Romanesque style bridge from the mid 1100s connecting Old Town to the Stadtamhof. For more than 800 years, it was the city's only bridge across the river. It was the major trade route being the only crossing over the Danube between Ulm, Germany, and Vienna, Austria.

The bridge boasts 15 arches and three towers once connected to the bridge, but one damaged by ice was torn down in the late 1700s, and another was damaged during the war in 1810 and torn down. One tower remains, Schuldturm, on the city side of the bridge and is now a museum. They ambled along the pedestrian and bicycle bridge dodging a couple of electric scooters, obviously in more of a hurry than they were.

Peter's stomach growled; with all the commotion Anne hadn't noticed they'd missed lunch. The unassuming one-story sausage kitchen sits right along the river serving the city's traditional finger-sized sausages, grilled over beech wood, and dished up with its own tangy sauerkraut and sweet grainy mustard since 1135. It rightfully claims the world's oldest sausage kitchen. Stepping inside for a late lunch instead of sitting outside the Besucherzentrum Welterbe, they saw Carol and Jim who were eating some delectable German food.

Anne ordered four grilled sausages and kraut. "Is that all?" the friendly waitress asked. Peter ordered eight, adding mashed potatoes. A woman sitting by herself overhearing the conversation chuckled and said, "I don't mean to eavesdrop but I live about 20 miles from here and come several times a year." The woman appeared to be a runner, fit and trim. "I order a dozen each time; after every bite you'll want a few more." Anne increased hcr order to six, Peter to ten, and the local expert was correct, each bite tasted better and better.

Longships and other types of boats lined their return

walk to their floating home. A sculpture of a large gold catfish with its tail pointing toward the river catches most people's attention. With the plaque written in German they could only imagine its significance. One man mumbled, "Modern art."

Several tables and food trucks were doing a great business. Gourmet speisekartoffel, in other words, baking potatoes, were sold in two-kg brown bags. Baskets of plump strawberries, blueberries, and cherries were snapped up by locals. Three food trucks sold fried or grilled fish, meat, veggie kabobs, and an assortment of drinks and snacks.

Around 3 that afternoon Nora, one of the *Var's* housekeepers, called her supervisor. "Brina, the Do Not Disturb sign is still out on suite 341. Can you call the room to see if they answer please, I'd like to tidy their room. I haven't been in there all week." Standing outside the closed door, Nora could hear the phone ring seven times.

"No answer."

"Knock again then enter," Brina said, "I'm on my way."

Nora unlocked the door to the Explorer Suite and said loudly, "Housekeeping. Hello, anyone here? Sorry to disturb you." The room looked spotless. Now that's odd, she said to herself.

Brina arrived within moments and stepped in. "Did someone already clean this room?"

"Not that I'm aware of."

"Let me check the logs; I'll be back shortly. Stay here."

Brina stopped by the front desk explaining what they were seeing in the room. Checking the computer, Erik said, "I don't see that Mr. and Mrs. Smith left today. They are here somewhere."

Nora observed the flashing message light on the phone and radioed Brina, "Listen to it."

"It's from a woman named Cathy in 212 checking on them for not showing up for breakfast. They were supposed to go with them for the day. There are two messages from the same woman."

Brina nervously reported, "We have two guests who haven't been seen today." Erik made a ship wide announcement. "Would Mr. or Mrs. Robert Smith from stateroom 341 please come to the reception desk?" He repeated it. Neither showed up. Erik notified Guest Relations Manager Brandt, who notified the captain, whose response was "Contact the police."

"Done," replied Brandt, who rushed into the Lounge and notified the police still on board from the morning episode.

Reaching suite 341, two officers slipped on gloves looking like they were preparing for German Warfare in their blue hazmat garb. A detective picked up a pen and slipped it into a clear bag, writing the date and evidence number on the top, then sealed it. They found no clothing in the closets or drawers; no toiletries in the bathroom; no toothbrushes, hairbrushes or anything belonging to the Smiths. The suite was too perfect and too clean. Glasses were washed and no prints seen. Officers bagged them anyway. "Get forensics in here now," they heard from the police chief.

One officer flipped through a notepad on the desk, and noticed three pages down a slight indentation on the blank page. "Maybe we can get something from this," he commented.

"Hopefully they'll get lucky and find some hairs in the bedding," one stated waiting for the forensic team to arrive.

The door of the small black safe was open, and an officer's flashlight showed nothing inside.

Two navy passports lay on the counter. An officer opened the first, "Mr. Robert David Smith." Second one, "Mrs. Deborah Suzanne Smith."

"Why would they leave their passports?" one asked.

"I've heard about this and some other similar cases. They are letting us know that their job is finished."

Another replied, "Probably because they are using their original passports and have left the ship. Smith could be assumed names."

"Do you think they're involved with the earlier death?"

"It certainly seems coincidental."

"You know Gina is highly suspicious about the death of the elderly man from this morning. This may be the work of generational groups dealing with WWII war criminals."

"That's a giant leap, don't you think?"

"Maybe, but I just read an article about these small groups eliminating criminals since governments won't do anything about it anymore. It just happened somewhere in Central America."

"We've never had anything like this happen before, have we?" a Viking employee stationed outside the door asked to another delivering a carafe of coffee.

"Keep searching and let the ship's captain know they are not departing anytime soon."

Detectives combed over every inch and took pictures of every nook and cranny. A man and woman from forensics entered. First impressions—they were seeing an extraordinarily clean room, too clean, obviously the work of professionals. Meticulously they opened each drawer picking up lint, specks of this or that, and searched under the bed for any trace evidence, following their standard quadrant grid. A smaller area than they were used to, it still took them many hours to go over every surface.

One officer said quietly to the other, "Do you think we will find them? Obviously they didn't fall overboard."

"Not unless we find fingerprints or DNA; it's immaculate. Probably the best we have are a few fibers from the sheets. We'll have the lab run tests ASAP."

That afternoon back onboard, Cath reminded Anne that the Smiths were a no-show that morning. "Right…maybe they're still not feeling well. If we don't see them soon, I'll check with the front desk. Even though they're not part of our group, it's like they've adopted us. I'll see if they can tell me anything."

Then it hit her, a full body hot flash starting at the tips of her toes, and in a couple of seconds soaring to the top of her head. The same reaction happened when she had contracted the nasty norovirus; she felt like throwing up. Her heart raced. Pushing a terrible thought away, it must be a coincidence. She would not mention her suspicions to anyone, not even Peter. *I'm swearing off reading or watching mysteries from now on, she told herself.*

Deciding not to wait, Anne approached a person at the front desk and explained her concern. With an alarmed look on her face, the employee said, "Please wait here." After stepping into a small room off the reception area, speaking with somebody behind the door, she returned. An employee pointed Anne out to a police officer. "She's the one who saw him earlier."

The officer approached Anne and led her to a corner. "I'd like to ask you some questions."

"Regarding?"

"Dmitry Rudolph."

"Of course. I do have a few things I can share with you, but I've been told I have a vivid imagination. There are several others who might be helpful, too, saying their names as she pointed to Julie, and Casey and Cath, except Cath's chair was vacant. Anne mouthed, "Where's Cath?" Casey pointed up the staircase as she'd made a beeline to stateroom 341 to find out if something might be wrong with Rob and Debbie.

The door swung open as she got there and shockingly a police officer stepped out. She saw other uniformed people in the room. She backed away shaken, returning to the Lounge.

———

The officer took a drink of coffee and said, "Now, about Mr. Rudolph."

"Well, I just learned his last name this morning before we left. First though, can I mention something?" Anne asked. He nodded.

"Several of us are really concerned about our friends, the Smiths. We haven't heard or seen them all day; that's who I was asking about at the front desk. Oh, and how's Mr. Rudolph?"

"Deceased."

"What?" Julie and Anne said at the same time gazing at each other.

"We will get to the couple next."

Cath returned whispering to Casey and Julie, "There's a policeman in Rob and Debbie's room. I'm so worried, what if they are dead?"

"Let's not jump to conclusions, Cath," her sort of reassuring husband lowered his voice.

Anne filled in the officer in chronological order seeing

the elderly man along the trip as Julie, Cath and Casey sat quietly. Anne tried not to elaborate or interject her *Something is fishy in Denmark* theories. After about 15 minutes back and forth, and the officer scribbling notes, he thanked Anne and said, "Now what about this Mr. and Mrs. Smith?"

Anne sat back in the chair. A video ran through her head of the past week. Her face turned pale as she turned to say something to Julie. "Anne, you're white as a ghost and you're scaring me."

"Mrs. Wellsley?" the detective asked. Anne couldn't answer.

"Madam, are you all right? Get her a drink of water, please. Now!"

"Sir, can I speak with you, privately?" as jumbled memories of brief encounters of Rob and Dmitry played like a movie in her head. The officer motioned for a second detective to join them.

Anne and one detective moved to another area and she told him everything flowing from her memory. Anne was quite sure she'd seen Rob in close proximity to Dmitry on several occasions in Budapest before the cruise started. She hadn't realized it until that very moment. "I thought I recognized Rob," she mumbled.

"They were supposed to join us at breakfast, then we were going on a tour together," Cath told the officer. "Debbie specifically said "If the Creek don't rise, we'll meet you at 8 o'clock." I laughed because I hadn't heard that before. I went to their room to check on them and the door was open."

"You didn't see them?" Julie asked concerned.

"No, I saw some commotion and a police officer coming out, so I backed away."

A third officer approached and asked Casey to come with him.

Anne rejoined Cath and Julie who sat side by side as the detective said, "Spell her name, please."

"Debbie Smith."

"Debi Smith."

"Debby Smith." The friends each answered recalling the way Debbie entered her contact info in each one's phone.

"It's spelled differently for each of you? Check the contact info and read it to me, please." Smith was spelled the same with an address in Alabama. Debbie, Debi, Debby, each was different. "What type of things did you discuss?"

Julie said, "I spoke with her about dogs. She loves dogs as do I. They have two."

"But we all love dogs, that's not so unusual," Anne interjected.

Cath mentioned, "I don't, I'm a cat lover. We talked about grandchildren a lot."

The women recalled discussions having many things in common with Debbie from Alabama. "They love to stroll down their driveway lined with Live Oaks dripping with moss," Julie mentioned. "And I learned the difference between Live Oaks and other oaks."

"We talked about fundraising events. They are very southern. How can we all have so much in common?" Anne asked.

"It's likely that you really don't. She could be a pro at *reading* to people," the official answered.

"What are you talking about?" one of the women asked.

"I'm not at liberty right now to explain this," the second officer said, "but we suspect that this couple is not who they purported to be."

Sitting in a corner with his officer, Casey mentioned, "Rob is a sports fanatic and a major football fan. We talked sports for probably hours. He's exceptionally knowledgeable with stats and knows zillions of records won by dozens of teams."

"Does he drink a lot?"

"Not really, maybe a couple in a row but it didn't seem to affect him."

"What about her? Did she drink?"

"I didn't notice; you would have to ask the ladies," Casey replied.

The three friends were deep in conversation with the detectives. "Sure, we had some drinks over the week. I ordered a White Lady, something Debbie drank a few times that appeared refreshing and clear like there was nothing in it. Anne faked a gag, "I about spit it out; it was all alcohol and nothing else."

"Any behavioral changes when she drank?"

"Nothing really, just about the same whether she drank or not. I think the bartender made the White Lady pretty strong though. She also drank Coke."

"Children?"

"She told me two."

Julie said, "Three; two daughters and one son."

"I heard about just one daughter." Each woman again gave a different answer.

"Sir, where do you think they are?"

"Madam, we don't know. We are trying to piece together a timeline."

"And whether or not this fits into the death of Mr. Rudolph?"

"Can't say. Did anyone get any photos?"

"Are you saying Rob and Debbie are dead or what?"

"No, I am not. We just know they are not on the ship. Back to photos."

"Oh yes, I'm sure I did," Anne replied, picking up her phone swiping through her photos. "We did lunch yesterday in Passau at a German restaurant, and I know I took a few there." Finding the grouping from the day before there wasn't one picture on her camera of Debbie or Rob. "That's really strange, there are none of them in the restaurant."

"Really?" Julie asked. "I know you did because you told us all to scrunch together as we lifted those hefty beer glasses. Two of us ordered lemonade and beer, but remember, she and Rob both drank the dark beer."

"Do you ever leave your phone unguarded?"

"No, I always carry it with me. Well maybe not always, like when going to the bathroom or something, but it's locked with my 4-digit code."

"Hmm," the officer said, "Well, maybe it's not as secure as you think."

The three women glanced at each other with eyebrows raised.

"Well, I don't believe any of this. He worked for, for, for, you know, oh for Pete's sake, I can't remember where. Casey, where did Rob work?"

"I don't think I ever heard where he worked."

"I thought they were both retired."

"Well, it just can't be," Cath said.

"I'm so confused," Anne admitted.

Julie said, "I think that's actually true."

"What? Why?"

"Now that I think of a few more episodes, it's like they were too perfect, maybe staged. You know how she invited us to see their suite?"

"Yes, because I haven't seen a suite before on this cruise line."

"She made a point of saying that they were both really messy people but there were hardly any clothes around."

"Well, that's because they got a last-minute deal on Facebook and that's why they were in the suite. And, probably why they hadn't packed much," Cath defended.

It was getting dark outside and coming up on dinner time, but the foursome stayed with the detectives.

An hour later sitting down at the final dinner on *Var* several weren't all that hungry after what transpired earlier. However, Anne's favorite dessert wouldn't be passed up, Key Lime Pie, although probably not made with real key limes from Florida. She didn't care. She ordered a mojito, heavy on the lime juice, light on the alcohol, and two pieces of pie.

Sitting on their veranda, she texted her two brothers, and BFF Peggy, at 10 o'clock their time. At home it was 2 in the afternoon.

The first response from Peggy, **Nooooooo, Anne. Not again. I am sooooo sorry.**

What? You're kidding me, Sis from her brother Max.

His wife Lola sent Anne a separate one: **Anne, Max just told me. R U ok? I just can't imagine what U and Peter R going through. Call me if U need me. Do U need us 2 pick U up at the airport?** with three heart emojis added at the end.

Anne's reply to Lola: **U R always so sweet and caring; we're fine but thx. Just so weird.**

Her sheriff brother Will responded: **I have a buddy, Bruno, who I met in Quantico at the Academy. He's a captain for a police department in Austria. I don't recall the name of the city where he lives but he showed me pictures of himself snow skiing to work in the winter. I can contact him.**

Anne responded: **We're fine. No need yet Will, but thx. I'll tell the folks when we get home. Don't want to worry them. Again.**

Anne admitted to herself that one of her first thoughts was about "Deputy Tall Dark and Handsome," Clay Malloy. He'd been a part of their family's discovery of a body at the headwaters of the Metolius River when she was barely a teenager. And her summertime crush. Then there was the serendipitous encounter almost three decades later in Juneau, when Anne discovered the infamous boot on Mendenhall Glacier. Malloy retired and moved his wife Twyla and their two children from Central Oregon to Juneau years earlier, then un-retired and started a second career as captain for the city's police department.

After their encounter and visit in his office, she stayed in touch with him randomly over the years mostly through emails, and about their upcoming Alaska cruises. They sent Christmas cards and became friends with the family and would see them on their Alaska visits. Clay was included in the Machu Picchu discovery, as was Peggy and her brothers. Clay kindly offered help from a retired police officer friend living in Cusco.

Texting the current situation, Clay responded back: **Right place at the wrong time. Again. Other than this episode, are you and Peter OK?**

Yes, we've had another marvelous adventure even with this. I'll let you know if we hear anything. THX. Give my regards to Twy.

An hour later, she took half a Xanax, which helped her fall asleep undisturbed for seven hours.

Will emailed Bruno anyway and the return text read, **I am here should she need assistance. And Hans lives in Munich if necessary.**

CHAPTER TWELVE

After their *final* breakfast, *final* farewell to helpful and sympathetic *Var* staff, and *final* goodbyes to their lovely stateroom, they boarded a bus to the train station that would take them to Prague.

Mike read the *Nautical Term of the Day, To Know the Ropes. There are miles and miles of cordage in the rigging of a square-rigged ship. The only way of keeping track and knowing the function of all of these lines was to know where they were located. It took an experienced person to know the ropes.*

"Is that the *final* nautical term of the day?" Anne teased Mike. "We'll see."

She couldn't wait to get back to one of her favorite cities. She loved seeing Gothic structures and spires, charming parks, cobblestone streets, stately palaces and bridges, ornate cathedrals, street shows, cute cafés, and impressive theaters.

When she thought about Dmitry, she couldn't help wondering what could have happened to him, but she'd forced herself to wait a several days before emailing her nice contact in the office on the *Var*. Obviously Dmitry was elderly, so probably a heart attack, she expected to hear. She felt sad for his poor wife.

The farmland and rolling hills looked much the Willamette Valley where they lived, except for the homes with red roofs and steepled churches that appeared often. She noticed the *Tschechische Republik* sign on the side of the road.

———

Prague reminded Anne of the charm of Paris, but without the costly price tag. The Czech Republic, or as more were calling it Czechia, belongs to the European Union, but the Euro isn't used. Anne pulled out her wallet with plenty of CKZs to spend.

Prague, also known as Praha, is the capital of the Czech Republic. In school their age group learned it as Czecho-slovakia before that changed in 1993, splitting with Slovakia. Having just been in Bratislava for the day, she recalled how the guide said the Slavs felt like they were sort of stepchil-dren to the people in the Czech Republic.

Anne started to read to Peter about Prague's history and he said, "Give me the condensed version, please." She laughed and skimmed through a guidebook.

"Okay, ready?" With his nod she said, "Prague's origins can be traced from a Princess Libuse, who married a man named Premsyl and they founded the Premsyl Dynasty. Good King Wenceslas, you know from the Christmas song, was some descendant. Yikes, poor guy, was assassinated while campaigning for Bohemia to have equal rights.

"Then Charles the 4th helped Prague become the third most populated city in Europe and became the capital of the Holy Roman Empire in 1315. He founded Charles Bridge, Newtown, and St. Vitus Cathedral.

"Emperor Franz Joseph established the Austro-Hungarian Empire which was then defeated during WWI and led to the creation of the country Czechoslovakia with Prague chosen as the capital.

"Oh dear, now it's the Germans. From 1939, Germany took over Czechoslovakia where the citizens of Prague were oppressed by the Nazis. The city was bombed leaving large parts of it damaged or destroyed. On May 8, 1945, the Germans left Prague as the Soviets came to liberate the city.

"Gosh, then in 1968 the city was invaded by the Soviet Union. In 1989, during the fall of the Berlin Wall, Czechoslovakia was liberated from communism and the Soviets, becoming its own separate country in 1993 and Prague became the official capital of the Czech Republic. What a history. That's good enough."

Each person pulled their luggage from the train through the historic station to where a charter bus drove them to their hotel, the Grand Hotel Praha in the Old Town Square. Driving by Gothic cream, gray, and beige buildings on narrow streets lined with trees and vehicles, dodging red and white electric trams, and going around the last corner, the driver parked the bus half a block from the hotel because of the vehicle-free square. Anne pointed to an outdoor market with dozens of booths and stalls in the middle of the square.

"How cool and perfect timing!" she squealed with delight.

"Great." Peter feigned.

She warned everyone there was a small elevator. Instead, most climbed two flights of steps to Reception where potted palms and vases of flowers added a welcoming touch. About ten minutes worth of bumping sounds of luggage hitting each step to the second landing, they reached a friendly face who greeted them by saying "do-bree-den" or "Good Day" in Czech.

Receiving a key, an old-fashioned real brass key, everyone

headed off to various rooms to unpack for three nights. According to the hotel brochure, *This three-story historic hotel offers luxurious furnished rooms with preserved historical atmosphere, featuring numerous interesting architectural details, together with comfort, offering a splendid view of the historical center.* The hotel is perfectly located close to everything, and includes a breakfast in the Mozart Café, complete with a full bar.

Peter opened the door to room 211 leading into a dim hallway with a wooden wardrobe on the left for hanging clothes, a round table with a lime tablecloth, and a couple of chairs. Peeking into a large bathroom to the right with two sinks, a large shower, nice amenities, plush towels, and marble walls, it was big enough to have a party. Straight ahead they entered the bedroom, about the size of their living room at home, with views of the famous clock and the square below from their window, with hundreds of people moseying around the craft market.

Unpacking a few items that they would use for the next several days, they left the front of the hotel and stood at the foot of the magnificent clock as it chimed 12 times, watching the six-minute presentation. "Even though it's our second visit I still don't understand that clock," Anne muttered. "Maybe our guide tomorrow can explain it to us in English."

Heading out, they wandered through craft and food stalls, smelling delicious aromas, perusing selections of jewelry and homemade crafts, seeing hundreds of bright yellow marigolds surrounding the base of a large statue. A group of elementary kids, likely from a local school, stood on a grand-stand readying themselves for a concert.

"Let's head that way and go to St. Nicholas Church," Sharon said pointing at its chartreuse dome. Phil read from a brochure he picked up in the lobby of the hotel, *The most famous baroque church in Prague stands along with the former*

Jesuit College in the center of Lesser Town Square. A medieval parish church consecrated by Prague Bishop Tobias in 1283 stood at the site until 1743.

Today's Church of St. Nicholas is one of the most valuable baroque buildings north of the Alps. Construction lasted approximately 100 years, and three generations of great baroque architects —father, son, and sons-in-law worked on the church.

The Church of St. Nicholas is a superb example of high baroque architecture, a building that astonishes visitors with its size and monumental interior. As the most prominent and distinctive landmark in Lesser Town, no panoramic view of the city would be complete without its silhouette.

Entering, the size of the building and statues felt almost overwhelming. The height inside the church to the top of the Lantern is 187 feet, making it the tallest interior in Prague.

Anne took a seat and Peter joined her. "This could easily be in the top five cathedrals we've ever seen," he said. The most ornate church they'd ever been in took about 100 years to complete. The pink stripes of artificial marble, really stucco columns, are affixed with four life-size statues of the church elders. They marveled at the gold altar, richly decorated arched rooms, over 50 statues, hundreds of icons, the ceiling done in frescoes and wonderful paintings, long corridor, and organ in the back where a plaque reads "Mozart played in 1787."

Not far from their hotel, they entered Oliva Verde for dinner. Tabletops were decorated with placemats designed with different colors and sizes of olives. "It reminds me of the woman on the cruise on the olive diet," Peter noted. Bottles of olive oil and various size drinking glasses were set on the tables. Warm bread was delivered before they were all seated. Anne tried a bowl of goulash, this version with a dark gravy instead of the redder types in Budapest.

That night, while Anne was standing in her pj's at the

window, Peter was already in bed checking the news apps on his phone, and people loitered below pointing at this and that, mostly watching the intriguing Astronomical Clock. With their accommodations smack dab in Old Town Square, she assumed it might be a bit noisy that night. She gently pushed in the foamy blue earplugs. Noise nor anything else was an issue that night.

CHAPTER THIRTEEN

A nne arched her back, slightly achy from the new hotel bed. "At least I managed to sleep through the night." Peter padded down the hallway and made a cup of coffee as she moved into the bathroom, and not recalling any bad dreams pleased her.

Her first thoughts went back to the longship wondering about Dmitry and what in the world happened to Debbie and Rob.

Anne gazed out the window. Below stood a couple hand-in-hand. The woman wore a poofy white wedding dress and held a bouquet of brightly colored flowers. "Wedding photos are sure popular in front of the clock," she mentioned to Peter coming out of the bathroom dressed and ready to go.

Stepping into the Mozart Café for a buffet breakfast, Anne spotted Judie doing a 360. It was an art gallery of plates, figurines, and artwork on the walls, not to mention the desserts in a glass case.

"This is about the coolest breakfast place I've ever seen," Anne overheard a guest say. Before taking in the café's gallery, they filled their stomachs from trays of pastries, chafing dishes of meats, bowls of mixed fruits, plates of vegetables, and about anything anyone could want.

They all joined up under the arch in the hotel lobby before heading out for the day. Anne had arranged for two local guides to take her friends around.

A woman approached Anne saying "Ahoj," pronounced "a-hoy." Lenka, their guide said, "It means 'Hello.'" They split into two groups, some with Lenka and others with Marek, both groups starting in front of the famous astronomical clock.

"Before we head out, I'm confused if we say Czech Republic or Czechia?" Mike commented.

Lenka said that both are commonly used, then turned her attention to explaining that the huge clock on the town hall was once far more complex than the current one. Originally it depicted the medieval universe divided into three spheres but it had been periodically rebuilt to correspond with the new advances in knowledge. In 1898, purists worked to restore it to its original state.

"Look up. Can you figure out how this works?" After one minute most impatient Americans give up waiting for her to explain. "Of the two giant dials on the top, the top one tells the time. It has an intricate series of revolving wheels within wheels but the basics are simple. The two big outer dials tell the time in a 24-hour circle. Of these, the inner dial is stationary and is marked with the Roman numerals I through XII. The colorful background indicates the amount of light at the different times of day. The black circle surrounded by orange at the bottom half is nighttime while the blue top half is daytime and the shades of gray and orange between them represent dawn and dusk.

"Meanwhile, the outer dial with the golden numbers on

the back black band lists numbers 1 through 24 in Bohemian script. Because this uses the medieval Italian method of telling time where the day resets at sunset, the number one is not at the top but somewhere in the lower right quadrant of the Roman dial. The Roman numeral with the Bohemian one lines up to tell you the time of last night's sunset, typically between 4:00 and 7:00 p.m."

"Umm, I'm totally lost," Anne whispered to Peter. Several others were perplexed like her.

Lenka continued, "The big hand with the golden sun on it does one slow sweep every 24 hours marking the time on both dials. Now pay attention to the offset inner ring marked with the Zodiac sign. This ring both rotates on its own and moves around the outer dial so the sunny big hands also land on the Zodiac signs, and then the little hand with the blue moon appears in this month's Zodiac.

"If it all seems complex to you, just think of the marvel during the 1400s when the clock was installed. The second dial, below the clock, was added in the 19th century. It shows the sign of the Zodiac, scenes from the seasons of rural peasant life, and names of saints. There is one for each day of the year.

"Four statues flank the upper clock. As the hour approaches keep your eye on death. First death tips his hourglass and pulls the cord ringing the bell while the moneylender jiggles his purse. Then the window opens and the 12 apostles move past. Finally, the rooster at the very top crows and the hour is rung but the hour is often wrong because of Daylight Saving Time, completely senseless in the 15th century." "And now," an Oregonian grumbled.

"The astronomical clock was intentionally destroyed by the Nazis in WWII. Today's version was rebuilt in 1953 by the communists so this one-of-a-kind clock is made in the socialistic style with chemists and historic mothers rather than saints."

Lenka said if we were here at noon it is marked by a parade on the clock. For six minutes the mechanical line of milkmaids, clerks, blacksmiths, medics, and teachers are celebrated as everyday champions.

"We saw it yesterday, the entire show," Rolland mentioned.

"The clock designers were optimists. The year mechanism on the bottom is capable of spinning until AD 9999," Lenka said.

"This is still the coolest clock ever even though I still don't understand it," Anne remarked as they moved closer to the fountain in front of the clock where a model town is designed for blind people to touch.

At the circle to the left of the town hall, they stopped at another fountain, this one with an equestrian statue of Julius Caesar. This is dedicated to the legendary founder of the town. Excavations found that it actually originated in the 3rd century AD, centuries after Caesar.

Lenka told them that within one day of seeing buildings in Prague, they were going to be whisked through almost 2,000 years of amazing history and unique architecture.

She said, "The town hall is a testament to the city's 600 years of prominence in Monrovia. The three wings around the rectangular courtyard once served as both city council chambers and market halls. The town hall is booked with local weddings. If you see a festively decorated car parked in the square, it's probably waiting to take a bride and groom away."

One of the statues features *Neptune the God of Water* and another that Lenka pointed out shows Hercules as a guardian holding the Bavarian checkered eagle in his left hand. She detoured their group around the throngs of tourists on a parallel route toward Maria Square.

Tucked in the corner of the square, Darth Vader lookalike captured their attention. "Darth Vader from *Star Wars?*" someone asked Lenka, while others were snapping photos.

She explained the statue retells passersby of the legend that is associated with the building that previously stood on this spot. According to the folklore, a war-weary knight in black armor had been seen wandering around Prague. He ended up on this street to get some work done on his armor that was worn and chipped after long battles. The craftsman he found had a lovely daughter who the knight fell in love with. She repeatedly rejected his advances infuriating the knight who then stabbed her for refusing him. As she lay on the street she cursed him causing the knight to turn into stone.

Supposedly, every hundred years on the same day at the same time as the murder, the ghost of the knight appears seeking absolution which can only be given by an innocent girl. Many years later a widow and her daughter moved into this building which was no longer a workshop. The ghost appeared to the young girl and explained what he needed from her and he would return the next night. The following evening the ghost appeared and was mortified to find the mother rather than the innocent girl as he expected. He received 100 more years to wait and has yet to be seen again.

As they strolled along the lovely cobblestone avenue, they all did a double take as a man was hanging from the top of a building. Lenka pointed to the hanging man explaining he is actually a seven foot tall statue of Sigmund Freud. He's been there since 1996. It's really not as bad as it seems. She told them to look closely. While dangling by one hand, the other hand is tucked in his pocket. He literally appears to be hanging out like the statue's name implies, "Man Hanging Out."

Lenka promised some out-of-the-way stops knowing they'd enjoy them even though they were not on the top tourist list of things to see. One was the hard-to-find municipal library next to the National Library. Having seen photos of the infinite tower of books, they wanted to see this and the humongous stack of books.

It was quiet inside. They waited their turn to get photos of the optical illusion within a circular column from the first floor to the two-story ceiling, with an upside-down V so one could peer up. Anne stuck her head in. Millions of books stacked on top of each other created a dizzying effect. Yet it felt sort of magical, like Alice-down-the-rabbit-hole kind of magic. Concerned about someone's demise should they fall in, Lenka pointed out that there's a mirror inside the tower to make it look like infinity.

Peter pointed out a gumball machine, but instead of containing sugary treats, the sign read, "Ear Plugs." Anne raised her eyebrows in a *I don't have a clue—ear plugs in a library*, look.

Along Vezenska Avenue, they stopped at an interesting statue of a walking man with no head, no hands, no chest, but a gaping hole in his jacket. He is Franz Kafka and also carries a man in his shoulders. The statue is about 13 feet high and depicts Kafka sitting on the shoulder of an empty suit. There are several versions to his story, but none made sense to Anne.

Cars can drive through the arch in the tower, a Gothic fortification used as a gunpowder store and the starting point during the procession of Czech king's to Prague Castle. Several sparkling clean white and fuchsia convertibles were lined up offering scenic rides around the city.

Observing her travelers' slowing pace, Lenka suggested it

was time for a break so they stopped at one of her favorite places. It looked open and light with floor-to-ceiling windows and massive chandeliers. White vases painted with three towers held a bird's nest with three white eggs. Lenka selected a variety of her favorite coffees, teas, fruit tarts, and other sweet treats that appeared on the table.

Fortified, the group headed back outside. They went past two short structures joining two buildings. "Similar to the Bridge of Sighs in Venice," Peter observed.

Stepping into the National Theater, the first mind-blowing thing they saw was the magnificent chandelier where rainbows were shooting out from hundreds of crystal prisms. A sweet lamb statue sits on top of a burgundy marble base. The interior is richly embellished with gold, huge statues, gorgeous moldings, a grand staircase, and paintings on the ceiling of the amphitheater.

Outside around the corner is a piece of Prague's history. The John Lennon Wall has been adorned with countless messages and graffiti since the death of Beatles musician, John Lennon in 1980. Initially, these were mainly critical of government and demanding freedom, but today they focus primarily on peace and love plus some political opinions.

The graffiti and messages are constantly replaced by new ones over the course of time. The original portrait of John Lennon, with which the story of the wall began, has long been covered under layers of art. The Wall is an open-air gallery that preserves the memory of him as well as a symbolic history. Covering the wall with layer upon layer of every color of paint imaginable are peace signs, hearts, flowers, political statements written in Czech, and people's names like Arthur, Vivi, and Bianca. A sign made of insects spelled out THE BEATLES with a large flying creature making the cross on the "T."

On Mala Strana or "Little Quarter" not far from Charles

Bridge, they stopped at the John Lennon Pub, boasting "Open Daily" with patio seating serving beers, cocktails, appetizers, pizzas, soups, and sandwiches, about anything for anybody. Between the pub and the restaurant buildings is Prague's line of demarcation for floods, with the highest line in 2002. The pub and the rest of the buildings were all under water in this neighborhood from a 500-year, massive flood raising the river from its usual six feet to over 30 feet. The unique bar is called the Wall Bar now, the change due to the proximity of the John Lennon Wall.

At a bridge over a stream stand two large panels of fencing opposite each other. They were crammed full of love locks. One read Omer & Lilo. Lenka said the locks were so popular that now portions of bridges have become unstable and cities are installing these displays to encourage lovers to hang their locks in a less destructive location.

Something moved. Anne noticed a creepy little statue hanging over the edge peering at them. According to Lenka, "Folk legend describes the Water Sprite as a friendly, kind-hearted ghost who lives up the stream near the Charles Bridge. He can be found coming up from the water to beg passersby for a pint, and those who show him kindness he rewards with fresh fish." The movement that caught Anne's attention was a bird splatting its last meal on the sprite's head.

They hopped on an electric tram, scrunched in with locals, passing an original city stone wall and oddly, a hot pink car parked in the middle of a large grassy yard off the side of a four-story military-looking, sprawling building. A white, blue, and red flag moved slightly in the breeze.

They thanked Lenka but before she departed Anne asked, "Is there a St. Stephens Cathedral here?"

"Oh yes, it's located in Newtown. It's truly outstanding

and founded by Knights of the Cross. It's Gothic style is impressive. Go if you can."

Returning to their square, a vendor roasted dough around a long dowel. He turned it quite a few times over charcoal as they watched the dough turn golden brown. He sprinkled on some rock sugar and cinnamon and told them it's called a Chimney Cake. The caramelized crust and chewy soft interior tasted like comfort food.

They admired the five- and six-story buildings painted in buttery yellow, soft pink, light gray, and creamy beige, with each window and doorway either ornately squared or arched, painted in clean, bright white.

Glancing down one street, each building seemed to be topped with a tower and spire. The Church of Our Lady was constructed from the mid-14th to early 16th centuries and built in the Gothic style.

In their hotel, the Mozart Café dessert display case held about a dozen round and square cakes, fruit and custard tarts, and much more. A two-layer cake with almonds pressed into the frosting was covered in six-inch, oblong egg-shaped pieces of marzipan creating the base of a pyramid. Anne lost count at 26 marzipan cookies on the bottom, then 25 created the next layer. The third layer maybe 15, then ten, ending with five at the top. Wedged on the top were five pieces of golden nut brittle. Each of the oval shapes were dusted in chocolate powder. "Stunning" was an understatement.

One rectangular cake with cream frosting all trimmed in gold displayed a gold plaque of marzipan with a picture of Wolfgang Amadeus Mozart 1756-1791. A case was chock full of colorful figurines dressed in finery. Another display held fancy plates. The café is its own art gallery.

Sitting at the window, Judie pointed out another bride dressed in a creamy, billowy gown. Anne looked out the third-floor café windows directly at the clock. What a view, she said to herself—the historic clock where hours earlier Lenka tried to explain it all. Anne still felt mystified by the gold faces. They ordered a light chilled soup, Caprice salad, and chocolate crêpes with sliced strawberries on the top.

That night in bed trying to relax, Anne's thoughts went to Dmitry's wife and their mysterious "friends," Debbie and Rob. It took some time for her to fall asleep.

CHAPTER FOURTEEN

After an earlier than normal breakfast, several friends cut across Old Town Square toward the Charles Bridge. Rolland reminded them of what Lenka told them the day before. The bridge is made of sandstone blocks connected by sandstone stucco mortar and lime.

Just south of the bridge, laughter caught their attention. At Kampa Park they spotted statues of three bronze faceless giant babies crawling on their hands and knees. A man easily 6 feet tall, stood level with the baby's nose, if there had been a nose, but there wasn't. He placed his hands on the baby's cheek as someone took his picture.

"What's the thing with the faces?" Judie asked. "Each one is like a barcode."

"I don't really know what to think about these crawling babies in this pretty park. They're sort of intriguing yet kind of bizarre," Julie observed.

"How about disturbing?" Sharon replied.

"True. Unconventional, but it's sort of comical. See those children crawling up the bronze butts of those barcoded faceless babies?" Casey added.

Rolland said, "Probably some drunks, too."

Judie mentioned, "Modern Art, certainly in the eye of the beholder here."

Mike said, "Do you want to see some more modern art? Follow me."

In the river they spotted adorable plastic penguins with broad bellies standing in single file on a metal beam that stretched out into the river. An onlooker announced, "There are 34."

A plaque explained that the exhibit was created by the Cracking Art Group, a Milan-based art movement. *The yellow penguins are all made from recycled bottles. The penguin is a social animal and has a strong ecological meaning. Its survival is affected by global warming and ice melting. The group's choice to use plastic is not only for its aesthetical appeal and malleability but also to show how the world is becoming increasingly artificial. By repurposing plastic, the group hopes to inspire new dialogues surrounding plastic waste and its impact on the environment.*

They heard plenty of "How Cool," "I Love It," and "What a Great Way to Get a Message Across." Anne agreed with all the statements.

A few blocks away they ambled to a neighborhood called Starmesto. Peter read, "This is one of the oldest squares in Prague and represents the medieval heart of the city."

With the backdrop of the Charles Bridge and Prague Castle, historic houses and churches, cobblestone streets and squares, statutes, and stone towers, all blend surprisingly well together with modern structures. "This is definitely my favorite area," Cath declared.

Toddlers sat sipping from cups and munching on sandwiches at the base of the bronze Charles IV monument. Standing a commanding 13-feet high, the neo-Gothic statue shows a robed and crowned King Charles leaning on his sword with one hand. The other hand is holding a letter or a document. The pedestal is adorned with four faculty on each corner: theology, medicine, law, and philosophy. Charles served from 1316 to 1379. Peter pulled out a 100-krona bill. "I thought he looked familiar. It's worth about $4, not too impressive. He should be on the 1000 or 5000."

Anne read from her Rick Steves' from his *Prague and Czech Republic* book, *Charles was born in Prague, raised in Paris, crowned in Rome, and inspired by the luxury-loving Pope. Charles returned home bringing Europe's culture with him. Founding the university, he built the Charles Bridge and Charles Square. Much of Prague Castle and the St. Vitus Cathedral and Newtown are modeled on Paris. He expanded his empire through networking and shrewd marriages not war.*

The Charles Bridge connecting the two halves of the city across the Vltava River and lined with statues of Czech saints is one of Europe's most famous bridges and one of its best public places. Day and night the bridge bustles with performers, tourists, vendors, school groups, impromptu concerts, and occasionally a few Czechs. The Vltava River is better known by its German name Moldau. It bubbles up from hills in southern Bohemia and runs 270 miles through the diverse landscape like a thread connecting the Czech people.

Before heading across the bridge, Rolland pointed to the top of the hill at the Prague Castle along with the prickly spires of St. Vitus Cathedral. "We're heading that way," he announced.

They took photos of the nearly seven-football-fields-long remarkable Charles Bridge adorned with lanterns and stat-ues, all held together by medieval towers at each end. Before going onto the bridge, the friends stood off to the right at a black iron fence laden with love locks and flowerbeds of bright yellow marigolds. With the castle across the river, they took each others' pictures.

Judith's Tower is built in Romanesque style, with the

newer and higher Old Town Bridge Tower, at the other end. Judie was forced to pose for numerous photos with her tower.

Walking onto the oldest stone bridge in Prague, they made their way slowly across and checked out the different statues on the right side. The statues on both sides of the bridge depict saints. Half of the statues are replicas with the originals safely located in the City Museum safe from the polluted air and in some cases, people. They dodged walkers, joggers, children in strollers, and dogs, and noticed the stalls of tempting jewelry and crafts on the other side that they would catch on the return trip.

Following a printed layout of the bridge, Peter pointed out that the first of the 30 baroque statues is *St. Wenceslas,* patron saint of the Czech Republic.

The statue of *St. John of Nepomuk*, the most important statue of Charles Bridge, is the only one made of bronze. It was installed on the 300th anniversary of the throwing of Father John's body off the bridge. He has five golden stars circling his head. Father John was a 14th century priest to whom the queen confessed all of her sins.

According to 7th century legend, the king wanted to know his wife's secrets, but Father John dutifully refused to tell. Peter pointed out the shiny plaque at the base of the statue showing what happened next. John was tortured and eventually killed by being thrown off the bridge. Evidently, when John hit the water five stars appeared signifying his honor.

Each saint depicts something extraordinary. St. Francis of Assisi caught Anne's attention. If she had a favorite, he would be it. He was founder of the benevolent Franciscan order. More and more saints line the bridge.

They hopped on a tram to the top of the castle. They were greeted by a stoic guard at the main entrance standing in a gray and white wooden structure, with a large flag overhead. Anne thought that he looked darn handsome dressed in navy with red epaulets, Tom Cruise sunglasses and stark white gloves. There were embroidered patches on his arms, and a thick red, white, and blue braided cord hung from his right shoulder across his broad chest to his waist.

They entered the west end of the castle square at a gateway with a golden arch guarded by two fighting giant statues, and two real life human soldiers, dressed in blue and black, standing in the white guardhouses. "I wonder if there's a booby hatch where he can drop down through the bottom," somebody joked.

Mike said, "That reminds me. Did you know that booby hatch is one of those nautical terms? It is a sliding cover, like a hatch or lid, that must be pushed away to access a passage."

His wife suggested they could be done with the nautical terms for the trip.

In the center of the complex sits St. Vitus Cathedral with its prickly steeples. They turned around to survey the broad expanse of the castle square. A musical group played in the square and turned out to be the Prague Castle Orchestra.

Excitement mounted because the Changing of the Guard would be happening soon. "Here they come," a little boy said as he hopped up and down. Men wore navy coats, gray slacks, and shiny black shoes, while carrying a gray rifle topped with a shiny spear glistening in the sun. They goose-stepped in unison, as people fell in behind them, walking under an ornate gold iron railing between two pillars. They changed out the guards and disappeared through an arch in the building.

Today the castle is an art museum with collections of Baroque-era pieces, Czech paintings, and sculptures. On the left side of the square, the building with a steep gable roofline is Schwartzenberg Palace, where the aristocratic

Rozmberk family of Ceský Krumlov, stayed when they were visiting from their country estates.

"What an awesome exterior," Judie said pointing to the envelope-shaped patterns stamped on the outside of the building. She read, "These are Renaissance-era adornments called *sgraffito* etched into wet stucco that decorate buildings throughout the castle and all over Prague plus the country."

In the second courtyard, a black baroque sculpture in the middle of the square is a Plague Column erected as a monument of gratitude to Mary and the saints for saving the population from diseases. After almost two weeks and several towns, they realized these columns are an important part of the main squares of many towns.

Through another passageway they walked into the third courtyard facing the impressive cathedral with two soaring Gothic towers. They saw pointed arches, a rose window, statues of saints, and creepy gargoyles making funny faces. Four men in modern suits are carved into the stone as if they are supporting the big round window on their shoulders. They're the architects and builders who finished the church six centuries after it was started. Prague's top church was finished in 1929 for the 1,000[th] Jubilee anniversary of St. Wenceslas.

They stepped inside the church entryway to view the nave. This Roman Catholic Church is the Czech National Church and where kings were crowned and buried, and the crown jewels are on display.

"This place is huge!" exclaimed Phil. "It's more than 400 feet long and 100 feet high. Look at the ceiling especially at the far end."

By now there were quite a few tourists and they zigzagged through the crowds to the third window on the left which was worth a closer look according to their informative *Rick Steves'* book. The 1931 Art Nouveau window was designed by the Czech artist Mucha and created by a stained glass craftsman. The window features two women dressed in aqua and teal with modern spirals floating above them.

Cath mentioned she wanted to make sure they visited the Mucha Museum in Newtown and several said they wanted to go with her. In the church, the main scene has four central panels that show Wenceslas as a child kneeling at the feet of his Christian grandmother, St. Ludmila. With arms spread, she teaches him to pray. He would grow up to champion Christianity uniting the Czech people. Above Wenceslas are two saints who brought Christianity to the region. Cyril, the monk in the black hood holds the Bible, and his brother, Methodius, has a beard. He was the bishop's guard.

They moved along reading their Rick Steves' book following the story of the side panels starting with the upper left around 886 when Ludmila was just a girl. These two Greek missionary brothers arrived in Moravia to preach. The pagan Czechs had no written language to read the Bible so Cyril sits at his desk to design the necessary alphabet which later developed into Cyrillic while his brother meditates. In the next three scenes they travel to Rome and present their newly translated Bible to the Pope. Cyril falls ill and Methodius must watch his younger brother die.

Methodius carries on, becoming a bishop of the Czechs. Then he's arrested for heresy for violating the pure Latin Bible and is sent to a lonely prison. When he's finally set free, he retires to a monastery where he dies, mourned by the faithful.

On the bottom center panel are two stunning Mucha pictures of young women representing the bright future. Anne stood mesmerized. Cath pointed out, "See how he uses colors with sapphire on the outside gradually turning to green then peach? The gold of the woman and the crimson of the boy in the center? In his colorful language, blue stands for the past, gold for the mythic, and red for the future. Besides all the colorful meaning, his art is simply a joy to behold."

The cathedral went on and on. The chapel walls were plastered with big slabs of precious and semiprecious stones. The jewel-tone stained glass radiated a soft light. The chandelier was exceptional. The entire place felt medieval.

Next, they stepped into one of the oldest structures in Prague. Basilica St. George is the best-preserved Romanesque church and was the burial place of Czech royalty before St. Vitus Cathedral was built. The church, founded by Wenceslas's father around 920, dates from the 12th century. Its baroque façade came later. Inside Anne felt calm, maybe because of its simplicity. They saw thick walls and rounded arches and some smaller exhibits, then left the church.

Outside across the lane was a building with columns and a curved portico. Maria Theresa's Institute for Noble Women, established in the 1750s, was created to empower and educate aristocratic but impoverished ladies.

The Old Royal Palace is big, big, big. Vladislav Hall is 200 feet long with an impressive, vaulted ceiling of vine-shaped designs. It served many purposes; it could be filled with market stalls and was big enough for jousting competitions. Even the staircase was designed to let a mounted soldier gallop in. On the right they saw two small Renaissance rooms known as the Czech Office.

They re-entered the impressive main hall and went to the end standing on the balcony for stunning views of Prague. It opens into the Diet Hall with a Gothic ceiling, a crimson throne and benches for the nobility who once served as the high court. Portraits on the walls depict Habsburg rulers in their finest dress. After seeing replicas of the Czech crown jewels, they returned to the Vladislav Hall and walked down the equestrian stairs, which once served as the entrance to tournaments for knights on horseback.

Outside, they turned and got a great look at the sheer size of St. Vitus Cathedral, its 325-foot lettuce-green tower, and the Republic's biggest bell at 16.5 tons, from 1549, nick-named Zikmund. They passed on viewing the bell close up. Having to climb 687 steps to the tower's observation deck was not on anyone's "must do" list.

They paced themselves going down about half of the 700 some steps to visit the gardens below Prague Castle. After paying to enter, they marched up about 20 tile steps to an area called the Small Fürstenberg Gardens. Fürstenberg is the name of a Swabian noble house in Germany, based primarily in what today is southern Baden-Württemberg, the source of the Danube River.

"I'm a Fürstenberg on my mother's side of the family, way, way back!" Anne almost shouted.

Rolland asked, "Didn't you get some pictures on the Rhine cruise, when we passed by the dilapidated Fürstenberg castle?"

"Uh-huh, sadly, now privately owned. Remember, I attempted to see it but there were no roads and no admit-tance." She had been known to climb over or under fences and walls but this was out of her realm of breaking and entering.

The sweet-smelling garden overflowed with pink roses. Hanging from the fence above them and trailing down the rock walls, more roses burst forth completely surrounding a black iron bench where Anne sat under an arch. Red and white roses climbed the trellis on the opposite side. The combination of scents would undoubtedly cause some to sneeze, but she took in a deep breath.

To their left were ruby roses and climbing pink roses with pots of greenery above. Leaving "Anne's" garden, they stepped up several dozen stairs while smelling more delicious climbing roses under a black trellis.

Sprinkler droplets dotted large leaves. Statues of stone guards protect the veranda. Below are terraced planters, and Anne took a photo of curly vine ivy in the foreground with Prague's rooftops of red tile, pokey spires, and towers artistically cluttering the skyline. The light clouds created a fan pattern. She took way too many photos of pink baby's breath, and snowy daisies with pops of dramatic, tall red roses in a corner. The azalea bushes in front were on fire with color, and there were flowers in many shades from pink to purple bursting out the window boxes and the borders along the pathway.

A tall Atlas cedar grows on the West side of the first terrace. Flowerpot plants were placed along the steps. Walking by the statue of Hercules and The Well, plus the fountain at the eastern wall, they were back where they began.

The fragrance wafting from the terraces and alcoves of 2,200 rose bushes, and over 3,500 flowering plants, made her think she might have ascended to Heaven to be with her ancestors.

Cath looked at a map showing that there were some gardens just across the street through the Czech Senate grounds—the gardens of Baroque Wallenstein Palace. A maze of manicured grass and hedges with statues dotted each corner. A turtle sat at the feet of a darling statue of a toddler blowing a horn.

They made a loop starting at the Sala Terrena, then another version of The Well and sculpture of Hercules, and the eastern wall of Parterre. Walking under the corridor's highly decorative ceiling, arches and walls, the middle fresco shows Wallenstein as the God of War in a horsedrawn chariot.

Following the hoot-hoot sounds, Anne came to a dark wall that seemed to be a more current addition, but it's part of the original baroque complex that houses the palace. Anne stood quietly at the grotto, the first drip stone wall she'd seen, created by things or dripping skulls. *Creepy*, she thought to herself. Walking closer she discovered the wall was made from a collection of stalactite-like rocks.

She was right to hear owls, the only birds she spotted were housed in a large enclosure. Peter stepped closer to the wall peeking through an open slot expecting to see something, maybe a hidden chamber, but there was nothing to see. As Anne looked closer, she realized they didn't represent anything in particular. A plaque stands in front of the wall to describe it, and its purpose. In total contrast are decades-old bushes of pretty purple, bright pink, and lush white hydrangeas that soften the eerie ambiance.

They exited through a scenic winding vineyard down to the base of the Charles Bridge walking back across seeing more sculptures and statues. They stopped at each stall to select jewelry, some framed art, chocolates, and a few other treasures.

With a blend of fatigue, the heebie-jeebies, and a dash of nausea, Anne needed protein. Her mind kept switching to thoughts about Dmitry then Rob and Debbie.

Marina Ristorante, a floating building at the base of the bridge, has terrific views of both sides of the city. A brief glance at the menu revealed Italian, Mediterranean, and European fare, something for everyone. One extraordinary dish was the bream. Fortunately, the waiter filleted it, but left the bony remains. Linguini with capers, a red sauce dish with mussels and a crawfish, and multiple Italian dishes were devoured.

Dessert for Judie was a scoop of vanilla gelato and a round chocolate ball of 72% chocolate fondant. Peter didn't even speak while consuming panna cotta with Kahlúa and salted caramel. He was torn between that and his favorite Tiramisu, which someone else had ordered. Sharon ordered ricotta dumplings with plums, marsala, and walnut ice cream. Anne observed how quiet her friends became when consuming the desserts, as she had been while enjoying every bite of crème brûlée with a pistachio biscuit.

Departing, each one petted the head of the restaurant's mascot, a bronze life-size Labrador Retriever, the top of his head and nose, bright and shiny.

At an open-air market locals were snatching up overflowing baskets of strawberries, red raspberries, thumbnail-size blueberries, blackish-red dark cherries, sugar peas, green beans, and potatoes by the bag. Kilograms instead of ounces and pounds at first glance seemed really inexpensive until they realized 2.2 kg equals about 5 pounds. Anne paid for a container of strawberries and shared. One of the Kathys mentioned all they needed was some chocolate for dipping.

A shop caught Julie's attention with an eclectic display of ceramic and pottery including a variety of mushrooms of different shades of browns and greens, in all shapes and sizes. Anne bought an assortment for her mushroom garden she'd create at home. The whimsical bright red ones with white polka dots and the grassy green with white dots were her favorites.

Midafternoon, a few weary men and women headed to the hotel while several made a beeline to the Mucha Museum. "We're going to be gone several hours," Cath told Casey. "You guys are on your own for dinner. We will be back by dark." Anne waved farewell to Peter. "They can handle one meal on their own," Cath said. Her enthusiasm felt contagious. Anne knew they were in for a treat with their own art teacher/guide with them.

After paying the entrance fee and picking up their brochure for their self-guided tours, Cath read that Mucha was an enormously talented Czech artist who impressed the art world as he developed the emerging style of Art Nouveau. Mucha's artsy theater posters which graced the streets of Paris at the turn of the century earned him international fame. He could have done anything, but instead he chose to return to his home country and use his talents to celebrate and promote Czech culture.

They looked to the left in front of the window seeing the timeline of Mucha's life, along with photos showing the artist, his wife, and some of the rich and famous they hung out with. Directly across from the photos were several decorative posters, some of his earliest works. These pieces defined his style throughout his career—slender tall women with flowing long hair with flowers pinned throughout, silky gowns, and curvy poses.

Cath said to her friends, "Mucha believed that art wasn't to be elevated and kept at arm's length in a museum, rather he wanted it to be shared and experienced in everyday life. These panels were designed to be mass produced, to decorate everyday homes."

Through his collection of *The Four Flowers*, *The Four Times of Day*, and *The Four Arts*, Mucha enjoyed the idea that through his works people could enjoy flowers inside, even in the winter.

Cath pointed to *Gismonda* and explained that this is the result of an extremely lucky stroke for Mucha. He was in Paris on the day after Christmas 1894, and being the low man on the totem pole at his design firm, he was the lone artist on duty while the more senior designers enjoyed some holiday time off. Unexpectedly Sarah Bernhardt, perhaps the most famous theater actress who ever lived, asked for a poster to be designed to promote her new play. In just a week, working under intense pressure, Mucha cranked out this poster which was plastered all over town on New Year's Day. It became an overnight hit, and when Parisians started stealing the posters for themselves, it was clear Mucha was on to something. Bernhardt signed him to a six-year contract and he became the artist most in demand in town.

They moseyed by more posters advertising theater presentations, art installations, even tobacco. The posters are lithographs, a printing process popularized in the late 19th century Paris. Moving on, they noticed in the windows were photos of models that Mucha photographed and copied for his works.

The crucifixion that Mucha drew as an eight-year-old is on display as well. His mother claimed that he could draw even before he could walk. She gave him a pencil for scrawling artfully on the floor.

Anne stood for a couple of minutes taking in the poster of poppies with scarlet ones in the top section with black and whites next to it. The bottom portion has poppies reaching upward on long stems with a wood fence in the background. An entire wall collage of eye candy included *Chocolate Ideal*, with an extremely satisfied look on a woman's face; *Monaco* that Anne remembered seeing in Monaco on one of their previous vacations; *Biscuits Champagne Lefèvre-Utile*, Sarah Bernhardt, American Tour poster, and *Vin des Incas*, which she recalled seeing in Peru.

In a display case they saw banknotes and medals that he designed for the young nation of Czechoslovakia. Mucha also created all kinds of paper products, jewelry, cutlery, and other household items. His talent transformed everyday objects into pieces of art. Before leaving, they each purchased a variety of notes and postcards, bookmarks, and some frameable pieces for home.

Stopping under the fragrant blooming Linden trees, the scent smelled deliciously pungent. Achoo! "These tree pollens are getting to me," Anne mumbled blowing her nose.

Walking along a stream they paused under a stone arch as they watched an artist painting a scene of the buildings downstream. Then they stopped at a peaked arch with a second one directly behind it seeing amber, scarlet, coral, celery, and other colorful buildings down the street. "Everywhere you look in the city, it's gorgeous," Julie declared. They wandered by other places they'd already seen once or twice, knowing this was their final afternoon.

"Here it is!" Julie almost shouted. "We found it."

"Thank goodness, I'm exhausted, thirsty, and hungry," Cath sighed. After wandering an hour or so stopping at shops along the way, following instructions on Anne's phone, they finally stopped to ask a young man at a hotel. Tucked in a small street just off the Charles Bridge, they located a tiny restaurant some friends of Anne's heartily recommended, Wine O'Clock Shop. A man had just opened the front door.

The ladies stepped into a small establishment with seating for 12. The walls were lined with bottles of olive oil, colorful liquor, and glassware. A sign propped up by a bottle of Jorche Riserva reads, "Save Water Drink Wine." Two men introduced themselves—Paul and Martin.

Perusing the menu, they decided to try an assortment of items that they would share. Jars of green and black olives, red peppers stuffed with garlic, and pepperoncino ripieno lined the corner of the countertop. They watched chef Paul slice fresh tomatoes as their first nibbles arrived—green and black olives and cubes of feta cheese wrapped in prosciutto. Next appeared crispy bruschetta with chopped fresh tomato and basil.

To drink, Martin suggested a local brand of Starý Vrch called Cuvée Frizzante. The clear beverage tasted light and tangy. Sliced tomatoes and a ball of fresh mozzarella drizzled with homemade balsamic vinegar came next.

Anne finally took some time to study the décor. Dozens of solid-colored pink, green and white pots affixed to the wall held fresh orchids of all types and colors. No wonder it smelled so good along with the food.

Watching Paul prepare everything they got to eat was a real treat. Next decision: Dessert. Paul started with a rectangular black stoneware plate, placed a fork on it, then sprinkled powdered sugar. He removed the fork and its shadow remained, set off by the white powder. Then he placed a layered delicacy on top, also the house specialty: Tiramisu. It was large enough for each to have several bites.

Returning to their hotel by taxi, Anne gazed at the unique clock of blue, scarlet, gold, black and bronze. She still couldn't read it. She zoomed her camera in on the top of the clock, hoping one day when reviewing her photos that she would recall Lenka's instructions on how to tell time. The stone angel stationed above the clock looked equally confused.

Anne was quiet, not wanting to wake sleeping Peter. Lazing in the spacious bathtub, Anne soaked her weary feet. It had been a long and wonderful day. Falling into bed, she checked her walk-o-meter, just a tad over eight miles, not a surprise given how tired she felt.

CHAPTER FIFTEEN

At 8:05 a.m. Chief Haas got a text from Gina. **Come to me now. My office.**

He always laughed when he received texts from her as the sentences were short and choppy, much like she spoke in her Romanian accent.

He called first. "It's a busy time. Can't you just tell me?"

"No." She ended the brief conversation.

When he walked through the door 15 minutes later, Gina announced, "Well, I can tell you it's not Russian."

"Good Morning to you, too, Gina," he said trying to make a point of her lack of social etiquette. She frowned at him.

"How do you know?

"Russians are meticulous killers: drownings, mysterious falls from 10-story buildings, airplanes falling from the sky. He would have been poisoned with a nearly unnoticeable injection. They never stab, too messy. Even though I'm an extremely skilled pathologist, it would be difficult even for me to discover."

"See." She pointed out again to him the almost invisible poke in the skin of Dmitry's neck, both of them bending down closely inspecting the mark. Their arms touched. He felt electricity and wondered if she did, too.

She was all business. "See how red his skin is in these photos? Abrin is one of those nearly untraceable poisons and it doesn't take very much. He was probably injected between 4 and 5 a.m. Symptoms are breathing difficulty, nausea, chest pains, and low blood pressure. Respiratory failure follows, then death. Larger doses can begin in seconds and cause an immediate reaction such as gasps for breath before passing out. Many suffer seizures and cardiac arrest. My guess is he lingered for some time."

She continued. "At first I thought ricin, but no. It showed up through abnormal liver function tests along with multiple ulcerations and hemorrhages of the gastric and small-intestinal mucosa on endoscopy. Increased white blood cell count."

"English please."

"His heart collapsed. Everything gave out. Gruesome."

"So, you are listing his death a homicide?"

"Yes. Nobody commits suicide this way."

"Good work once again, Gina."

The smile on her face indicated she had some serious feelings for this middle-aged police chief.

"You know the reasons for murder: Money, lust, jealousy, greed, revenge. You get to determine which one. I look forward to your findings, *Chief.*" He could have sworn she smiled when she said chief.

Anne and Peter ate a leisurely breakfast before going with some of their friends to Lobkowicz Palace. It is a Privileged Access tour, meaning extra special, that only Viking offers. Walking through a modern entrance with red carpeting and red walls either papered or painted, their guide looked striking—pale skin, long blonde hair in zillions of waves, and tall. Her clothes were maximum country squiress: a man-style white shirt, black slacks, black boots, with a cashmere peachy pashmina around her shoulders.

The tour began upstairs in private quarters. Walking on a navy carpet along the corridor of rooms, they were led to a small music hall with an incredible fresco on the ceiling. Here they were treated to their own private concert. Three men played an assortment from Haydn, Mozart, Beethoven, Schubert and Dvorák. One piece was particularly soothing as Anne discovered when her chin dropped to her chest.

After the concert, they strolled by portraits of a family dressed appropriately for the period in which they lived. In display cases, the family's crest on dishes and silver sparkled in the light with not a speck of dust. Another room with red walls held spears, guns, and a full-size armor encircled by rifles. The music room seemed more up Anne's alley, with a grand piano in one corner.

In one room the walls were covered with pictures of birds, but these weren't like any pictures they'd seen before. Giving it more attention, they could see that actual feathers were used along with the artist's painting. The sign read *The Bird Room. A very unusual and rare series of images of birds circa 1800 decorate this room. The outlines of the birds themselves are drawn and partially colored in watercolor and then finished with real feathers on public display for the first time. The restoration of these watercolors have been made possible by the support of friends of the Heritage Preservation in Los Angeles CA. Examples of birds from the family's extensive ceramic and other collections also can be seen in the showcase.*

Their love for dogs, especially dachshunds, were show-cased in another room. Standing outside on the terrace, the river and city lay before them.

They were escorted to a dining room with parquet wood floors and a round table set for eight with chairs covered entirely in white linen. Pictures of historical scenes lined the walls, some larger than others. Out the window below is the city of Prague. Having their own family wine on the label with the palace wasn't a surprise. The lettering was burgundy with gold fleurs-de-lis that matched the tablecloth.

Today's Menu displayed on a music stand read:
  Mixed salad with aceto balsamico and cherry tomatoes
  Lobkowicz-style Czech goulash served with dumplings
  Homemade cheesecake with wild berry sauce
  Drink of your choice: wine/beer/soft drink/coffee/tea

Departing the palace and walking down hundreds of cobblestone steps, a black stone statue of a man leans against the wall. One lone orange poppy grew up from the ground, squeezing through a crack between the wall and steps. Several groups of young people played instruments and sang. Anne placed some coins into the open guitar case on the ground.

They stopped at a fruit stand where plastic cups held watermelon chunks, grapes, Kiwi, and strawberries. Multiple fresh juices were available for sale as well. They shared a cup of watermelon.

Most of the women had serious shopping to do so they marched off to find the perfect gifts to take home. Running of out of vacation time, they stopped for a *Traditional Czech Trdelník* ice cream in a waffle cone with whipped cream and one strawberry on top. A skinny green hotel called Clementin has two windows on each of the three floors facing the street. Cath suggested next visit they should stay there. It is squeezed between two buildings, one boasting The Best Italian Pizza.

Anne heard a chirping bird, meaning a text. Pulling her phone out of her purse, it showed an unknown foreign number. The detective she talked with while in Regensburg identified himself.

Do you recall seeing Mr. Rudolph with anyone other than his wife?

Once. A young woman approached him but I didn't watch that encounter.

Where?

Heroes' Square Budapest.

Thank you were his final words.

"You know I hate this," as Anne packed up their clothing, wrapping and taping delicate souvenirs in bubble wrap that she always took with her. Then tucked smaller items down safely in shoes. She always looked forward to going home; there's no place like home but getting back wasn't nearly as enjoyable as the departure before a trip.

"All good things must come to an end," Peter noted.

"I know but I'm still bummed."

Peter set the alarm on his phone for 2:30 a.m., for their 6 o'clock airport check-in. Then he set the alarm on the nightstand clock. Anne set her alarm, too. As tired as they were, they didn't want to have something go awry before an international flight.

CHAPTER SIXTEEN

Captain Haas read the detective's report he'd taken home six days later. The DNA divulged one hair belonged to a female, another hair was from a male. Nothing matched in their database. No fingerprints were viable. It would have been a dead end except for the fact it had been discovered that Dmitry Rudolph was born Aleksandr Pushkin and a Nazi war criminal. Speculation was the two accomplices could likely have had family who were murdered in Nazi concentration camps. Revenge was always a motive for murder.

He'd knew that charges of murder and being an accessory to murder aren't subject to a statute of limitations under German law.

Haas read the recent headlines regarding a 98-year-old man who had been charged with being an accessory to murder as a guard at a Nazi concentration camp between 1943 and 1945. He was accused of having supported the cruel and malicious killing of thousands of prisoners as a member of the guard detail. He was charged with more than 3,000 counts of being an accessory to murder. An elderly female who worked as a secretary in a camp was recently found guilty of the same crimes.

German prosecutors had brought several cases under a precedent set in recent years that allows for people who helped a Nazi camp function to be prosecuted as an accessory to the murders without direct evidence that they participated in a specific killing.

Should Aleksandr Pushkin have been arrested and ended up in court instead of dead, the captain pondered. He came up with no answer but thought it would be an interesting discussion to have with Gina over drinks.

He pondered if 10 p.m. was too late to call. His index finger touched seven numbers on his cell phone. He smiled when he heard her say, "Yes, Arno?"

CHAPTER SEVENTEEN

At home about a week, Anne skipped one day out of seven from pestering her brother, Will, asking if he'd heard anything from his police-friend in Vienna. Her phone rang.

"Hey Sis," she heard her brother say. "I've just gotten an email from my buddy Bruno in Austria. You sure got yourself involved in some intrigue and espionage this time."

"What do you mean?"

"Well, he reports that the man who died was murdered by a poison injected in his neck. His real name was Aleksandr Pushkin, a Nazi guard in a concentration camp. He had it changed right after the war and lived as Dmitry Rudolph for 70+ years."

"What? Like on the news where the Russians eliminate journalists, politicians, and people that don't tow their party line?"

"Nope, not the Russians. Most likely two people on board posing as a married couple from the US, who are really assassins. Bruno says evidently they feel justified because of the atrocities during WWII to the Jewish people, along with thousands of others. People over the decades have picked up the cause from groups after WWII who captured former soldiers, camp guards, and anyone associated with the Nazis or SS."

"Like payback?"

"Righteous retribution, I guess one could say."

"How do they know about the couple from the US? Did he mention their names?"

"Yes, something common and unsuspecting; get this, Smith is their last name, complete with fake passports and..."

She butted in, "Holy moly," as she flopped down in a chair, "great accents, and stories, too. I know who he is referring to. I really liked them. They sure fooled us for the entire week."

"He said several strands were found from a wig ; that obviously didn't help. They didn't find fingerprints or anything else usable. These people are obviously pros and he said the room looked spotless. One detective found a human hair on the floor under the bathroom sink and another in the bed sheets but no database match.

"They suspect the duo has completed other jobs, but no one has ever been able to track them down. The disguises they use are never duplicated. They aren't the only ones who do these well-planned out, clandestine hits. There is a group of unknowns who continue to hunt down and eliminate proven war criminals no matter their age or sex."

"Maybe they are doing what the justice system can't or governments won't," she stated.

"Possibly but citizens can't take the law into their own hands," her sheriff-brother stated matter-of-factly. "Bruno reports the case is closed."

"This is so depressing," Anne sniveled against Peter's chest. "If Will hadn't gotten verification I would never believe it. Casey, Cathy, Julie, and others won't either. Well, they will since now it all makes a bit more sense about Rob and Debbie, or whoever they are, and their sudden disappearance from the cruise. I don't know if I'll be able to trust a stranger ever again. I really liked her, so did Julie and Cathy."

Anne called both women who repeatedly said, "I can't believe it." She emailed the rest of their group with the conclusions and got similar responses.

Back and forth, back and forth. *Make up your mind*, the woman in Poland scolded herself. The past ten days she'd concluded it could be a huge error in judgment. What she was contemplating broke every rule, code, and regulation. But unlike any other women she'd met over the decades, she really cared for Cathy, Julie, and Anne. She felt that under normal circumstances, they all would have been real friends.

Goshia had never done anything like this, looking at the burner phone she picked up at a store in Kraków. It must be untraceable. She could never explain why they'd done it but she felt compelled to say something. And she would never, ever tell anyone what she'd done. Would it be a simple goodbye or an apology? It took her two more days to figure it out.

At 3 a.m. staring at the phone she tapped in three cell numbers, took another drink of wine, and typed one word, **SORRY**. Goshia took another sip and hit send.

Fifty-four hundred miles and nine time zones away, Julie stepped in the door from a walk with Ollie, her beloved Australian Labradoodle. Cathy and Casey were enjoying a glass of vino on their patio and Anne was at home reclining while reading a mystery before starting dinner. Each woman heard a ping or chirp indicating a text on their phones. Each read one single word…**SORRY,** in all caps.

Seconds later, Anne's phone rang and seeing Julie's name, "Hey did you just get an odd text? What in the world is this?"

"I don't know."

"I wasn't even going to look at it since it's from an unknown international number."

"**SORRY**. That's it from some mysterious number, like 20 numbers long?"

"Cathy is calling," as Anne connected the three into a group conference call. Their conversation bounced around.

"Did you just get…?" as Anne interrupted her.

"Yes, we both did. It's gotta be Debbie or whatever her name really is."

"Okay, is it nice or creepy? "

"Are you going to respond?"

"No, I'm not."

"I'm ticked and sad."

"I think we should."

"Really?"

"What are you going to say?"

"Not sure."

"We should do it now though."

Three minutes later, Goshia read:

Thank U

Apology accepted

R U really married to Rob? Goshia burst out laughing at Anne's question.

She removed the sim card and hammered it into dozens of pieces. She wished she could tell her gal-pals the truth.

And that she and Rob were meeting up next weekend and hoped they'd be making some more permanent arrangements.

Anne had been feeling uneasy for the past week and now she felt worse. Peter knew her love for adventure and that she'd snap out of this funk, although it might take some time. This seemed the worst of all the unfortunate incidents that happened to her over the decades. Probably due to the betrayal of the Alabama so-called friends.

"Hon," Peter said. "I bought you a new book on Ireland. You've wanted to return since we went 20 years ago. Let's grab a few friends and sign up for a Collette tour and go."

"Great idea. But you know, we've also talked about an adventure in Africa for years. Maybe we should do that before we get any older?"

CHAPTER EIGHTEEN

That night Anne dreamed of dramatic crashing waves as she stood at Malin Head, mainland Ireland's most northerly point, overlooking the long stretch of spectacular emerald North Atlantic coastline hundreds of feet below.

An imperial stormtrooper, a bad-guy soldier in the *Star Wars* sagas, darted through her idyllic scene. Anne heard a female scream. The trooper started to remove the shiny white helmet.

She turned and saw the face of a famous golfer, Rory McIlroy, painted on the side of a building with an elephant munching on the emerald grasses and giraffe nibbling on treetops.

She woke wondering where in the world that crazy mish-mash came from. It had to be the spicy Mexican food she'd had for dinner while they were watching a rerun of the high-energy *Star Wars: Episode VII–The Force Awakens* or maybe paging through the *National Geographic* magazine on exhilarating African safari adventures.

RECIPES

Hungarian Goulash is a thick, hearty soup spiced with sweet paprika. Serve with a dollop of sour cream.

- 2 T oil
- 1 large onion, finely chopped
- 2 pounds lean stewing steak
- 3 carrots, chopped
- 3 celery stalks, chopped
- 2-3 cloves garlic, chopped
- 1 green bell pepper, deseeded and chopped
- 2 large tomatoes, skinned and chopped
- 3 pints beef stock
- 2 tsp sweet paprika
- 1 lemon
- Salt and pepper to taste
- 3 large white potatoes, peeled and chopped
- Sour cream

- In a large pot, heat the oil, then fry the onion for about five minutes until softened. Add the beef and sauté, stirring constantly, until completely browned (add more oil if necessary).

- Add the carrots, celery, garlic and chopped bell pepper, then sauté for another 5 minutes.
- Stir in the tomatoes, stock, and sweet paprika. Season generously with salt and pepper and add a good squeeze of fresh lemon juice.
- Increase the heat and bring to a boil, then lower the heat, cover, and simmer for about 90 minutes, until the meat is tender.
- Add the potatoes about 20 minutes before the end of cooking time.
- Serve in bowls and garnish with a large spoonful of sour cream.

Serves 4-6

Recipe provided with the cute bags of paprika purchased in Budapest.

Viennese Sachertorte

From a café in Vienna: *This famous dessert should be served with a mountain of whipped cream.*

- 5 oz butter, softened
- 3½ oz confectioner's sugar (powdered), sieved
- 8 eggs, separated
- 5 oz bittersweet (dark) chocolate
- 2¾ oz all-purpose flour
- 3½ oz sugar
- 2 T apricot jam

- For the glaze:
- 8 oz bittersweet (dark) chocolate
- 2 T butter

- Preheat oven to 375 degrees.
- Grease and line a 9-inch cake tin.
- Cream together the butter and powdered sugar, then mix in the egg yolks, one at a time, until very creamy.
- Melt the chocolate in a heatproof bowl placed over a saucepan of simmering water. Do not allow the bowl to touch the water.
- Gradually add the melted chocolate into the creamed mixture, then fold in the flour.
- In a separate bowl, beat the egg whites until they form soft peaks then gradually fold in the sugar.
- Combine this mixture with the chocolate mixture.
- Pour the cake mixture into the prepared tin and bake for about 50 minutes to an hour until springy to the touch.
- Remove from the pan and cool on a wire rack.
- Heat the apricot jam and smooth over the entire torte, including the sides.
- For the glaze, melt the chocolate and butter together until smooth and glossy.
- Pour carefully over the cake, making sure it's completely covered, and allow to cool before serving.

Anne's eyes sort of glazed over reading all the details and thought to herself that she'd check their favorite extravagant dessert hangout at home called the Konditorei. If any place had something this extraordinary, they would.

———————

Viennese Coffee

A cup of fancy coffee that's part hot chocolate and part coffee contains espresso, chocolate syrup, chocolate ganache, and a whole lot of whipped cream and toppings like cinnamon, chocolate sprinkles, cocoa powder, whatever you like.

- 3 regular shots of espresso, hot
- 1 c of heavy cream
- 3.5 oz milk chocolate
- 3.5 oz chocolate syrup

- Separate ¾ of the heavy cream and set it in a metal bowl.
- In a larger pot bring water to a boil and set the metal bowl with the heavy cream just above the water. After the heavy cream has gotten hot, keep it over the hot water and add the chopped-up chocolate into the cream.
- Keep stirring and be patient.
- The chocolate will take a few minutes to melt but it will melt. Once it's melted and you've gotten your ganache, set the bowl on the counter.
- If you've got an espresso machine, make 3 shots of espresso. Add them directly onto the ganache and stir. It will take a minute, but the mixture will become thinner and resemble just a thicker, smooth coffee.
- Get 4 warm cups and portion the coffee mixture into the cups.
- Separately, in a clean cold bowl whisk the ¼ heavy cream that is left over. Whisk as much as you like.

- Decorate the coffee with the whipped cream any way you like. Drizzle the chocolate syrup on top. Add any other toppings.

Serves 4

Recipe provided at a coffeehouse in Vienna.

To quench your thirst, an **Aperol Spritz**, in less than one minute.

- 2 oz Aperol
- 3 oz Prosecco
- 1 splash of soda water (about 1 oz)
- Ice
- Orange slice, for garnish

- Fill a festive (or any type) glass with ice and let chill for 30 seconds. Pour in Aperol, Prosecco, and soda water.
- Give it a few stirs to combine then garnish with an orange.

Recipe provided by one of Anne's favorite bartenders at home named Bruce.

Bon Appétit!

TRIP TIPS

- There are no clocks in your room. Telephone is programmable for wakeup calls.
- Hairdryer in the bathroom and high-quality toiletry products.
- Plenty of storage. Your luggage, opened flat, will slide under the bed.
- Take some cash for small purchases and two credit cards that don't charge you international transaction fees.
- Your stateroom will be dark at night. Leave the bathroom light on and close the door, or bring a nightlight, or take clothes pins to secure the drapes.
- Take plugs and adapters for each country. Viking voltage is 220V & 110V (US outlet) with plenty of USB ports.
- Use the laundry service; consider it part of your trip expenses.
- Consider ear plugs and sleep medication.
- Use a weather app to check the weather forecast.
- CLOTHING: Think about colors that go well together so you can mix and match. Dress is casual. Most wear jeans or casual pants. Some men wear a collared shirt at dinner. If you are attending an evening event such as a concert, bring a pair of black slacks and a nicer top or blouse. Mornings and evenings can be cool, so a jacket or sweater helps. A rain jacket. Comfortable walking shoes and one other pair for evening.
- Try to use two basic colors for pants and tops such as black or navy and khaki. Four pair of pants and each bottom has tops to match with both colors. Seven tops: four shorter sleeve and three longer, depending on the time of year. Try to bring items made of nylon or poly blend for easy washing, lightweight and wrinkle free.
- Leave room in your luggage for souvenirs.

- Spend time on your *myvikingjourney.com* to purchase extra excursions, prepay gratuities, and much more.
- Purchase a couple of good travel books and study up on where you are going and what you'd like to do in your free time.

REFERENCES

Budapest Photo Guide
ISBN: 978-963-87573-1-9

Lonely Planet *Pocket Budapest*
Second Edition
Published by Lonely Plant Global Limited
Printed in Malaysia
July 2017
ISBN: 978-1-78657-028-4

Rick Steves Germany 2019
Published January 2019
Avalon Travel
An imprint of Perseus Books
A Hatchette Book Group company
Berkeley, California
ISBN: 978-1-63121-830-9

Rick Steve Prague & Czech Republic
Eighth Edition
Published May 2015
Avalon Travel
A member of the Perseus Books Group
Berkeley, California
ISBN: 978-1-6312-055-6